# Fiber Menace

KONSTANTIN MONASTYRSKY

# Fiber Menace

THE TRUTH ABOUT FIBER'S ROLE IN DIET FAILURE,
CONSTIPATION, HEMORRHOIDS, IRRITABLE
BOWEL SYNDROME, ULCERATIVE COLITIS,
CROHN'S DISEASE, AND COLON CANCER

Ageless
Press

Published by Ageless Press
www.AgelessPress.com
U.S.A.

Monastyrsky, Konstantin
    Fiber Menace: The Truth About Fiber's Role in Diet Failure,
    Constipation, Hemorrhoids, Irritable Bowel Syndrome,
    Ulcerative Colitis, Crohn's Disease, and Colon Cancer
    p. cm.
    ISBN 0-9706796-4-5
    1. Fiber. 2. Constipation. 3. IBS. 4. Cancer. I. Title.
    2005

The content of *Fiber Menace* is intended solely for informational and educational purposes and not as medical advice. Please contact medical or health professionals if you have questions about your health.

# Acknowledgments

The completion of this book wouldn't have been possible without having had the luxury of uninterrupted time, since almost two years were needed to research, write, and publish it. My wife Tatyana has made endless sacrifices, and absorbed a great deal of family and business responsibilities to free this time up for me. This is in addition to all the other things a great wife provides—friendship, comfort, security, and confidence. Besides, Tatyana is a phenomenal cook. If not for her ability to turn a piece of meat into a piece of culinary art, I'd still be a vegetarian.

Transitioning from writing in Russian to English wasn't a trivial task, even though English has been my working language for the last twenty-five years. Dianne Belfrey helped me to find a confident tone and voice, and polished a raw manuscript into prime-time shape. I am doubly grateful to Dianne for her endless patience over blown deadlines. In the process, she became a true friend.

Amy Gillett proofread the finished manuscript and pointed to things that otherwise would have made me blush. Thank you, Amy!

# About the Author

Konstantin Monastyrsky graduated from medical school in 1976 with a degree in pharmacology. He emigrated to the United States in 1978 from Ukraine (the former Soviet Union), and chose to pursue a career in the high-technology field.

From 1985 to 1990, he worked at two premier Wall Street firms: at First Boston Corporation as a senior systems analyst and at Goldman-Sachs & Co. as a consultant to Dr. Fischer Black, the co-author of the Nobel Prize-winning Black-Scholes theory of options trading. Between 1990 and 1998, he was the president of a software company.

In 1996, Mr. Monastyrsky began to suffer from diabetes and a host of related ailments, including debilitating carpal tunnel syndrome. Unable to use the keyboard, he turned his attention back to medicine to find solutions for his rapidly deteriorating health. He applied the same analytical rigor to the study of his health condition as he had to technology, and within several years completely recovered from diabetes. In 1998, free from the ravages of carpal tunnel syndrome, he left the technology field to pursue a career in medical writing and research.

Since then, Mr. Monastyrsky has written two best-selling Russian-language books, entitled *Functional Nutrition: The Foundation of Absolute Health and Longevity*, and *Disorders of Carbohydrate Metabolism*. *Fiber Menace* is his first English-language title.

Mr. Monastyrsky lives and works in Northern New Jersey with his wife Tatyana, a literary editor and businesswoman, and their two whimsical cats, Dusik and Nosik.

To Tatyana, my wife, friend, student, and teacher

# Table of Contents

*Those who believed that the Earth was flat
had been staring at the exact same horizon
as those who discovered that it's round.*

Author

# INTRODUCTION

---

# THOU SHALT NOT EAT
# ANY ABOMINABLE THING[1]

---

Back in the 1830's, a Presbyterian minister named Sylvester Graham (1794–1851) crusaded against anything and everything that he considered the "playboy philosophy." According to Graham, men should abstain from sex until the age of 30 and have sex just once a month thereafter. To control lust, Graham prescribed a high-fiber vegetarian diet.

Besides sex, Graham campaigned against soft mattresses, hot baths, and other "sensual" things not worthy of "real men," because, according to Graham, they led to "venereal excess." That's how hard beds and cold showers entered into the American pantheon of manhood, and turned countless boys into rebellious neurotics, drug users, and alcoholics. Alas, substance abuse and mental disorders often follow even a mildly abusive childhood.

Graham preached equally hard against white bread because it lacked fiber and, presumably, caused constipation. In time, this rhetoric gave birth to Graham flour—a coarsely ground wheat made into Graham bread, Graham muffins, and Graham crackers, which eventually degenerated into the ubiquitous sugar-laden children's cookies made from refined white flour practically devoid of fiber.[2]

Ironically, Sylvester Graham was the seventeenth child of the Reverend John Graham, who was 72 years old at the time of his son's birth. Graham himself lasted for just 57 years and died alone and in obscurity, in large part because of his abrasive, irritable personality—a typical manifestation of acute protein deficiency and unstable blood sugar. Apparently, in Graham's own case, a strict vegetarian diet, harsh fiber, and prudish abstinence brought neither health nor happiness. Nonetheless, his message took hold. But it took another century to finally hook Americans on fiber for good.

John Harvey Kellogg (1852–1943) was everything Sylvester Graham was not—a practicing physician, a celebrated surgeon, a successful entrepreneur, a charitable individual, an author of numerous books, articles, and patents, an accomplished lecturer, a man of strong principles, and one of the most prominent and influential health reformers of his time. His impact on American dietary habits was far more profound (and far more damaging) than Graham's because he had the resources, the forum, the charisma, the conviction, and the authority to deliver his message over a long, long period of time and to lots and lots of people.

Just like Graham, Kellogg was obsessed with chastity and constipation. True to principle, he never made love to his wife. To "remedy" the sin of masturbation, he advocated circumcision without anesthetic for boys and mutilation of the clitoris with carbolic acid[3] for girls. He blamed constipation for "nymphomania" in women and lust in men, because, according to Kellogg, impacted stools[4] inside one's rectum were stimulating the prostate gland and the female vagina into sexual proclivity.

His prescription was part vintage Graham, part New World ingenuity—a coarse vegetarian diet, one-to-three ounces of bran daily, and paraffin oil with every meal. This regimen wasn't without a rational: as any nutritionist will tell you (and as Graham and Kellogg undoubtedly observed themselves), the decline of libido, functional impotence, and infertility are among the very first symptoms of chronic protein deficiencies prevalent among vegans.[5] For similar reasons, numerous religions prescribe vegan diets for monks and nuns. It isn't as radical a solution as clitoral mutilation or punitive circumcision, but it's equally effective.

The rational behind paraffin oil—the same oil used to light oil lamps—was different. Because all that fiber in the Kellogg's diet caused large stools and hemorrhoidal disease, the oil was prescribed as a laxative stimulant and lubricant to ease off straining, anal lacerations, and hemorrhoidal pain.

As with any "drug," you gain some, lose some more: constant anal leakage was one of paraffin oil's most immediate side effects; more serious—it was washing out already meager fat-soluble vitamins A, D, E, and K from the intestines, which caused blindness, infertility, birth defects, immune disorders, diabetes, cancers, osteomalacia (soft bones), and hemophilia (inability of blood to clot). Kellogg was just plain lucky that only the most stubborn diehards—too few to expose the quackery—could stick to the daily regimen of paraffin oil long enough to kill themselves.

Despite his obvious nuttiness, Kellogg lived and worked to 91. He could never accomplish this feat following his own counsel because to last that long, he would need a daily supply of primary (animal) proteins and fat, which can't be obtained from a vegetarian diet alone. And that's even before taking into account the devastating vitamin deficiency caused by the daily intake of paraffin oil. More likely, Kellogg was a typical hypocrite, who didn't practice what he preached, sex or no sex.

Even though Kellogg's delirious ideas had more holes than a fine sieve, his message took hold, and his namesake[6] company is still minting a fortune by peddling, among other things, sugared breakfast cereals fortified with fiber. In 2004 alone, the Kellogg Company spent over $3.5 billion[7] just on "promotional expenditures." No wonder fiber is still on everyone's mind and in everyone's stools, and remains as popular as ever, even though John Harvey Kellogg is long gone.

So if you believe that the introduction of fiber into the American diet came about as a result of thorough academic research, methodical clinical investigation, and penetrating peer reviews, I'm sorry to disappoint you, but it didn't. It's actually based on profane sacrilege,[8] fanatical misogynism, medieval prudishness, common quackery, crass commercialism, incomprehensible medical incompetence, and, by the legal standards of today, negligence and malpractice.

Even when a few legitimate attempts were made to validate Graham's and Kellogg's rational for fiber in regard to constipation and intestinal health, according to the American College of Gastroenterology Functional Gastrointestinal Disorders Task Force, they amounted to nothing at best:

---

Specifically, there are 3 RCTs [randomized controlled trials] of wheat bran in patients with chronic constipation,[7–9] but only 1 is placebo-controlled.[7] This trial did not demonstrate a significant improvement in stool frequency or consistency when compared with placebo—neither did 2 trials[8–9] that compared wheat bran with corn biscuit or corn bran.[9]

---

At worse, according to the same source, fiber "has been associated with bloating," "mechanical obstruction of the esophagus and colon," and, in the case of psyllium, "will likely worsen symptoms in an IBS patient," effects "similar to placebo" and "anaphylactic reactions"—a euphemism for a toxic shock few survive.

All that and much, much more is the subject of this book—a penetrating investigation into the menacing role of dietary fiber in your health and nutrition.

***

# Footnotes

[1] Bible, King James Version; Deuteronomy.14:3.

[2] Nabisco Graham Crackers; 21 g of carbohydrates and 1 g of fiber per one 28 g serving; NDB No: 18617; USDA National Nutrient Database for Standard Reference; http://www.nal.usda.gov/fnic/foodcomp/search/index.html

[3] John Harvey Kellogg, MD; Treatment for Self-Abuse and its Effects: Plain Fact for Old and Young; F. Segner & Co.; 1888.

[4] For impacted stools to happen, a person must experience rectal impaction, which is an abnormal accumulation of hard stools inside the rectum. This is a condition usually associated with toddlers, paraplegics, the bedridden, infirm, and very old—not exactly a group of characters with sex on their minds.

[5] Strict vegetarians (i.e. vegans) don't consume dairy, eggs, fish, seafood, fowl, or meat of any kind. Their diet consists of nothing but carefully combined vegetables, fruits, grains, and legumes. Protein malnutrition among vegans is common, and widely described in medical literature. Many Westerners consider themselves "vegetarians" even though the only food they exclude from their diet is red meat and pork. Nonetheless, the lore of "healthy vegetarians" is quite popular. I've yet to meet a person who didn't know one, even though only 1% of adults in America (under two million) are practicing vegans, and most of them take prodigious amounts of supplements— vitamins, minerals, essential fatty acids, and free-form amino acids needed to maintain half-decent health.

[6] Kellogg Company of today was the result of an acrimonious split between John Kellogg and his brother and business partner Will, who insisted on adding sugar to the cereals. Sugar won. True to his principles, Dr. Kellogg never spoke to brother Will again.

[7] Kellogg Company Annual Report 2004; Page 30; http://investor.kelloggs.com/downloads/AR_2004.pdf

[8] Although fiber wasn't explicitly mentioned in the scriptures, even God couldn't have foreseen that some people would be crazy enough to consume indigestible substances and wash them down with lighting oil. Besides, Graham's and Kellogg's anti-sex crusade is a willful desecration of the sanctity of marriage.

[9] Philip S. Schoenfeld, MD, MSEd, MSc; Guidelines for the Treatment of Chronic Constipation: What Is the Evidence?; Medscape Gastroenterology. 2005;7(2) ©2005 Medscape; http://www.medscape.com/viewarticle/507545. This quote refers to the following studies:

(7) Badiali D, Corazziari E, Habib FI, et al. Effect of wheat bran in treatment of chronic nonorganic constipation. A double-blind controlled trial. Dig Dis Sci. 1995;40:349–356.

(8) Anderson AS, Whichelow MJ. Constipation during pregnancy: dietary fibre intake and the effect of fibre supplementation. Hum Nutr Appl Nutr. 1985;39:202–207.

(9) Graham DY, Moser SE, Estes MK. The effect of bran on bowel function in constipation. Am J Gastroenterol. 1982;77:599–603.

## Part I

# Truth, More Truth, And Diet Failure

*Get the facts, or the facts will get you.*
*And when you get them, get them right,*
*or they will get you wrong.*
Dr. Thomas Fuller (1654—1734)

# PART I. INTRODUCTION

## FIBER MADNESS OR
## MADNESS FROM FIBER?

While studying the history of Japanese cuisine, I came across a remarkable historical fact: in the name of Buddhism, which postulates strict vegetarianism, the Samurai class prohibited ordinary Japanese citizens from hunting, fishing, and keeping livestock. They didn't, however, apply that prohibition to themselves. If you're a fan of Akira Kurosawa's movies, you must remember the striking visual results of that social policy—huge, well-endowed, Samurai masters vs. diminutive, hunched peasants and servants, who subsisted mainly on rice.

Just like the powerful Samurai warriors, early humans flourished on abundant meats, fish, and seafood. This is apparent from looking at a human dental chart—protruding canines, razor-sharp incisors, rock-hard premolars, and massive molars are not exactly the implements intended to slurp bananas. Had humans had an evolutionary predisposition for eating fibrous plants, their teeth would have evolved along the lines of sheep and cows, and we wouldn't have become the canine-wielding predators that we really are.

If you continue analyzing the evolutionary functions of each digestive organ, you'll find the same pattern: the functionality of each organ matches the specific food group: the mouth to macerate and masticate flesh; the stomach to ferment and digest proteins; the duodenum (the first section of small intestine) to mix chyme with enzymes and absorb water; the gallbladder to store bile needed to break down and assimilate fats; the jejunum and ileum (the last two sections of small intestine) to complete digestion of proteins, fats, and carbohydrates, and absorb their basic components (amino acids, fatty acids, monosaccharides); the large intestine to recover remaining water, nutrients, and electrolytes, convert liquid chyme to semi-solid stools, and expel them.

If you interfere with this natural order by matching each organ with the wrong food group or specific constituent, the organs will eventually get dysfunctional for the same reason a luxury car may stall on cheap, regular gas—they're not meant for each other. So to keep the digestive organs functional (i.e. healthy), you should pair them with foods that match their functionality (the stomach with proteins, small intestine with digestible carbohydrates, gallbladder with fats, and so forth). Otherwise...

Otherwise, if you feed cows with meat, first they get mad (the condition is called "mad cow disease"), and then they die. If you feed humans with only carbohydrates and fiber, first they get bloated, then emaciated and mad (the condition is called *marasmus,* which means a physical and mental wasting from protein-energy malnutrition, or PEM[1]) and then they die too. It just takes longer because, unlike cows, humans are omnivorous, and can, for a while, subsist on a carbohydrate-only diet.

That's why we raise cows for meat and dairy rather than just grazing on the greenest pastures ourselves. And that's why fiber is a relatively new phenomenon in human nutrition. As little as a few hundred years ago—an eye blink on the evolutionary timeline—people couldn't consume fiber because there were no industrial mills, no stainless steel grinders, and no high-temperature ovens to convert (process) what is really livestock feed into foodstuff fit for human consumption.

Since we now can mill, grind, and bake fiber with the push of a button, its advocates may argue that it's suitable for people, but the simple fact that humans don't have digestive enzymes to break down fiber inside the intestines speaks volumes for itself. Hence, for anyone who aspires to remain healthy, adapting to evolutionary realities is far more practical than to wait for evolution to adapt to oneself.

Some people attempt to cheat evolution with digestive aids, such as Beano®, but even a fistful of Beanos can't change the goings on inside one's mouth, stomach, and intestines. Besides, breaking down fiber into glucose with factory-made enzymes may prevent bloating and flatulence, but only at the expense of even more weight gain and related metabolic disorders from digesting even more carbohydrates.

Other people, upon hearing that fiber is a menace, assume an ignorant or naive posture: "I (we, they) eat plenty of fiber and nothing happens, therefore everything you say is nonsense." Well, if you smoke, abuse alcohol, cheat on taxes, or run red lights, nothing happens for a while, either. That's exactly why fiber is so insidiously and maddeningly menacing. After reading the next three chapters you'll be able to make your own judgment on just how menacing it really is:

- Chapter 1. *Fiber Carnage.* Describes the role of fiber in nutrition and disease in layman's terms. It concludes that fiber is an addictive substance, meaning that after you begin consuming fiber specifically for its "health benefits," you'll need more and more fiber with every passing year to get, literally, the same "kick in the ass." If you abuse any organ too long and too hard, it eventually breaks down. The list of fiber-related fault lines is so long, the chapter takes over thirty dense pages just to describe the major ones.

- Chapter 2. *Water Damage.* The widespread popularity of fiber brought with it another menace: increased consumption of water. Not because more water is actually needed, but because the advice to "eat more fiber" invariably accompanied the advice to "drink more water." Water is every bit as addictive as fiber, but for a different reason—the more you drink, the more you urinate, the more you urinate, the more water you need to replace. Unfortunately, you don't urinate just water. Urine washes out minerals that are crucial for health, especially potassium. Potassium deficiency happens to be one of the primary causes of costiveness (hard stools) and constipation (irregular stools). When that happens, you'll be advised to increase fiber and water consumption. Imagine what happens next.

- Chapter 3. *Atkins Goes to South Beach* illustrates the connections between fiber and obesity, and fiber and diet failure—two of the most pressing public health problems of our generation. Public health authorities' incessant urging that we consume more natural fiber in the form of bread, pasta, cereals, fruits, and vegetables precipitated an obesity epidemic, because fiber-rich foods contain ten to twenty times as much carbohydrate as they do fiber (5% to 10%). Unfortunately, by the time you're ready to jump on the low-carb bandwagon, dropping carbs cold turkey doesn't work, because your body is already addicted to fiber. If you throw the shortcomings of the Atkins and South Beach diets into this mix, you end up with diet failure. If you didn't get major anorectal damage from the "hard landing," consider yourself lucky. For anyone who aspires to lose weight and preserve health, this chapter alone makes it worth reading this book.

\*\*\*

# Footnotes

[1] Protein-Energy Malnutrition; The Merck Manual of Diagnosis and Therapy; 17th ed,; Section 1, ch. 2;
http://www.merck.com/mrkshared/mmanual/section1/chapter2/2c.jsp

*Many patients starting [out on] fiber complain
of flatulence, distention, bloating, poor taste,
and are unwilling to continue.*

Rome II: The Functional Gastrointestinal Disorders
Ch. 7. Constipation[1]

# CHAPTER ONE

# FIBER CARNAGE

## Fiber's role in disease: A lifelong demolition derby

If you consume minor quantities of fiber from natural, unproces-sed food, there isn't anything wrong with it, because (a) small amounts of natural fiber (which is mostly soluble) will not obstruct your intestines or cause diarrhea, (b) most of it will get fermented in the large intestine, and (c) the reminder will not bulk up the vol-ume of stool high enough to cause any damage from "roughage." But that's not what most Americans do or are urged to do:

**Average recommended fiber intake (grams per day)[2]**

| Age | Children | Boys | Girls | Men | Women | Pregnant |
|---|---|---|---|---|---|---|
| 1–3 | 19 g | | | | | |
| 4–8 | 25 g | | | | | |
| 9–13 | | 31 g | 26 g | | | |
| 14–18 | | 38 g | 26 g | | | |
| 19–30 | | | | 38 g | 25 g | 28 g |
| 31–50 | | | | 38 g | 25 g | 28 g |
| 51–70 | | | | 30 g | 21 g | 28 g |
| Over 70 | | | | 21 g | 21 g | |

These are the standing recommendations from the *Food and Nutrition Board,* a division of the *Institute of Medicine of the National Academies,* which is the body that establishes the nutritional policy guidelines of the U.S. Government. Let's analyze those recommendations:

- *Children from one to eight:* The recommended amount is sky-high even by the standards of the *American Dietetic Association.*[3] It isn't based on the actual need, but on the fact that up to 25% of children in this age group suffer from constipation related to the abuse of antibiotics, lack of breastfeeding, poor toilet training, inadequate nutrition, frequent diarrhea, and other factors. In this case, fiber is used as a hard laxative instead of correcting the primary causes of constipation. The large intestine of a one-year-old is about one-tenth the size of a fully-grown adult's, but the recommended dose is only half of the adult's (19 g vs. 38 g or 0.7 vs. 1.3 oz). With that much fiber in the diet, the child will be irritable from abdominal pain, bloated from a large volume of stools, flatulent from gases, prickly with food because eating causes cramps, and prone to frequent bouts of diarrhea alternating with constipation from all of the above. That's a direct path to malnutrition, stunted growth, poor development, and academic mediocrity.

- *Teenagers and adults:* Similar amounts of fiber are recommended for teenagers and adults—from 26 to 38 g (0.9–1.3 oz) daily. If you consume that much fiber, it means large stools, inevitable anorectal damage, and eventual dependence on fiber to move the bowels.

- *The elderly:* As people get older, less fiber is recommended (not more, as one may think) because the digestive organs are no longer as agile and healthy. Unfortunately, this is not what most constipated elderly patients hear from medical professionals. The majority urge seniors to increase fiber consumption in order to relieve constipation. Even so, 20 to 30 g (0.7–1.0 oz) of fiber for people over 50, half of whom already suffer from hemorrhoidal disease (and from diverticular disease by the age of 60) is a prescription for trouble.

As the dynamics of "broken telephone" transform already bad advice, it gets worse, much worse. Here are the "enhanced" recommendations from what is considered one of the best medical and research institutions in the nation, *The Mayo Clinic*. The article is entitled "Fiber—A Good Carb":

---

The June [2004] issue of Mayo Clinic Women's HealthSource suggests ways to increase fiber in your diet:

- Eat a high-fiber cereal or add a few spoonfuls of unprocessed wheat bran to your cereal.
- Add bran cereal or unprocessed bran when making foods such as meatloaf, breads, muffins, cakes, and cookies.
- Choose whole-grain bread instead of white bread. Look for breads made with 100 percent whole-wheat flour.
- Substitute whole-wheat flour for half or all of the white flour when baking.
- Experiment with whole grains and whole-grain products such as brown rice, barley, whole-wheat pasta, and bulgur.
- Try adding canned kidney beans, garbanzos and other beans to canned soups or salads.
- Eat snacks that are high in fiber, such as fresh and dried fruits, raw vegetables, low-fat popcorn, and whole-grain crackers.
- Add barley to soups and stews.
- Eat generous quantities of vegetables and fruits.[4]

---

If you follow this advice, just one cup (60 g) of Kellogg's All-Bran Cereal With Extra Fiber[5] gives you 30 g of fiber, already the daily amount recommended for adults, and many more times for children. And that's just for breakfast, before adding in the recommended breads, salads, soups, stews, and "generous quantities of vegetables and fruits" throughout the rest of the day.

Think about it—just one cup of fiber-fortified cereal contains **three times more fiber than the maximum recommended daily dose for fiber laxatives**, such as Metamucil® (3.4 g up to three times daily[6]). Even that little, just under 12 g of fiber in Metamucil, may cause severe side effects:

---

**Side Effects**: Bloating, gas, and a feeling of fullness may occur. If these effects continue or become bothersome, inform your doctor. Notify your doctor if you experience: stomach cramps, nausea, vomiting, rectal bleeding, unrelieved constipation.[7] (Metamucil Powder; Rite Advice, Patient Counseling at www.RiteAid.com)

For all intents and purposes, the indigestible fiber in cereals isn't any different from the fiber in Metamucil's psyllium—fiber is fiber regardless of the source. People who aren't accustomed to a high-fiber diet may have identical side effects whether it is Metamucil or high-fiber cereals.

Shocked? Puzzled? Surprised? Bewildered? Here is a brief Q&A which explains why the side effects of various kinds of fiber consumption are identical:

Q. *Why does fiber cause bloating?*
A. Because (a) fiber fermentation inside the intestines produces gases, and (b) because the acidity from fermentation causes intestinal inflammation. Since the absorption of gases is the primary function of the intestine, the combined impact of (a) and (b) blocks their absorption, and causes the intestines to expand just like an air balloon.

Q. *Why does fiber cause gas?*
A. The intestines are colonized with symbiotic bacteria (normal intestinal flora), which are essential for many health-sustaining functions. Normally, mucin—a component of mucus—provides bacteria with the nutrients they need. But when fiber—soluble as well as insoluble—reaches the lower intestine, the bacteria go wild, ferment everything in sight, and multiply prodigiously. The fermentation is accompanied by lots of gases, just as with yeast-rising dough or aging champagne. If you don't experience gas after ingesting fiber, it means that your intestines lack normal bacteria, and you are affected by disbacteriosis, a serious pathology which is explained in Chapter 4, *Disbacteriosis*.

Q. *Why does fiber cause "stomach cramps"?*
A. Actually, not stomach cramps, but abdominal cramps. The cramping is a pain sensation in the abdominal region that results from gases, inflammation, acidity, intestinal obstruction, and large stools, or that stems from regular contractions of affected

sections of the small and large intestines.

Q. *Why does fiber cause nausea and vomiting?*
A. Once inside the stomach, fiber lumps together and may cause mechanical stimulation of the receptors that activate the vomiting center in the brain. The lumped fiber may also temporarily obstruct the path between the stomach and duodenum, and cause vomiting related to the stomach's overload or delayed emptying. If you have gastritis (inflammatory stomach disease) or ulcers, the likelihood of fiber-related nausea and vomiting is even higher because of the fiber's contact with extra-sensitive impaired tissues.

Q. *Why does fiber cause "rectal bleeding"?*
A. Doctors, nutritionists, and dietitians refer to fiber as "bulk" or "roughage," because it makes stools rough and bulky. When large stools pass through the narrow anal canal, they may lacerate its delicate lining, and cause bleeding. Large stools and the straining needed to expel them are also behind hemorrhoidal disease and anal fissures—lacerations inside the anal canal that won't heal. Far more dangerous bleeding may result from ulcerative colitis, caused by the prolonged contact of undigested fiber and large stools with the colorectal mucosal membrane. Ulcerative colitis raises the risk of colorectal cancer by 3,200%. The mechanical and chemical properties of fiber and large stools are also the most likely causes of precancerous polyps.

Q. *Why does fiber cause "unrelieved constipation"?*
A. For the same reason it causes anorectal bleeding. When stools become large from excess fiber, many people, particularly children, seniors, and those affected by hemorrhoidal disease or anal fissures, simply can't pass them. If this condition isn't quickly resolved, it may lead to fecal impaction. The continuous accumulation of impacted stools may cause diverticular disease (the bulging of the colorectal wall), megacolon (permanent stretching of the colorectal walls), and colorectal perforation (the spilling of intestinal content into the abdominal cavity), which is usually lethal.

Q. *Why there are no fiber warnings printed on the boxes of fiber-fortified cereals?*

A. Cigarettes didn't have any warnings either for a long, long time. It takes a while to change a belief system.

Q. *I am young, fit, and healthy, and I consume lots of fiber. And it causes me no harm. Why?*

A. Fiber is very much like a bomb with a time-delay fuse. For a while, it will not visibly affect you, because young people are still active enough to burn off all excess carbs, their intestines are still supple enough to process fiber, and young anorectal organs are still strong enough to handle large stools. Alas, if you keep consuming lots of fiber, your youthful bliss may soon be over. Just ask your parents and grandparents.

Avoiding dietary fiber in food isn't an easy task. It is often hidden behind obscure names such as cellulose, β-glucans, pectin, guar gum, cellulose gum, carrageen, agar-agar, hemicellulose, inulin, lignin, oligofructose, fructooligosaccharides, polydextrose, polylos, psyllium, resistant dextrin, resistant starch, and others.

These ingredients are factory-made from wood pulp, cotton, seaweed, husks, skins, seeds, tubers, and selected high-yield plants that aren't suitable for human consumption without extra processing. They are widely used to add texture and volume to ersatz food. For example, guar gum or cellulose gum are added to water and dry milk in order to fake yogurt or sour cream consistency, carrageen gives texture to cheap ice cream, and pectin thickens fruit preserves.

The only reliable way of avoiding hidden sources of fiber is this: read the labels! if you didn't learn the name of the ingredient on the product's label by the first grade, it doesn't belong on your plate and inside your gut.

So let's stroll along the mouth-to-anus pathway and check out the damage from this fiber orgy.

**Fiber's affect on the oral cavity: As sticky as glue**

The human mouth is primarily intended to cut and chop flesh, not grind indigestible fibers. Unlike humans, cows have so-called *hypsodont* teeth, which extend very far above the gum line to accommodate a lifetime of wear-and-tear from grinding fibrous grasses. We aren't as lucky—our teeth are *brachydont,* and aren't intended for chewing fiber, otherwise, after a decade or so, you simply wouldn't have any teeth left to argue this point with clarity.[8] That's why the fiber for human consumption is crushed, milled, or ground first, and requires little or no chewing. But even after processing, it affects the oral cavity with a menacing vengeance:

- *Obstruction of the salivary glands.* Fiber, especially in dry-roasted cereals, has a tendency to obstruct the salivary glands. When that happens, the tongue senses a polyp-like protrusion. Though unpleasant, this benign problem may, in some instances, cause acute inflammation and require treatment with antibiotics.

- *Dental caries.* Powdered (well-milled) fiber of any kind has a natural tendency to lodge itself inside the abrasions both on the chewing surfaces and between the teeth. Once there, it provides perfect feed for normal oral flora. The bacterial fermentation in the mouth produces lactic acids that bind with the minerals that form the enamel mineral matrix. In turn, the weakening of the matrix causes dental caries. That's why all kinds of fiber-rich products, especially cereals, are exceptionally destructive for dental health. Not surprisingly, tooth decay is the second most common disease in the United States. The common cold is the first. Weak immunity related to disbacteriosis happens to be one of the leading causes of most colds as well.

- *Periodontal disease (*gingivitis, necrotizing ulcerative gingivitis, periodontitis*).* Pulverized fiber lodges easily inside the gingival sulcus, a pocket that exists between the teeth and the gums (gingiva). The bacterial fermentation inside the sulcus causes inflammation of gingiva, periodontal ligament, and alveolar bone, and eventual tooth loss. Gingivitis—the initial stage of periodontal disease—is easily recognized by bleeding gums. A receding gum line, even without bleeding, indicates the progression of periodontal disease.

**Fiber's affect on the esophagus: If not plugged, then burned**

The esophagus is the narrow muscular tube that transports chewed food and water from the mouth to the stomach. A chewed mass is called *bolus.* The bolus travels the entire length of the esophagus in just a few seconds. This unassuming organ is quite vulnerable to the vagaries of indigestible fiber. The impact is indirect, through the digestive disorders of the stomach, such as heartburn, but the suffering is real—millions of people suffer from *dysphagia,* the difficulty or inability to swallow food. The other prominent fiber-related complications are:

- *Esophageal obstruction.* Supplemental fiber may rapidly expand and cause an obstruction when not accompanied by a lot of liquid. It isn't likely to happen in healthy adults, but is probable in small children, people with a narrowed esophagus or affected by dysphagia (difficulty swallowing), as well as the mentally disabled, old, and infirm.

- *Heartburn* is the most common symptom of gastroesophageal reflux disease (GERD)—a spilling over (reflux) of the stomach's content back into the esophagus. The burning sensation emanates from the esophageal mucosa, unprotected from digestive juices and enzymes.

- *Barrett's esophagus (change of mucosa, precursor to cancer), dysphagia (difficulty swallowing), ulceration, bleeding, and esophageal cancer.* Indirectly through the GERD, indigestible fiber is a primary causative factor behind these conditions.

**Fiber's affect on the stomach: The luck stops here**

The digestion of protein is the exclusive provenance of the stomach. When gastric digestion commences, the contents of the stomach are churned[9] inside, until it's completed (i.e. solid particles of food larger than 2 millimeters, or 0.08," are no longer detected).

Fiber's specific properties—water absorbency, expansion, stickiness (congregation)—interfere with digestion and may cause an array of gastric disorders. Fiber-related problems become more pronounced with age because of the inevitable wear-and-tear of the internal organs. Insoluble fiber affects the stomach particularly hard because it tends to congregate and form lumps, and its rapid expansion fills the stomach with idle bulk.

You don't even need to consume that much fiber to feel its punch. For example, TV commercials for antacids are commonly shot inside Mexican restaurants because beans—a main staple of Mexican cuisine—commonly cause heartburn, even though a 100 g (0.22 lb) serving of beans contains a paltry 4 to 5 g of fiber. Just imagine the cumulative impact on the aging stomach of 30 to 40 grams of fiber consumed daily. Here are the most prominent problems:

- *Nausea and vomiting.* The congregated lumps of fiber may cause mechanical stimulation of the receptors that activate the vomiting center in the brain. That much, as you recall, is stated in the side effect section of common fiber supplements.

- *Obstruction (Gastric outlet obstruction, Duodenal obstruction).* The lumps of expanded fiber, primarily from supplements, may temporarily obstruct the path between the stomach and duodenum. If there are no other pathologies, the situation resolves itself with nausea and vomiting.

- *Gastroparesis (delayed stomach emptying).* The stomach's peristalsis and digestion are completed when specialized receptors no longer detect undigested components over 2 mm. The undigested lumps of fiber may considerably extend the duration of the gastric phase of digestion because the stomach can't distinguish between an undigested chunk of meat and a lump of fiber. This problem is particularly acute among older individuals, who may have weak peristaltic contractions of the stomach. The digestion can extend from the customary 4–6 hours to 10, 12, and beyond. The extended exposure of the stomach lining to digestive juices and enzymes, particularly while laying down, may cause inflammation and ulceration of the esophagus and upper stomach regions (*cardia* and *fundus*), that aren't as well-protected as its lower regions (*antrum* and *pylorus*).

- *Gastroesophageal Reflux Disease (GERD).* Simply speaking, GERD results from two primary factors: overloading the stomach with food and liquids, and delayed digestion (indigestion). Because indigestible fiber expands four to five times its size, it is the largest contributor to the stomach's overload. Absence of indigestion, heartburn, and reflux is one of the most immediate and pronounced benefits of low- or fiber-free diets.

- *Dyspepsia.* A general term that describes non-specific pain and discomfort that emanates from the stomach (upper middle abdominal region). The sensation of pain may result from conditions described above and below. The pain may become more pronounced after a meal. Meals heavy in all kinds of fiber cause more pain because of the volume and the extended duration of digestion. Some medical writers refer to dyspepsia as "indigestion." Well, guess what substance doesn't digest in the stomach?

- *Gastritis.* All of the above conditions, related to fiber interfering with or extending gastric digestion, are the primary causes of gastritis—an inflammation of the stomach's mucosa, caused by the inability of the stomach's lining to withstand its own aggressive environment. The risk of gastritis goes up exponentially if you're under a great deal of stress (it inhibits digestion); consume alcohol (in small amounts it stimulates digestion, but inhibits in large); drink coffee, chew gum, or smoke (all three stimulate digestion); regularly take aspirin and other NSAIDs drugs; or are infected with H.pylori bacteria. The fiber adds to this mix far more than the proverbial two cents. Please note that there is nothing wrong with stimulating digestion when appropriate. The problems develop when the digestion is stimulated inappropriately—between meals, before going to bed, while experiencing reflux, dyspepsia, and similar circumstances.

- *Gastric Ulcer (Peptic ulcer disease).* A perforation of the stomach's mucosa causes ulcers. Gastritis commonly precedes ulceration and bleeding. All of the causative factors behind gastritis apply to ulcers as well. Fiber extends digestion. The longer the digestion lasts, the more difficult, if not outright impossible, for the ulcers to heal. That's why people who are admitted to a hospital with a bleeding ulcer are placed on a liquids-only diet. If a zero-fiber diet helps ulcers to heal, a low-fiber one isn't as likely to cause them.

- *Hiatal (Hiatus) Hernia.* The *diaphragm* (midriff) is a muscular membrane that separates the heart and lungs (thoracic cavity) from the digestive organs (abdominal cavity). The esophagus connects with the stomach through the *esophageal hiatus*—an opening in the diaphragm. A pathological protrusion (herniation) of the stomach's upper wall above the diaphragm through that opening is called *hiatal hernia*. This condition affects over 40% of the population[10] in the United States. When the stomach capacity is exceeded by food and fluids, the upward pressure created by peristalsis (at the bottom of the stomach) causes its upper walls to prolapse into the opening. Fiber is the only food that expands four to five times its original size once inside the stomach. This expansion creates strong volumetric pressure long after the meal has already been consumed. Neither proteins, nor fats, nor soluble carbohydrates can expand beyond their initial volume. A horizontal position (i.e. while lying down) is likely to contribute to herniation. You may have heard that herniation contributes to heartburn, dyspepsia, gastritis, and peptic ulcers. It isn't so—the hiatal hernia simply mirrors a state of the affected stomach, and these conditions are already present there, regardless of the hernia. Unless patients stop recklessly stuffing their stomachs with fiber, the majority of surgeries to remove hiatal hernias are also useless.

As you can see, the relationship between the stomach and the fiber is awkward at best, ruinous at worse. Well, what else would you expect when matching a primary digestive organ with an indigestible substance?

### Fiber's affect on the small intestine: Not welcome at any price

The journey of food from the plate to the large intestine—that is, through the mouth, esophagus, stomach, and small intestine—normally takes about 24 hours, depending on what was on that plate.

The small intestine is long and thin—about 7 meters (23') of coiled tubing laid out in a tight serpentine shape (3.5 to 4 cm wide in adults), which is about the width of a half-a-dollar coin.

The more insoluble fiber there is in the meal, the longer the trip, because of the bottlenecks in the small intestine, which is an organ nature intended for moving along liquid chyme, not lumps of heavy fiber. If you doubt this, just visualize the following experiment:

- To replicate chewing action, use a fork to crush a serving of

high-fiber cereal in a bowl;
- To reproduce the stomach's churning, add water or milk to the bowl, mix thoroughly, and let the crushed cereal soak in the liquid;
- To imitate the small intestine, cut a piece of garden hose, about 7 meters long, and lay it down into a serpentine shape—a good approximation of the small intestine's architecture;
- To simulate the propulsion of food through the small intestine, keep adding the "digested" cereals through a funnel on top until it appears at the other end of the hose. Or will it appear?

It's highly unlikely. The more fiber in the cereal, the faster this dense, thick, semi-liquid mass will clog the hose (intestine) at the bottom of its very first bend, and there are quite a few more bends left to go. To propel the cereal to the end of the hose, you'd need to keep adding more of the mixture from the top, in order to push out the jam in the middle—a process strikingly similar to pressure-stuffing homemade sausages with ground meat.

Unlike the clumps of cereal, any liquid poured through the funnel, no matter how thick, will soon reach the end thanks to the inescapable laws of gravitation. As long as the exit is located below the entrance, no clogging occurs, even if the hose is old and worn out.

If you chew your food thoroughly, and your stomach digests it well, it's transformed to *chyme*—a thick liquid without any solids. And the first organ to greet chyme is the duodenum.

*Duodenum.* Literally twelve fingers' breadths, the duodenum is the first and the shortest (18–25 cm) section of the small intestine. The pyloric valve (sphincter) separates the stomach from the duodenum. When the gastric phase of digestion is completed, this valve controls the transfer of chyme into the duodenum. Once inside, the chyme is neutralized with bicarbonate, mixed with bile and pancreatic juices, and the intestinal phase of digestion begins.

Fiber is particularly hard on the duodenum, because, unlike the stomach, the duodenum isn't expandable, but a small, narrow, and easy-to-clog circular tube shaped like the letter C. That's why duodenitis (a condition identical to gastritis) and duodenal ulcer (a condition identical to gastric ulcer) strike their victims in their early twenties, twenty to thirty years ahead of the peak occurrences of gastritis and gastric ulcer.

It's a well-known fact among military doctors that duodenitis and duodenal ulcers are quite common among recent recruits. No surprise there—beans, legumes, whole grain cereals, whole wheat pasta, and bread make up the largest share of military rations, and young soldiers are particularly prodigious eaters after the daily grind of military life.

The duodenum possesses a few specifics that make it particularly vulnerable to obstruction with fiber. The ducts from the liver, gallbladder, and pancreas congregate into the common bile duct and terminate inside the duodenum. They supply a prodigious amount of bile (400 to 800 ml daily) and pancreatic juice (up to 1500 to 3000 ml daily). It doesn't take long to cause considerable damage to the liver, gallbladder, and pancreas by blocking, even partially, a considerable outflow of those fluids.

The blockage of billary and pancreatic ducts can be purely mechanical or caused by duodenitis, an inflammation that affects the lining of the duodenum and the common duct itself. Again, the prolonged contact of a fibrous, acidified mass with duodenal mucosa is the most likely cause of both inflammation and blockage. The conditions that follow are quite common:

- *Pancreatitis* (inflammation of the pancreas). Besides fiber there isn't any other substance in human nutrition that enters the duodenum not only *as is,* but also expanded many times its original size. Lo and behold, the recent (17th edition) of *The Merck Manual of Diagnosis and Therapy* confirms this fact: "recent data indicate that obstruction of the pancreatic duct in the absence of billiary reflux can produce pancreatitis."[11] *Acute pancreatitis* is quite common in toddlers, who are placed on solid food, which means loads of fiber from cereals, bread, pasta, fruits, and vegetables. The condition itself often remains undiagnosed, while its most prominent symptom—the onset of juvenile diabetes (type I), a failure to produce insulin because of acute inflammation—manifests itself almost immediately. Here is yet another ruinous aspect of fiber that strikes so early in life.
- *Cholecystitis* (Inflammation of the gallbladder). Gallstones are the primary (90%) cause of acute (sudden, severe) and chronic

cholecystitis. Gallstones are formed from concentrated bile salts when the outflow of bile from the gallbladder is blocked. The gallstones cause inflammation either by irritating gallbladder mucosa or by obstructing the duct that connects it to the duodenum. The gallstones are the secondary factor, because before they can form, something else must first obstruct the billary ducts. Just like with pancreatitis, that "something" is either inflammatory disease or obstruction caused by fiber.

Women are affected by gallstones far more than men, because they are more likely to maintain a "healthy" diet, which nowadays means a diet that is low in fat and high in fiber. Since the gallbladder concentrates bile pending a fatty meal, no fat in the meal means no release of bile. The longer concentrated bile remains in the gallbladder, the higher the chance for gallstones to form.

*Upper (jejunum) and lower (ileum) small intestine.* The duodenum transitions into the *jejunum,* which comprises the upper two-fifths of the small intestine. It's distinguished from the ileum by its larger width and thickness, slightly more pronounced mucosa structure, and deeper color, because it embodies more blood vessels.

It's somewhat ironic that the name *jejunum* is derived from the Latin *fasting,* because during dissection this particular segment of the small intestine was always found empty. Apparently, the fathers of anatomy, who named the internal organs, hadn't yet been confronted with the scourge of indigestible fiber; otherwise this particular section of the small intestine would be called *intestinum repletus* (filled intestine).

The final three-fifths of the small intestine are called the *ileum* (from Latin's *groin,* meaning near groin). The ileum is narrower (3.5–3.75 cm), has thinner walls, and is not as vascular. At the very end, the *ileocal valve* terminates the small intestine and prevents the content of *cecum* (the first section of large intestine) from spilling back into small intestine.

One look at the small intestine, laid out inside the abdominal cavity like a tangled, convoluted garden hose, makes it apparent that this organ was designed to move fluids only, and that it's remarkably easy to jam with solid, undigested stuff. There is only one substance that can get down there undigested and expanded many times its size—indigestible fiber. And when that happens, here are the possible outcomes (a partial list):

- *Mechanical obstruction.* The medical term for an undigested mass that forms inside the stomach or intestines and gets stuck there is *bezoar* (pronounced *bízor*). Indigestible fiber is the only consumable substance that doesn't digest, and has the potential to form bezoars, which cause mechanical obstructions of the small intestines. When bezoars are lodged beyond the reach of the endoscope, abdominal surgery is the only option available to remove the obstruction. Bezoars are rare among healthy adults, but more common among children (whose intestines are comparatively tiny and underdeveloped). Old and infirm individuals, whose intestines lack the muscular tone needed to propel anything but fluids, are also vulnerable. That's why indigestible fiber should be taboo for children, or very old, infirm, and bed-ridden patients.

- *Enteritis* (inflammation of the small intestine). The insides of the small intestine are covered with a pinkish mucosal membrane, superficially similar to the insides of one's mouth or vagina. The assimilation of digested nutrients into the bloodstream is the sole function of the intestinal mucosa. It can only assimilate nutrients dissolved in liquid chyme. It isn't intended to transport anything other than mildly acidic chyme (pH 6.0 to 6.5). Once inside the stomach, undigested fiber soaks up acid and enzymes like a sponge. When expanded fiber enters the small intestine, the permanent contact with the delicate mucosa causes mechanical and chemical damage, which in turn causes mucosal inflammation (enteritis). Once inflamed, the mucosa can no longer absorb the nutrients and gases formed during digestion, and the intestines expand, causing bloating and cramping, which is often accompanied by severe pain.

- *Crohn's disease.* If left unchecked long enough, enteritis progresses into Crohn's disease. The mucosal inflammation gets so severe that it may cause intestinal obstruction—a condition similar to a stuffy nose during a cold, flu, or allergy attack, all of which cause acute inflammation of the nasal mucosa. The inflammation may happen at any point along the length of the small and large intestines, but it's most commonly localized in the bottom section of the ileum—the place where clogging with undigested fiber, bacterial fermentation, and fecal reflux is likeliest to occur. According to *The Merck Manual of Diagnosis and Therapy:* "Over the past few decades, the incidence of Crohn's disease has increased in the Western populations of Northern European and Anglo-Saxon ethnic derivation, third-world populations, blacks, and Latin Americans."[12] What else happened during "the past few decades?" A substantial increase in the consumption of indigestible fiber, of course.

- *Hernia.* When intestines protrude through the abdominal wall or inside the scrotum, they cause hernias. About 5 million Americans suffer from this unpleasant, potentially lethal condition. Coughing, straining, or lifting weights isn't generally enough to push the intestines so hard that they pierce the abdominal muscles or squeeze down into the scrotum (inguinal hernia). Intestinal bloating from inflammatory diseases caused by indigestible fiber is the primary force capable of expanding the intestines so much that they don't have enough room inside the abdominal cavity, and may ripple through the abdominal wall. The physical exertion that causes the actual herniation is a secondary force. Straining to move large stools (caused by fiber) is one of the major causes of hernia as well.

- *Malnutrition, and vitamin and mineral deficiencies.* All the hard work that the body did breaking food down into basic nutrients—simple sugars, amino acids, fatty acids, vitamins, and minerals—is wasted unless they get assimilated into the bloodstream to become energy, electrolytes, hormones, enzymes, neurotransmitters, tissues, and other substances that keep our bodies functional and healthy. That final act of digestion takes place throughout the entire length of the small intestine, unless it's affected by inflammation. In this case, the essential nutrients will not digest, even if your diet contains plenty of them. Since indigestible fiber is the major source of intestinal inflammation, it is also a major cause of malnutrition and mineral and vitamin deficiencies. *Pernicious anemia,* which is a chronic shortage of dietary iron, folic acid, and vitamin $B_{12}$, related to gastric and intestinal inflammation, is one of the most common forms of such a deficiency. It's also the most difficult to overcome, because regular oral supplements won't digest, no matter what the dose, unless the fiber is completely withdrawn and the stomach and intestines permitted to heal.

### Fiber's affect on the large intestine: Demolition completed

The *large intestine* (a.k.a. gut, colon, bowel, entrails, and viscera) is a bona fide digestive organ. Its time is primarily taken up with the fermentation of undigested carbohydrates and assimilation of nutrients, water, and electrolytes. In the process, the large intestine converts the remnants of liquid chyme into stools and expels them. The more indigested fiber there is in the chyme, the larger and harder the stools become.

The adjective "large" next to the word "intestine" is misleading—the *large intestine* isn't that large vis-à-vis the *small intestine,* but wide. In Russian, for example, the intestines aren't *small* or *large,* but, respectively (and correctly), *thin* for small and *thick* for large. Length-wise, the large intestine is under 1.5 meters (5'); width-wise, it's 6 to 9 cm (2.3–3.5") at the base, narrowing down at the end.

The large intestine is made up of four functional sections that encircle the small intestine. It starts with a sac at the bottom that metamorphoses into a tube that looks like the letter "U" upside down. At the opposite end of the tube, another sac, terminated by a tight sphincter, completes the U-turn. Respectively, these are the *cecum, colon, rectum,* and *anal canal.*

*Cecum.* The *cecum* is a large pouch at the bottom of the ascending colon, also known as the *blind gut.* It is called blind because it only has one exit, just like a blind alley. The cecum is located at the lower-right-hand side of the abdomen. It collects chyme from the *ileum,* which is the final segment of the small intestine.

The cecum can hold up to 1.5 liters (1.58 quarts) of chyme. A sphincter (*ileocecal* valve) prevents chyme from spilling back into the small intestine whenever you lie down, bend down, or stand up on your head.

As water, electrolytes, and micronutrients get absorbed into the

bloodstream, the chyme is slowly propelled up the ascending colon. By this stage, it begins transformation into what we call stools
or feces.

The cecum's most famous sibling—the appendix—is attached to
the cecum's inside wall, further to the left, just under the intersection with the small intestine. Despite what you may have seen in
pictures, the appendix is pointed upwards, not downwards, and its
orifice faces sideways, not down.

*Colon.* The terms *colon* and *large intestine* are often used interchangeably, although technically this isn't correct. Actually, the colon is the tubing between the cecum and rectum, and it is divided
into four parts: the first three are named for their direction: *ascending, transverse, descending,* and the fourth—*sigmoid*—for its
*sigma*-like shape.

This is why medical professionals use the term *colorectal* in connection with such words as cancer, exam, surgery, x-ray, etc., because saying "an exam of the large intestine" is cumbersome, while
"colon exam" is incorrect: doctors must pass and examine the rectum before reaching the colon, hence the term "colorectal exam."

The word colon gave birth to numerous related terms, none of
them particularly pleasant, such as *colic* (abdominal pain emanat-
ing from the colon), *colitis* (inflammation of the large intestine),
*colonoscopy* (examination with an optical scope), *colonics* (a type
of generous two-way enema), and *colonic* (specific to the large intestine, as in *colonic bacteria*).

Fecal mass goes up through the *ascending* colon, makes a sharp
left, passes the *transverse* colon, turns down into the *descending*
colon, and then makes a slight right into the *sigmoid* colon—the
ramp leading into the rectum, and the last stop before being
dumped. The mucus secretion (binding factor), water removal
(drying factor), and bacterial action (volumetric factor) solidify the
remnants of liquid chyme into solid stools before they reach the
descending colon. The descending and sigmoid colon essentially
perform a storage function for ready-to-be eliminated stools.

*Rectum.* The rectum is a stretchable, muscular sac, 10 to 15 cm
(4"–6") long, situated at the end of the sigmoid colon. It's right

above the anus, and it shares a central space inside one's pelvis with the reproductive organs. Not romantic, but it works. The term *rectal ampoule* is often applied to the rectum's shape, because it's narrow at the bottom and dilates further up to form an *ampoule*-like appearance.

*Anal Canal.* This is the least appreciated organ, and usually the first to get into trouble because it's so tiny. The anal canal's maximum aperture is tight and narrow—3.5 cm (1.37"). The anal canal itself is about 3 cm (1.18") long, and is encircled with two taut muscular sphincters—internal and external. Both sphincters perform in concert to keep the stools safely inside the rectum. We can consciously control only the external sphincter, while the internal is controlled autonomously, by the body itself.

The elimination of stools is the final act of digestion. Technically, it should be as easy as eating—the first act of digestion. When everything works just right, it is, but when it doesn't, it becomes a long and awful ordeal, first because of large stools caused by undigested fiber, second because of all the damage caused by large stools.

As with everything else in life, timing is everything with digestion: the mouth is busy chewing an average meal for 15–20 minutes; the healthy stomach digests an average mixed meal in 5 to 7 hours; the small intestine takes about 24 hours to transport chyme down to the large intestine; and the large intestine processes stools in about 72 hours.

In young, healthy people, indigestible fiber slows down stomach digestion and the transport time in the small intestine, but considerably speeds up the transport time (motility) in the large intestine, sometimes down to 24 hours. When this happens, the person may experiences diarrhea and cramping, which are usually "diagnosed" as irritable bowel syndrome. The word "diagnosed" is in parenthesis, because what's happening isn't a disease, but a natural reaction of a healthy colon to unhealthy content. If caught early, the "syndrome" disappears a few days after the fiber is removed from the diet.

When a person is no longer young, or digestive organs aren't in perfect shape, everything takes longer—the digestion in the stomach, the transport of chyme through the small intestine, and colonic motility. And when fiber is added, it takes even longer:

*The Functional Gastrointestinal Disorders:* Those with defecation disorders or slow transit respond [to fiber] much less favorably. Those with severe colonic inertia may not be helped by fiber, since there is decreased smooth muscle contractile activity.[13]

That's why fiber affects the large intestine the most, earlier than any other organ, why its impact becomes much greater and more obvious, and why the list of associated diseases is so much longer. Here are the conditions that one may get, or have already, from consuming too much fiber:

- *Appendicitis.* Appendicitis is the sudden swelling and inflammation of the appendix. It generally follows the obstruction of the appendix by undigested food or a large accumulation of hardened stools (fecal impaction). There is only one type of food that reaches the cecum undigested, and that's plant fiber, including seeds and husks. The swelling occurs because the bacteria trapped inside the appendix continues to divide, grow in volume, and generate refuse that has nowhere to go. Inflammation follows the swelling, and then sharp pain and other symptoms ensue. Without prompt surgical removal, the swollen appendix may burst and spill the cecum's "dirty" contents into the sterile *peritoneal* cavity, and cause *peritonitis*—an infectious inflammation of the membrane (peritoneum) that lines the insides of the abdomen. Without rapid and competent surgical treatment, the chances of recovering from acute peritonitis are slim.

  Appendicitis is more prevalent among children precisely because their tiny cecum and appendix are so much easier to clog with undigested fiber and large stools. When infected appendixes are removed in children, in many cases the source of obstruction and infection are undigested seeds, nuts, and grains.

  Think twice before force-feeding your child fiber-rich food or supplements. Most children dislike raw, cooked, or pureed fibrous vegetables, such as broccoli, cauliflower, carrots, cabbage, and spinach, because their reaction to fiber, literally and figuratively, is visceral (by the gut): discomfort, flatulence, cramps, -

and sharp pain. And these "veggies" aren't even that fiber-rich (just one or two grams per serving) until you recognize that just five grams of fiber for a three-year old is about the same as thirty to forty grams for an adult, which is almost twice the amount of the average daily fiber intake for people in the U.S.[14]

The combination of fecal impaction and fiber laxatives may also cause appendicitis in adults. It just takes longer to "stuff" a much larger adult's bowel with fibrous stool, until the cecum is completely clogged with undigested fiber. It takes about two to four weeks to fill the large intestine to capacity, depending on the amount of fiber in the diet and the degree of distention.

(The overviews that follow are shorter than those above because these conditions are discussed in greater depth in Part II of this book.)

- *Disbacteriosis.* The fermentation of undigested fiber causes acidity inside the large intestine great enough to damage intestinal flora. The damage isn't likely to occur with minor amounts of fiber, but is highly probable when fiber is consumed in excess. This and other causes of disbacteriosis are discussed in depth in Chapter 4, *Disbacteriosis.*
- *Bloating and flatulence.* The fermentation of fiber by colonic bacteria creates gases. The gases in excess of normal vital activity cause abdominal distention (bloating). Gases are normal in human digestion, excess gases aren't.
- *Abdominal cramps.* A high volume of chyme, large stools, and gases (all related to fiber action) cause mechanical pressure on the intestinal walls, which is especially pronounced after meals, when peristalsis commences.
- *Diarrhea.* Soluble fiber is a known causative factor of osmotic diarrhea and is commonly used as a laxative. The laxative/diarrhea effect depends on the amount of fiber taken and the status of intestinal flora. The absence of normal intestinal flora (disbacteriosis) contributes to diarrhea.
- *Constipation.* Indigestible fiber has a pronounced laxative effect in healthy people because it increases stool size and stimulates motility—the propulsion of stools through the large intestine. In

people who already have colorectal disorders related to age, medication, disbacteriosis, or other causes, the enlargement of stools has the opposite effect: it causes anorectal damage and even more severe constipation. In healthy people, anorectal damage caused by large stools is gradual, and the onset of constipation is delayed.

- *Hemorrhoidal disease.* By some accounts, over 50% of Americans suffer from hemorrhoidal disease by the age of 50, and by other accounts, over two-thirds do. Large stools related to fiber are the primary cause of this self-perpetuating condition. As it develops, enlarged internal hemorrhoids permanently constrict the anal canal. The narrowing of the anal canal requires more straining to move the bowels. The more the person strains, the more the hemorrhoids become enlarged, and the need for straining increases.

- *Straining:* Normal defecation requires no more effort than urination. Large stools caused by fiber (and resulting constipation) require additional external force to move them because they exceed the width of the anal canal. This action is accomplished with the help of the abdominal and pelvic muscles. The applied force and pressure on the intestinal lining and walls from large stools causes inevitable damage to the rectum and anal canal. The resulting conditions are extremely painful, because the anus has the highest degree of innervation among all of the alimentary canal's organs:

  - *Anal abscess.* An injury of the anal canal mucosa lining may cause small ulcerations. The spontaneous healing of the ulcer may leave encapsulated pus inside the wound. This condition is extremely painful, because of the continuous pressure of the pus on the upper skin layer. This condition may require treatment with antibiotics and/or surgery.

  - *Anal fissures*—a tear in the skin lining the anus. Fissures are particularly hard to heal, because each consecutive hard stool damages newly grown tissues and breaks the wound apart.

  - *Anal fistulas (non-congenital)*—permanent ducts (passages) from the anal canal into the perianal (around anus) region or vagina. Fistulas form as a result of ulcerations, fissures, or abscesses inside the anal canal. The fistulas cause the continuous spillage of stools, which is particularly unsafe when the fistula terminates inside the vagina. In almost all cases, elimination of fistulas requires surgery.

– *Rectal prolapse.* This condition is likely to affect older people, and is characterized by the protrusion of the rectal wall or just the rectal mucosa through the anus (to the outside). Rectal prolapse requires urgent medical intervention.

– *Withdrawal of stools.* This problem is particularly acute among children, and it happens in response to pain and discomfort related to the above complications. The withdrawal of stools causes fecal impaction, which usually requires manual disimpaction, because laxatives are no longer effective. The most dangerous thing one can do (and often does) in this case is to give a child more fiber. In this case, there is a high probability of stools spilling into the small intestine, and fiber causing obstruction.

There is just one solution to straining-related complications—elimination of fiber from the diet, resulting in the semi-soft or even watery stools that will allow healing, and soft, small stools thereafter. (See Chapter 11, *Avoiding the Perils of Transition.*)

▪ *Diverticular disease (diverticulosis).* When fiber increases stool size beyond the normal confinements of the large intestine, it causes the outward protrusion of the intestinal wall. The pouches that are formed are called diverticula (plural). When the diverticulum (singular) gets inflamed, the condition is called diverticulitis. The diverticulitis is localized to specific diverticula because they may retain fibrous fecal mass indefinitely. The eventual inflammations inside the diverticula are caused by the same mechanical, chemical, and bacteriological factors that are behind IBS, ulcerative colitis, and Crohn's disease. (See Chapter 9, *Ulcerative Colitis and Crohn's Disease.*)

▪ *Irritable bowel syndrome:* Along with undigested fiber's mechanical properties, increased acidity causes irritation of the mucosa lining inside the colon, hence the term *irritable bowel.* In most cases, before the onset of ulcerative colitis, the removal of fiber from the diet reverses IBS within a few days. A reintroduction of fiber into the diet brings this condition back as soon as it reaches the large intestine.

- *Ulcerative colitis.* Disbacteriosis and fermentation-related acidity strips intestinal mucosa of its protective properties and leads to ulcerations of the intestinal walls. The healing of ulcers is further complicated by a pronounced deficiency of vitamin K (blood-clotting factor), which is caused by disbacteriosis. The removal of fiber and reinoculation of the large intestine with bacteria is often all that is needed to reverse both conditions.
- *Megacolon.* The stretching of the large intestine by expanded, impacted fiber compromises colonic motility (the normal peristaltic transport of stools inside the large intestine), resulting in a condition known as *colonic inertia,* which is a precursor to *fecal impaction* (an abnormal accumulation of compressed stools, which stretch the colon and rectum even further); hence, *megacolon.*
- *Anorectal nerve damage.* The irreversible stretching (distention) of the rectum, and anorectal nerve damage (both caused by large stools from fiber) diminishes defecation reflexes, and in turn requires even more stool volume (obtained from fiber or laxatives, of course) to stimulate defecation. At one point the reflexes may disappear altogether, which is a problem that can be alleviated only with even more fiber and/or laxatives.
- *Fecal Incontinence.* The loss of anal sphincter control causes an uncontrolled escape of stools. The condition is further exacerbated with excess gas, because the sphincter tone isn't sufficient to contain it, and the release of gas provokes spillage. Both problems—anal sphincter damage and excess gas—are caused by, respectively, large stools comprised mainly from fiber and bacterial fiber fermentation. Obviously, the exclusion of all types of fiber is the first step in combating this devastating problem.
- *Precancerous polyps.* The normal bacteria that reside in the intestinal mucosa (epithelium) provide non-specific immune defense against external pathogens and internal cellular pathologies. Disbacteriosis strips the epithelium of its protective properties. Mechanical abrasion from large stools (caused by fiber) and chemical damage from fermentation-related acidity (from too much fiber) contribute to cellular damage, and the formation of polyps—neoplasms (new growth of tissues) that protrude from the epithelium, and have a high risk of becoming malignant tumors.

- *Colon cancer.* A single polyp increases the risk of colon cancer by 2.5% at 5 years, 8% at 10 years, and 24% at 20 years.[15] Ulcerative colitis alone increases the risk of colon cancer 3,200% (32 times). Both conditions—polyps and ulcerative colitis—are connected by the same common denominators, fiber and disbacteriosis.

**Fiber's affect on the genitourinary organs: Unlucky neighbors**

The bladder and reproductive organs (collectively, *genitourinary* organs) share common space at the bottom of the abdominal cavity with the small and large intestines. The sigmoid colon bend is situated right next to the bladder; a thin wall separates the female rectum from the vagina; the uterus and ovaries are enveloped by intestines; the male prostate gland is located in the immediate proximity of the rectum. You get the picture.

This layout may offend your sense of sexual esthetics, but it has been working quite well for millennia, except when the intestines are expanded by large stools and gases "courtesy" of fiber. The resulting outward pressure of distended intestines on reproductive organs, even slight pressure, causes symptoms identical to genitourinary disorders, such as prostatitis, endometritis, cystitis, and urethritis—respectively, an inflammation of the prostate gland, endometrium, bladder, and urinary canal.

Unfortunately, modern day gynecologists and urologists aren't trained to recognize the impact of intestinal disorders and large stools on the genitourinary organs, and may prescribe potent pain relievers, antibiotics, diuretics, or antidepressants to treat these phantom conditions instead of advising patients to eliminate fiber, large stools, or treat constipation. Here are some of the results:

*Premenstrual Syndrome* (PMS). The impact of fiber's side effects is particularly profound prior to menstruation. The physical metamorphosis that precedes menstruation—water and sodium retention, enlargement of endometrium and ovaries, egg movement through the fallopian tube(s)—predisposes women to premenstrual syndrome. The ensuing symptoms, such as Mittelschmerz (*middle pain,* a condition related to the enlargement of ovaries during ovu-

lation), cramping (primary dysmenorrhea, a condition not related
to physical anomaly), abdominal pain, and backache, are often related to undue pressure by distended intestines on the uterus, fallopian tubes, and ovaries, which become hypersensitive during ovu-
lation.

Correspondingly, the emotional aspect of PMS isn't related to
hormonal changes so much, but to the constant presence of pain
and discomfort, which trigger the continuous release of stress hormones. In turn, stress hormones cause migraine headaches and patterns of social interaction typical for PMS sufferers.

PMS is often accompanied by intermittent constipation and diarrhea. Evidently, both conditions are usually already present before
menstruation. They simply become more pronounced and noticeable during this period.

*Nausea and Vomiting during Pregnancy (NVP).* If fiber causes so
many problems during menstruation, imagine its impact during
pregnancy, especially the last two trimesters, when NVP can no
longer be written off on hormonal changes. That's why many pregnant women unconsciously switch to liquid-only diets, in most
cases with deleterious effect for both themselves and the fetus, as
these diets lack essential proteins, fats, and micronutrients.

NVP is easy to understand: the metamorphosis that is taking
place in the abdominal cavity to accommodate the expanding
uterus affects the stomach's ability to expand and accommodate fiber; the outward pressure on the small intestines increases the
chances for intestinal obstructions by fiber. A pattern of diarrhea
and vomiting caused by all of the above causes a predisposition to
constipation.

If you're planning to become pregnant, study this book and wean
yourself off fiber in advance of your pregnancy. If you're already
pregnant, and suffer from NVP, just follow the guidelines in later
chapters to restore the normal physiological functioning of the
large intestine, so you can get off fiber without incurring the wrath
of constipation, that comes with sudden fiber withdrawal. It will
not only reduce or eliminate NVP altogether, but will also prevent
you from developing numerous gastric disorders, related to persistent vomiting, diarrhea, and constipation.

Restoring normal intestinal flora in advance of pregnancy and maintaining adequate nutrition will improve the quality of your breast milk and enhance your ability to breastfeed. And, of course, all of the above will have a positive impact on fetal development, and the health, growth, intellect, and future life of your child.

*Rectocele.* The prolapse (herniation) of the rectal wall into the vagina is another common affliction related to fiber consumption (around 18.4% prevalence[16] in the general population). Rectocele is most likely related to large stools and severe straining. Most, if not all, medical texts on this topic don't mention the rectal connection, and write off rectocele on abnormal childbirth, weakness of the pelvic support system, and unspecified congenital conditions. These are doubtful assertions, because rectocele affects women who have never been pregnant, the incidence of rectocele increases with age—which means the condition wasn't congenital, and the rectum wall can't simply prolapse into the vagina unless some external force pushes it down there. In most women, fiber-laden stools and straining are most likely these forces. To avoid corrective surgery and enjoy sex into the wee years, cutting out fiber, and avoiding constipation and straining, is the best prescription to preventing rectocele.

*Vaginitis.* An inflammation of the vagina's mucosal lining related to vaginal yeast infection *(vulvovaginal candidiasis),* which is characterized by an enlargement of the labia, inflammation of the external opening of the urethra, itching, vaginal discharge, odor, and pain during intercourse and urination. Candidiasis is directly related to disbacteriosis, that may be caused, contributed to, or sustained by excess fiber. The absence of normal flora causes an overgrowth of yeast bacteria (Candida albicans) and reduction of nonspecific immunity.

Candidiasis affects up to 75%[17] of American women during their lifetimes—a number which accurately mirrors societal dietary dogma. Fiber reduction by itself isn't sufficient to eliminate candidiasis. An affected person and her sexual partner must restore normal intestinal flora as described in Chapter 11, *Avoiding the Perils of Transition* (see page 211).

Candidiasis infects men via sexual intercourse with an infected partner or from contamination of the urethral opening with his own fecal matter. In this case, the condition is likely to be diagnosed as urinary tract infection (UTI) or *prostatitis,* and a harsh treatment with antibiotics may follow, which will only exacerbate disbacteriosis and its side effects.

*Urinary obstruction.* The male urethra, the canal that discharges urine from the bladder, passes through the prostate gland. An accumulation of large stools in the rectum (typical for organic constipation and fecal impaction) causes strong pressure on the prostate gland which in turn squeezes the urethra and blocks urine flow. This blockage of the urethra interferes with normal urination, may stimulate frequent urination, and cause pain typical of prostatitis and benign prostate enlargement.

*Sexual dysfunction.* Finally, keep in mind that just a thin wall separates the rectum from the vagina, and an equally thin wall separates the rectum from the prostate gland. That's why even the mildest intercourse is capable of stimulating the defecation urge or the release of gas in the least desirable moments. The fear of such an occurrence tenses the anal muscles in both men and women, inhibits erection and arousal, and precludes orgasms, particularly among affected women. Good sex ain't a laxative, though it often works that way. If you wish to enjoy relaxing, worry-free sex, cut out the fiber and finish reading this book.

**Fiber's affect on heart disease: A bargain with the devil**

Dietary fiber represents from 5 to 10% of the total content of consumed carbohydrates. For example, to get just the 30 grams of recommended daily fiber in natural form, you need to consume 300 to 600 grams of carbohydrates. But excessive carbohydrate consumption is the primary cause of diabetes, obesity, hypertension, elevated triglycerides, and hyperinsulinemia—the best researched and most obvious precursors of heart disease.

In this context, the idea of protecting yourself from heart disease with a high-carb, high-fiber diet is as preposterous as the suggestion to treat high blood pressure with bloodletting (less blood being equated with less blood pressure). That the patient would soon die from anemia or cardiac arrest caused by acute hypotension (extremely low blood pressure)—well, that's a problem for the undertaker. Nonetheless, the idea of using dietary fiber against heart disease got some traction, because certain types of fiber in combination with a low-fat diet slightly reduce LDL ("bad") cholesterol.

To avoid the onslaught of natural carbs, you may try to fool the system, and replace these carbs with just fiber supplements. Well here, courtesy of the American Heart Association's research, is a description of the probable outcome:

---

...a fiber supplement containing a mixture of guar gum, pectin, soy fiber, pea fiber, and corn bran lowered LDL cholesterol by 7% to 8% in hypercholesterolemic participants after 15 weeks compared with those taking a placebo. These reductions persisted throughout the 51-week follow-up period with continued use of supplements. Potential risks of excessive use of fiber supplements include reduced mineral absorption and a myriad of gastrointestinal disturbances.[18]

---

"Impressive," isn't it? "Reduced mineral absorption," meaning more hypertension, more arthritis, more osteoporosis, and a "myriad of gastrointestinal disturbances." Well, "myriad" is an understatement, a euphemism for gastritis, gastric and duodenal ulcers, enteritis, Crohn's disease, irritable bowel syndrome, colitis, diarrhea, bloating, flatulence, and, of course, constipation and its side effects. Besides, according to the same research by the American Heart Association, the fiber-heart disease theory is a fluke anyway. It appears to work on paper, but not in real life:

---

The rate of CHD [cardio-vascular disease] mortality was reported to be inversely associated with fiber intake across 20 industrialized nations, but adjustment for fat intake removed the association. Similarly, a 20-year cohort study of 1,001 middle-aged men in Ireland and Boston reported significant inverse association between fiber intake and risk of CHD, but the association diminished when other risk factors were controlled.[19]

---

Well, well, well. Since heart disease isn't a topic covered in this book, it's up to you to decide who's a devil's advocate, and who's not.

## Summary

This entire chapter in itself is a summary of the most prominent problems caused by fiber. Hence, the list of key points is brief:

- Fiber from plants wasn't consumed by humans during most of evolution because until very recently there was no means to process fiber.
- Sugars and starches are broken down in the small intestine, but the small intestine can't break down fiber because the human body lacks the necessary enzyme.
- There are two types of fiber—soluble and insoluble. Soluble fiber causes osmotic diarrhea, because it retains water inside the large intestine. Insoluble fiber absorbs digestive juices and expands four to five times its original size. The expansion of insoluble fiber may cause esophageal, gastric, and intestinal obstruction.
- Fiber interferes with gastric (stomach) digestion, and is the leading cause of indigestion, GERD, heartburn, gastritis, and ulcers.
- Fiber obstructs the small intestines throughout their entire length, and is the primary cause of intestinal disorders. Because intestines are responsible for the assimilation of nutrients, fiber-related inflammatory disease causes malnutrition, and an acute deficiency of vitamins and minerals.
- Children are particularly vulnerable to fiber, because their digestive organs are smaller than adults.
- Fiber is a primary cause of flatulence. The gases are formed during fiber's fermentation inside the large intestine.
- Fiber increases stools weight and size, and causes mechanical damage to colorectal organs. Even minor damage leads to constipation. When more fiber is added to combat constipation, more damage is incurred.
- Fiber's impact on the small and large intestine affects male and female genitourinary organs because of their proximity. Women

are particularly vulnerable because female reproductive organs occupy a large space in the abdominal cavity, and because of the specifics of menstruation.

- Fiber has no measurable affect on heart disease. If anything, it worsens the outcome because of the excessive carbohydrate consumption that comes with fiber.

- Patients who try taking supplemental fiber to reduce cholesterol levels develop a "myriad" of digestive disorders.

***

# Footnotes

[1] Functional Constipation; Ch. 7: Rome II: The Functional Gastrointestinal Disorders by Douglas A. Drossman (editor);

[2] Dietary, Functional and Total Fiber, Dietary Reference Intakes for Energy, Carbohydrate, Fiber, Fat, Fatty Acids, Cholesterol, Protein, and Amino Acids (Macronutrients) (2002), Food and Nutrition Board (FNB), Institute of Medicine (IOM); http://books.nap.edu/books/0309085373/html/265.html

[3] The American Dietetic Association recommends fiber for children only after two years of age, and no more than 5 grams + the child's age. That amounts to 7 to 13 grams of fiber for the two to eight-year-old age group. Health implications of dietary fiber, J Am Diet Assoc 2002;102:993–1000; http://www.eatright.org/Public/Other/index_adar2_0702.cfm

[4] Mayo Clinic; Fiber–A Good Carb; Consumer Health Tips and Products; June 11, 2004; http://www.mayoclinic.org/news2004-mchi/2309.html

[5] KELLOGG'S ALL-BRAN WITH EXTRA FIBER; NDB No: 08253; USDA National Nutrient Database for Standard Reference; http://www.nal.usda.gov/fnic/foodcomp/search/index.html

[6] Metamucil Psyllium Fiber for Regularity, Smooth Texture, Orange; Package Detail; www.dgustore.com

Metamucil Powder; RiteAid Patient Counseling; © First Databank; The Hearst Corporation; http://www.riteaid.com/pharmacy/monographs/monographs.php?edtn_cde=6 10904&lang_cde=E&lbl_name=Metamucil+Powder

[8] Weston A. Price, D.D.S. Nutrition and Physical Degeneration; 6th Edition. (Examples of tooth decay related to fiber consumption are provided through out the book.)

[9] There is still considerable controversy as to whether the pyloric valve is completely closed during gastric digestion or not, hence "locked" is written in parenthesis. Still, whatever the mechanisms, the stomach has a remarkable ability to retain its content until it is almost completely liquefied. For more information, see *The Pyloric Sphincteric Cylinder in Health and Disease* by A.D. Kleet; Internet edition: http://med.plig.org/index.html

[10] Hiatus Hernia; The Merck Manual of Diagnosis and Therapy; 3:20; http://www.merck.com/mrkshared/mmanual/section3/chapter20/20j.jsp

[11] Pancreatitis: Inflammation of the pancreas; The Merck Manual of Diagnosis and Therapy; 3:26; http://www.merck.com/mrkshared/mmanual/section3/chapter26/26a.jsp

[12] Crohn's Disease; The Merck Manual of Diagnosis and Therapy; 3:31; http://www.merck.com/mrkshared/mmanual/section3/chapter31/31b.jsp

[13] Functional Constipation; C3: p. 389; Rome II: The Functional Gastrointestinal Disorders by Douglas A. Drossman (editor);

[14] Dietary, Functional and Total Fiber—Summary; Dietary Reference Intakes for Energy, Carbohydrate, Fiber, Fat, Fatty Acids, Cholesterol, Protein, and Amino Acids (Macronutrients); Food and Nutrition Board; Institute of Medicine; 2002; 7:265; http://books.nap.edu/books/0309085373/html/265.html

[15] What are polyps; Colon Polyps & Colon Cancer; D. E. Mansell, MD; http://personalweb.sunset.net/~mansell/polyp.htm

[16] Pelvic Organ Prolapse in the Women's Health Initiative: Gravity and Gravidity; Hendrix SL., Clark A., Nygaard I., Aragaki A., Barnabei V., McTiernan A.; Am J Obstet Gynecol 2002;186:1160–1166.

[17] Vaginitis Due to Vaginal Infections; National Institute of Allergy and Infectious Diseases (division of National Institutes of Health); http://www.niaid.nih.gov/factsheets/stdvag.htm

[18] Linda Van Horn, PhD, RD; Fiber, Lipids, and Coronary Heart Disease; A Statement for Healthcare Professionals From the Nutrition Committee; American Heart Association; http://circ.ahajournals.org/cgi/content/full/95/12/2701

[19] Ibid (same as above).

*All truth passes through three stages. First, it is ridiculed.*
*Second, it is violently opposed. Third, it is*
*accepted as being self-evident.*
Arthur Schopenhauer (1788 - 1860)

# CHAPTER TWO

## WATER DAMAGE

The infatuation with fiber brought with it another menace—the proverbial eight glasses of water. Everyone and their dog insists that you MUST drink eight glass of water a day for health and beauty. Well, if you follow this advice, you're assured of disease and premature aging, which is just the opposite of the original intent.

### Water abuse: They play with words, you pay with health

Drinking more water does nothing to lower cholesterol, nothing to prevent colon cancer, nothing to make stools "wetter" or softer, and nothing to alleviate constipation. If anything, the more you drink, the worse all of those things are going to get, including fiber dependence and constipation.

Why, then, does the advice to drink more water invariably accompany the advice to eat more fiber? Apparently, because of associative word play: if a hard stool is *dry,* then water supposedly makes it *moist.* As it turns out, this is pure fiction, based on observational conjectures derived from several unrelated facts:

- Conjecture #1: *Because fiber absorbs water (true), it will in-crease stool moisture.* Wrong! Dietary fiber in stools doesn't re-tain water any better than other cellular components, except psyl-lium seeds in laxatives[1] (a mere 5% more). Word play: *dry/moist.*
- Conjecture #2: *Because fiber is so highly water-absorbent (true), it requires additional water.* Wrong for two reasons! First, up to 75% of fiber,[2] including insoluble fiber, gets fermented by intes-tinal bacteria and doesn't require any water. Second, the remain-ing fiber gets all the water it needs from up to seven liters of di-gestive juices, which are secreted daily inside the alimentary ca-nal. Word play: *dry/wet, absorb/water.*
- Conjecture #3: *Water is needed to prevent intestinal obstructions from dietary fiber:* Wrong! Water, actually, expands the fiber four to five times its original volume and weight,[3] and if anything makes obstruction even more likely. Word play: *plug/solvent.*
- Conjecture #4: *Water is needed to prevent esophageal obstruc-tions with fiber laxatives.* True, water is needed to dissolve fiber powder before taking it, but this has nothing to do with regular food, bodily needs, or constipation, only with drug safety. Word play: *dumb/and dumber.*

If you still have your doubts (can't really blame you), here is a quote from a *Journal of American Dietetic Association*'s article, entitled "Health Implications of Dietary Fiber":

It is a common but erroneous belief that the increased weight [of stool] is due primarily to water.[4]

But that's not all. Too much water (with or without the fiber) causes more problems than you may realize. Besides, you may consume too much water even if you ignore the ubiquitous "eight glasses" advice altogether. This happens because our bodies re-plenish water from four principal sources:
- *From drinking water.* Tap, well, spring, and mineral are the pri-mary sources of unadulterated water. Its volume is apparent and easily measurable, because that's what you drink—100% water.
- *From fluids and drinks of all kinds:* colas, seltzer, coffee, tea, juices, dairy, wine, beer, milk, soups, sauces, and so forth. The

water content ranges from 85–99.9%, and most of it is all apparent and measurable as well.

- *Water hidden in solid food.* Water is the largest single component of most food, ranging from 50–70% in meats to 75–96% in fruits and vegetables. This water isn't apparent until you squeeze it out under the press or in the juicer.
- *Water from metabolic oxidation.* Water is formed as the by-product of many biochemical reactions that take place inside the body, and is actively reused. This water is hidden, completely out of view.

Hidden water happens to be as real as water from any other source. But because almost no one counts hidden water, the total daily intake may easily go through the roof. Keep reading!

### Eight glasses: Fountain of youth or fountain of death?

Though we look rather solid, and feel dry to the touch, anywhere from 41 to 84% of our body weight is represented by water alone. The spread is so wide because of age, fat (adipose tissue), and protein (muscles) content. In general, a frail old person will have the lowest ratio of water content to total body weight, while newborns and infants will have the highest. For adults (19 to 50 years of age) the water content ratio ranges from 43 to 73% for men, and 41 to 60% for women. The water content decreases in overweight people, because adipose tissue contains less water (10–40%) than does lean tissue (75%). For the same reason—more fat—women's bodies contain less water than men's. (Source: all figures.[5])

Certainly this leading component of body chemistry is extremely important for our health, and indeed, water's profound deficit may cause death, and death happens rather fast in its absence. But what about an excess of water? Can it cause a "slow death"?

Yes, it can, and it does. But before analyzing the meaning and implication of "slow death," let's establish a norm. In other words, what's the average daily water requirement for the average adult?

Since this question is so controversial, let's quote directly from a well-regarded academic textbook. (The abbreviation *ca.* means *circa,* academic speak for "approximately.") Hold on to your toilet seat:

A person weighing 70 kg [155 lbs] requires at least ca. 1,750 ml [59 oz] water per day. Of this amount ca. 650 ml is obtained by drinking, ca. 750 ml is the water contained in solid food, and ca. 350 ml is oxidation water. If more than this amount is consumed by a healthy person it is excreted by the kidneys, but in people with heart and kidney disease it may be retained (edema; pp 505, 771f).—*Human Physiology; Robert F. Schmidt, Gerhard Thews, 2nd edition*

As you can see, only 1,400 ml (47 oz), or about six glasses of water, are required every day from food and drink in almost equal proportion. The rest—the hidden oxidation water—is derived from the body's internal chemistry.

Also, please note one crucial point: 1,750 ml is equal to about seven-and-a-half glasses of water. This is where the initial round figure of "eight glasses" (1,890 ml) originally came from. What *Human Physiology* makes plain is that only 650 ml, or about two-and-a-half glasses of water, "is obtained by drinking." Not eight, as we have all been told to drink.

Here's another excerpt, this time from *The Merck Manual of Diagnostic and Therapy,* which is considered the gold-standard medical reference source and "must have" manual for any physician and researcher worth his or her salt. *The Merck* is even more miserly and specific:

...a daily intake of 700 to 800 ml is needed to match total water losses and remain in water balance...[6]

Just 700 to 800 ml, or about three full glasses of water, derived from all food and drink for the entire day. One average-sized Valencia orange contains 104 grams of water; one medium-sized tomato 200 grams; one eight-inch cucumber 286 grams. Essentially, two oranges, one tomato, and one cucumber will provide all of the water you need for the entire day.

Hard to believe, right? Then read *The Merck Manual* on the Internet (it's free), and verify for yourself that the quote above is accurate and taken within the proper context. Print that article, highlight the relevant passage, and show it to your doctors, dieticians, nutritionists, parents, partners, colleagues, spouses, or anyone who insists that you must drink eight glasses of water along with all other food and drink. Out of stubbornness some may dismiss my book, but not *The Merck.*

Now let's do the "eight glasses" math: eight glasses of water times 8 oz per glass equals 64 oz, or 1.89 liters. This amount of water alone is more than the total daily replacement needs for the average adult, by either *Human Physiology* or *The Merck*'s criteria. And this is just drinking water we're talking about. After adding up all of the water from beverages, water concealed in solid food, and water derived from invisible metabolic oxidation, you end up getting much, much more than your daily requirement.

And this is exactly what most Americans have been doing for several decades: consuming two to three times more water than they need. At the present time, the average daily water consumption by men in the United States stands at 3.7 liters (125 oz, or almost a gallon), and 2.7 liters (91 oz, or 11.5 glasses) by women.[7] And that's before adding the water from solid food and oxidation.

So why, despite the obvious facts and common knowledge, do most medical authorities think so very differently and urge people to drink more, and not less?

### Water requirements: In Big Brother's loving care

The reason lies in the approach. While this book relies on academic and medical references, medical authorities in the United States rely on *Recommended Dietary Allowances* (RDAs), a set of guidelines published by the *National Research Council* (NRC). The NRC is funded by the United States government, and it is chartered to determine and set the nation's paternalistic nutritional standards through the *Food and Nutrition Board* (FNB), its policy-setting arm.

The RDAs are best known from the serving tables that appear on all food and supplements labels. The goals behind RDAs were certainly honorable, but some of the results are typical by-products of a government bureaucracy that's answerable to no one: wrong policy, bad results, even more wrong policy to justify the results.

The very first suggestion to drink eight glasses of water came from the academic figures already cited. Unfortunately, the government's proxies failed to forcefully remind the scientists and public alike that the "eight glasses" was meant to include all water consumed daily—water from beverages, from oxidation, and hidden in solid food.

A few decades later, after most Americans started to heed that suggestion in earnest, the *Food and Nutrition Board* surveyed the average water consumption of people in the United States (the already mentioned 3.7 and 2.7 liters for men and women respectively), and presumed that this was the amount all the rest of us must drink. (Source: *National Health and Nutrition Examination Survey* (NHANES) III[8]; *2004 Dietary Reference Intakes for Water, Potassium, Sodium, Chloride, and Sulfate.*[9])

What's wrong with relying on population surveys? Well, for starters, surveys don't take into account a simple fact, that most Americans have been hooked on the likes of *Folgers, Lipton, Tropicana, Coke, and Budweiser.* The more you drink these beverages, the more water is required to replace the losses caused by caffeine, sugar, and alcohol, which are all potent diuretics. That's why water consumption in the United States is so high to begin with, even among those who ignore the "eight glasses" advice.

Next, for the sake of experiment, you can easily increase *water loss* by simply having a healthy person drink more water. Even a three-year-old knows that the more you drink, the more you pee, and the more you pee, the more you need to drink. In a nutshell, that's how the "finest" government-funded scientists arrived at their findings and recommendations—by measuring the end result of their initial bad advice to drink eight glasses of water in addition to all food and drinks.

### Overhydration: Too much of a good thing?

Now comes the "slow death" part. Can you wash away your health with too much water? According to *Human Physiology,* yes, you can:

*Overdosage symptoms.* If larger amounts of hypotonic solutions [water with low concentration of mineral salts] are taken within a short time into the body, or large amounts of salt are lost, there can be a transient influx of water into the intracellular space (pp. 771f). The resulting syndrome, called water intoxication, consists of impaired performance, headache, nausea or convulsions (symptoms of cerebral edema).

---

Translation into everyday English: long before the body starts twitching uncontrollably, too much water from food and drinks causes edema, fatigue, migraine, and symptoms of digestive distress (nausea).

But that's not all. Other side effects happen along the way, principally because of ongoing mineral loss from excessive urination. Here's a partial list:

- *Constipation.* Potassium is a principal electrolyte, responsible for water retention inside human, bacterial, and plant cells. Overhydration causes the gradual loss of potassium through urine. Potassium deficiency, not shortage of water, is the principal reason behind stool dryness. The dry stool causes constipation, because it is hard, abrasive, and difficult to eliminate.
- *Kidney disease.* It doesn't take a medical degree to understand that kidneys pumping two, three, four or five times more water than normal will wear out faster. (The resources of our internal organs was determined by evolution long before Coke, Pepsi, and Bud came on the scene.) Kidney stones in particular are associated with calcium deficiencies that may result from either a deficiency in one's diet or from loss related to overhydration.
- *Urinary disorders.* Urinary infections are a common side effect of overhydration. With too many carbs and too much water in the system, urine alkalinity drops, acidity goes up, and the bladder and urethra become hospitable to pathogenic bacteria, which have an affinity for an acidic environment. Elevated glucose in the urine from too many dietary carbohydrates greatly stimulates these infections by providing plentiful feed for pathogens—a warm, dark bladder becomes just as hospitable to bacteria as a sweet-and-sour Petri dish.
- *Digestive disorders.* The more you drink right before, during, or within the first few hours after a meal, the more difficult and time-consuming digestion becomes, because it requires corre-

spondingly more hydrochloric acid and digestive enzymes to bring their concentration up to the optimal level.[10] The high volume of liquid in the stomach is prone to causing heartburn, which results from the spillage of acidified content into the unprotected esophagus. Indigestion, or delayed digestion (gastroparesis) causes gastritis—an inflammation of the stomach's mucosa, which may eventually lead to ulcers. Chronic indigestion may also result from a chloride deficiency (hypochloremia), especially when excess water consumption is accompanied by reduced or salt-free diets.

- *Degenerative bone disease.* A loss of minerals in general, calcium in particular, leads to bone softening—*osteomalacia* in adults, *scoliosis* in young adults, and *rickets* in children. (Osteoporosis is a *bone tissue* disease, and not a *mineral deficiency* condition, as mistakenly thought by most people, including most medical professionals.[11] A loss of bone tissue—collagen that makes up the bone matrix—leads to bone brittleness, not softness, as from the loss of minerals.)

- *Premature aging.* Facial bones determine our overall appearance and create a perception of age that no makeup or plastic surgery can hide. Because of a comparatively low physical load, facial bones experience the fastest loss of bone tissue and minerals. I call this *Mick Jagger syndrome,* after the characteristic facial appearance of this famous performer. This isn't surprising—hyperactive stage performers perspire profusely, and drink gallons of water on and off the stage. It's just more apparent on Mr. Jagger's face because he's underweight, and has no fat to cover up a profound bone loss.

- *Muscular disorders.* Calcium and magnesium are key regulators of muscle contractions. A deficiency of these two minerals is broadly associated with fibromyalgia, fatigue, cramps, tremors, involuntary flinching, and many other conditions that affect not just body muscles, but also the eyes, blood vessels, intestines, heart, womb, and all other organs that are controlled by the muscles.

- *Unstable blood pressure.* Hypertension and hypotension naturally follow water binges. First, as the volume of blood plasma increases from absorbed water, blood pressure rises. As long as the kidneys remain healthy, the excess is quickly removed, along with the minerals. As the minerals become depleted, the volume of plasma goes down in order to maintain its chemical stability, and low blood pressure sets in. Even though low blood pressure isn't likely to cause heart attack or stroke, it is as dangerous, because it causes dizziness, drowsiness, and disorientation—not the most desirable state for driving a car, managing heavy machinery, or caring for a child.

- *Heart disease.* The heart is a muscular organ. Its health and efficiency mirrors the rest of the body, and anything that affects the muscles on the outside, impacts the heart on the inside. Over 400,000 Americans die annually from sudden cardiac arrest. Their hearts simply stop beating. Eighty percent of all cardiac arrests result from "electrical dysfunction"[12] of the heart muscles. Lo and behold, minerals—calcium, magnesium, sodium, potassium, and chloride—happen to be the major carriers and/or regulators of those electrical signals, and overhydration is the primary cause of their disbalance, be it an excess of potassium and magnesium, or a depletion of calcium and chloride.

Not surprisingly, cardiac arrest preceded the demise of Dr. Atkins, who was also an avid advocate for "eight glasses." He was fitted with a pacemaker to correct "electrical dysfunction," but died anyway a year later under mysterious circumstances. According to numerous press accounts,[13] his autopsy and medical records revealed a history of heart attacks, congestive heart failure, hypertension, and cardiomyopathy—a heart enlargement typical for overweight men who suffer from high blood pressure.

If you care to learn what kind of harm mineral deficiencies can cause, please review *The Merck's* "Mineral Deficiency And Toxicity" chapter[14] on the Internet. Once you learn how important these minerals are, and how profound their loss can be on your health, you'll understand why a blood test—which provides a relative[15] mirror of your mineral status—is such an important diagnostic tool. And nothing dilutes blood faster and leaches those important minerals out of your body more than too much water does, especially filtered, processed, devitalized, soft water that you're most likely to consume from the tap, bottle, or with factory-made refreshments.

## Moderation: Easy said, easy done

Now we're primed for the key question: what should your total water intake be? (I didn't write "how much do you need to drink" on purpose, because water comes from other sources.)

- First, thirst should be the first indicator that your body needs more water. But be careful here—the more you drink, the thirstier you become. So you need to bring down your water consumption gradually.
- Second, the guideline to obtain 1.4–1.6 liters of water daily from all sources—water, drink, and food—is a reasonable one (the equivalent of 5 to 7 glasses). The other 400–500 ml will come from oxidation.
- Finally, we've already established that additional water isn't required to "dilute" fiber or prevent constipation. You already have plenty of water inside the GI tract to keep your stools moist.

The kidneys don't lie. Under normal circumstances, a healthy person should urinate no more than three to five times daily, and zero times during the night, while asleep. If you urinate more often, if the urine is colorless or transparent, or there's a large volume of it, your cumulative water intake is probably too high.

As always, there are exceptions. Keep these important points in mind:

- *Physical activities.* If you are physically active, exercise strenuously, visit a sauna, drench in hot baths, or perspire heavily for other reasons, your water needs increase in order to compensate for the losses with sweat, urine, and vapors in exhaled air.
- *Medical conditions.* If you have kidney disease or diabetes, or experience diarrhea or vomiting, your water needs increase to compensate for losses related to frequent urination, vomit or stool.
- *Age.* The thirst reflex may be blunted in the aged and infirm, and their water intake must be closely monitored. Too much water in this situation is as dangerous as too little, because older hearts and kidneys can't expel excess water as fast, and may cause life-threatening edema, hypertension, arrhythmia, blood clots, diarrhea, kidney failure, and many other medical emergencies.
- *Environment.* High temperatures, high altitudes, and low humidity (dry air) lead to rapid water loss through the lungs and skin

(the technical term is *insensible losses).* The rate of water loss in these circumstances may be up to ten times greater than normal.

- *Infants and toddlers* require 1.5 times more water than adults for the following reasons: a higher physiological turnover of water, larger skin area relative to body weight, larger percentage of body water, greater need by the kidneys to remove metabolites, and the inability to express thirst. Don't confuse "inability to express" with "ability to sense." Unlike socially conditioned adults, children's instincts are finely tuned to their bodily needs. The role of a parent or guardian is to provide fluids, but never to force children to drink. Obviously, the fluid provided shouldn't be juices or soft drinks. Fresh non-carbonated mineral water, preferably from a glass bottle, like *Evian, Panna,* or *Vichi,* are the best sources of drinking water for a growing child. Adequately breastfed babies don't require additional water.

- *Pregnancy.* Despite what you may have heard from medical professionals, pregnancy doesn't impose additional water requirements beyond an additional 30 ml (about 1 oz) per day.[16] Overhydration, along with the chronic deficit of electrolytes and minerals often induced by drinking too much water, is one of the reasons so many pregnant women suffer from edema, nausea, anemia, constipation, and inevitable bone disorders: osteomalacia (soft bones), osteoporosis, degenerative arthritis, periodontal disease, cavities, and many others.

- *Lactation.* Since up to 86% of breast milk is water, lactating mothers must drink an amount of water equal to the amount of milk they produce, or about 750 to 1000 ml (3 to 4 glasses) extra. Interestingly, most women add water, but fail to replace all of the essential fats, proteins, minerals, and microelements that they excrete with milk. This omission impacts their own health, and compromises the health of their babies too, because the quality of milk goes down, and the milk volume may run short or disappear altogether.

The impact of rapid *overhydration* is comparable to poisoning. Consuming too much water than is necessary over a long period of time is as bad, except the problems aren't as immediately obvious as they are after five to ten liters of water are ingested in one sitting. Finally, here are the additional reasons why too much water makes fiber dependence more pervasive and constipation worse:

- *Human anatomy.* The digestive organs aren't a straight tube, so none of the water that you drink streams down into your large intestine to moisten or flush out feces.
- *Physiology of digestion.* All water from food, drinks, saliva, and digestive juices—about seven liters daily—gets absorbed back into the bloodstream in the stomach and small intestine (75% to 90%), and the rest gets assimilated in the large intestine.
- *Minimal requirement.* Only 1% of all water involved in digestion[17]—the sum of all intake and the secretion of saliva and digestive juices—is excreted with stool. I repeat, only 1% (about 70 ml, or 2 oz).

As you can see, drinking *too little* water isn't going to make much immediate difference in the stool's shape, weight, moisture content, and consistency, while drinking *too much* will eventually make the stool dry and hard because of potassium depletion. As stools get drier, people begin adding more and more fiber and drinking more and more water, instead of less.

## Underhydration: The opposite side of the coin

What's the difference between *de*hydration and *under*hydration? Underhydration is on the opposite side of overhydration, but not yet as self-evident as dehydration. And that's why it's as treacherous as overhydration.

The subject of water's role in health and well-being is inseparable from certain essential minerals that help maintain the tight water balance inside the body. You can drink plenty, and still be underdehydrated, or even dehydrated, when those minerals are missing because of an inadequate diet, heavy perspiration, diarrhea, vomiting, kidney disease, and certain medical conditions.

Even then, neither underhydration nor dehydration are likely to cause constipation, because so little water is needed to maintain stool moisture. However, the shortage of those minerals and related ailments may and will cause constipation and fiber dependence.

**Chapter summary**

- The dependence on fiber to maintain regular stools is partially a result of chronic overconsumption of water.
- The volume of water consumed daily doesn't play any direct role in forming the stool or causing constipation.
- The recommendation to drink eight glasses of water in addition to food intake is wrong, because it doesn't take into account the substantial water content of food and water produced by the body's own metabolism.
- Actual daily water needs depend on age, weight, health, gender, occupation, climate, diet, and some other factors. It's individual for each person, and can't be generalized.
- Stool dryness and hardness isn't caused by water deficiency, and can't be overcome by drinking more water. To overcome dryness, one must restore intestinal flora and mineral balance, primarily potassium.
- Stool weight, mass, and form doesn't depend on the amount of consumed water. At most, normal stool contains under 75 ml of water (per 100 g), about five tablespoons.
- Excessive fluid consumption from all sources leads to a depletion of potassium, and is one of the major causes of constipation and ensuing dependence on fiber.
- Overconsumption of water causes a broad range of other conditions and diseases related to depletion and deficiencies of essential minerals and microelements, and adds additional stress on cardiovascular, genitourinary, and digestive organs.

\*\*\*

# Footnotes

[1]  Health implications of dietary fiber, J Am Diet Assoc 2002;102:993–1000;
http://www.eatright.org/Public/Other/index_adar2_0702.cfm

[2]  Health implications of dietary fiber—Position of ADA; J Am Diet Assoc.
1997;97:1157–1159;
http://www.eatright.org/Public/Other/index_adap1097.cfm

[3]  Water. Dietary Reference Intakes for Water, Potassium, Sodium, Chloride,
and Sulfate, The National Academies Press. 4–56:2003; www.nap.edu

[4]  Health implications of dietary fiber; J Am Diet Assoc 2002;102:993–1000;
http://www.eatright.org/Public/GovernmentAffairs/92_adar2_0702.cfm

[5]  Dietary Reference Intakes for Water, Potassium, Sodium, Chloride, and Sulfate (2004), Food and Nutrition Board, Institute of Medicine; pp 4–2:5.

[6]  Water and Sodium Metabolism, 2:12; The Merck Manual of Diagnosis and
Therapy;
http://www.merck.com/mrkshared/mmanual/section2/chapter12/12b.jsp

[7]  Dietary Reference Intakes for Water, Potassium, Sodium, Chloride, and Sulfate (2004), Food and Nutrition Board, Institute of Medicine; p 4–1;
http://books.nap.edu/books/0309091691/html/67.html#pagetop

[8]  National Health and Nutrition Examination Survey Home;
http://www.cdc.gov/nchs/nhanes.htm

[9]  Dietary Reference Intakes for Water, Potassium, Sodium, Chloride, and Sulfate (2004); Food and Nutrition Board, Institute of Medicine;
http://books.nap.edu/catalog/10925.html

[10]  The stomach doesn't secrete properly diluted digestive juices directly, as is
commonly and incorrectly thought. Specialized glands secret hydrochloric
acid and digestive enzymes into the stomach's cavity until their concentration
in the already existing volume of liquid is brought up to the proper level. The
liquids come from saliva, water, drinks, and solid food. When liquids aren't
available, the stomach will secrete necessary water.

[11]  Definition of osteoporosis: "A generalized, progressive diminution of bone
density (bone mass per unit volume), causing skeletal weakness, although
the ratio of mineral to organic elements is unchanged."— 5:57; The Merck
Manual of Diagnosis and Therapy;
http://www.merck.com/mrkshared/mmanual/section5/chapter57/57a.jsp

[12]  Cardiac Arrest; 16:206; The Merck Manual of Diagnosis and Therapy;
http://www.merck.com/mrkshared/mmanual/section16/chapter206/206a.jsp

[13]  Dr. Atkins was overweight, had heart problems: report; U.S. National-AFP
News; Feb 10, 2004.

[14]  Mineral Deficiency And Toxicity; 1:4; The Merck Manual of Diagnosis and
Therapy;
http://www.merck.com/mrkshared/mmanual/section1/chapter4/4a.jsp

[15]  Blood chemistry, especially mineral balances, is maintained within a fairly
narrow range at the expense of all other organs. If a blood test indicates certain mineral deficiencies, the situation may be quite dire. Not all deficiencies

related to mineral stores—certain endocrine (hormonal) disorders, for instance—may be perceptible through a blood test.

[16] Water and Electrolytes. *Recommended Dietary Allowances.* National Academy Press. 10th Edition, p. 250.

[17] R.F. Schmidt, G. Thews; Water and Electrolyte Balance; *Human Physiology, 2nd edition;* p. 764.

*Self-conceit may lead to self-destruction.*
Aesop (620 BC - 560 BC)

*Oh what a tangled web we weave,*
*When first we practice to deceive!*
Walter Scott (1771 - 1832)

# CHAPTER THREE

## ATKINS GOES TO SOUTH BEACH

The number of overweight and obese Americans is mind-shattering—by the turn of the 21$^{st}$ century, 137 million adults out of 210 million adults were overweight. In this context, it isn't surprising that in the United States alone over 35 million people have read Dr. Atkins' books with the intent to lose weight.

And the facts are: when the original *Diet Revolution* was published in 1972, only 14% of Americans were overweight. When *New Diet Revolution* was released, in 1992, 56% of Americans were. In 2003, when Dr. Atkins passed away, the figure rose to an incredible 65%—a staggering 464% jump in just one generation. Some revolution!

True, some of Dr. Atkins' readers lost weight. Fewer kept it off permanently. The majority failed completely. Some of these dieters ended up with more health problems after the diet than what they started with, including Dr. Atkins himself.

After Dr. Atkins' cardiac arrest, unquestionably from obesity-related complications, and his mysterious death one year later, ever-hopeful dieters jumped onto the South Beach bandwagon. Still, permanent weight loss remained as elusive as ever for most do-it-yourselfers, and the shortcomings of this new fad diet were just about the same as the shortcomings of the Atkins diet.

Both the Atkins and South Beach diets share a common denominator—a low intake of carbs. Though Dr. Agatston, the author of the South Beach Diet, denies that his diet is low-carb, it absolutely is: around 100 grams (3.6 oz) of carbs are allowed on South Beach, which is still 300% to 500% less than what most Americans consume daily.

Food from plants—grains, legumes, fruits and vegetables—are the major source of dietary carbohydrates and fiber. Whenever the amount of carbohydrates in any diet goes down four to five times, so does the corresponding amount of fiber. Thus, someone who was getting 25 to 50 grams (0.9–1.8 oz) of fiber on a regular diet is now getting only 5 to 10 grams (0.17–0.35 oz) on a low-carb one.

Not surprisingly, an instant and dramatic reduction of fiber in the diet causes constipation among dieters, who depend on a high intake of fiber to move their bowels—a condition this book defines as *latent constipation*. Here are the reasons behind this grief-causing dilemma:

- *Zero-residue food.* Unlike *indigestible* fiber, protein- and fat-rich food—eggs, meats, fowl, game, seafood, and dairy—*digest* almost completely. Only minute traces of these foods reach the large intestine intact.
- *Reduction of stool volume.* With negligible residue from fat and protein, the volume of stool gets proportionately smaller.
- *Decreased rectal sensitivity.* Because the large intestine adapted its elimination reflexes to a far larger stool volume, the defecation urge diminishes or disappears altogether.
- *Insufficient retention of moisture.* As stools keep accumulating, they compress, harden up, and dry out because the fiber that was retaining water (instead of bacteria) is no longer present in stools.
- *Pain and suffering.* Finally, straining and hard stools cause anorectal pain and discomfort, which, in turn, leads to unconscious avoidance or delay of defecation, and so the severity of constipation grows exponentially.

These cumulative problems are even more acute for someone who already has a prior history of constipation and anorectal disorders, such as hemorrhoidal and diverticular diseases, which are present in over half of the adults over, respectively, the ages of fifty and sixty.

When constipation becomes unbearable, most people just drop the diet and resume a high-carb, high-fiber lifestyle. Others may do so only after belatedly following Dr. Atkins advice to add fiber laxatives. Supplemental fiber forces out hardened stools with considerable pressure, often strong enough to cause hemorrhoidal prolapse and/or laceration of the anal canal. That's enough pain and suffering to stop any diet dead in its tracks.

We know, of course, that other people (including my family and many readers of my early books) embraced a low-carb lifestyle, lost weight, and weren't perturbed by constipation a tiny bit. These people belong to three distinct groups:

- The lucky ones who have intact intestinal flora, good toilet habits, and healthy guts untouched yet by anorectal disorders, such as hemorrhoidal disease or...
- People like myself, who take some or all of the steps described in this book to manage prior anorectal disorders and who overcame their earlier dependence on fiber, or...
- Those who take supplemental fiber laxatives, such as Metamucil or Citrucel, as Dr. Atkins recommended in his books.

Keep in mind that taking supplemental fiber isn't a question of having your cake and eating it, too. It is a man-made laxative medicine, and just as with all drugs, it comes with a price, which is amply described throughout this book. Still, a lot of people would gladly tolerate constipation for the fleeting chance of getting back into their prom gowns and tuxedos. But even that wasn't happening—they weren't losing weight or they couldn't keep it off beyond the first few weeks. Here are the reasons why.

### A diet empire built on crap, literally

If a diet doesn't work, the blame is always passed onto the dieter: you aren't strong-willed, you aren't committed, you aren't this, you aren't that. That's—forgive my bluntness—certified bull! The reasons diets don't work have little to do with will power, commitment, and other personal characteristics. All it really means, is that:

## IF THE DIET ISN'T WORKING FOR YOU, IT'S A BAD DIET!

If one lacks the know-how necessary to develop an effective diet, or the integrity to tell the hard truth that losing weight is very hard, all that's needed is a gimmick that shows at least some weight loss. The *induction* stage of the Atkins diet and *phase one* of the South Beach diet, both lasting the same 14 days, became these faultless gimmicks for their respective promoters, a Three-Card Monte of sorts, that suckers people in even if they sense a con.

The deception is right there, on the back cover of *The South Beach Diet,* stated in no uncertain terms:

---

Dr. Agathston's diet has produced consistently dramatic results (8 to 13 pounds lost (sic) in the first 2 weeks!) [...] Now you, too, can join the ranks of the fit and fabulous with *The South Beach Diet.* (Hardcover edition, 2003)

---

And right on the front cover of *Dr. Atkins' New Diet Revolution:*

---

Experience in 14 days the unique metabolic edge the Atkins Diet provides. (Hardcover edition, 1992)

---

Inside, Dr. Atkins provides specifics: depending on gender, current weight, and metabolic resistance, one can expect to lose between 2 and 16 lbs in 14 days (p. 172, Chart 17.2).

Indeed, who can resist an easy loss of 5–10–15 lbs in just two unforgettable weeks, when fat is melting like butter, pounds are dripping off, and the waistline is shrinking!

Actually, it wasn't fat that was melting, but "crap." It wasn't pounds that were dripping off, but body water. And it wasn't the waistline that was shrinking, but bloated intestines. And none of these are just "figures of speech" to grab your attention, but actual physiological occurrences behind *phantom weight loss*—a phe-

nomenon, I believe, that is defined, described, deciphered, and debunked for the first time in this book.

To fathom what I'm talking about, let's begin with a simplified
overview of energy metabolism, so you can perceive the difference
between real and phantom losses, as well as understand and appreciate the dynamics that drive the processes of weight loss and gain.

The body needs a continuous supply of glucose to fuel energy
metabolism. To maintain tight glucose homeostasis—stability
within a corridor of about 70 to 90 mg/dl—the body converts digested nutrients into cellular energy from carbohydrates or synthe-
sizes glucose in the liver from fatty and amino acids by means of
*gluconeogenesis.* These processes complement and back each
other up in case any one raw nutrient—carbohydrates, fats, or protein—is temporarily unavailable.

While fasting and at relative rest, a 155 lbs (70 kg) individual requires approximately 200 g (7 oz) of glucose during a 24-hour period. The formula to calculate the demand for your particular
weight is 2 mg of glucose per kg of body weight for each minute
(2 mg/kg/min).[1]

These 200 g, are, of course, approximate. The actual number
changes depending on the body and outside temperature, levels of
additional physical and intellectual activity, and some other factors.
"Additional" means above and beyond the body's regular functionality, such as heart function, breathing, walking, vision, hearing, thoughts, etc. Obviously, the additional activities increase energy needs, and that's why exercise, physical as well as intellectual, will accelerate commensurate weight loss.

Beyond the glucose for energy metabolism, the body needs a
continuous supply of fatty and amino acids to build new cells, synthesize hormones, enzymes, vitamins, and other critical substances. Those needs are called *plastic, organic,* or *replacement,*
meaning *to rebuild* or *to replace* dead cells and the substances lost
with feces, urine, perspiration, and exhaled air.

The amount of replacement fatty and amino acids isn't as simple
to determine, because, unlike glucose, the body stores considerable
amounts of fat (adipose tissue) and protein (muscle tissue), and can
synthesize what it needs on demand. However, according to the
U.S. RDA, the rule of thumb is:

- 30% of caloric intake must be fat[2] to stay in balance (to compensate losses). For someone consuming 2200 calories a day—a pittance by the U.S. customary "standards" of daily food intake—that's about 75 grams of fat.
- 0.75 g of reference protein[3] per kg of body weight per day for both sexes, or 53 g for 70 kg adult. Please note one very important distinction: a 2 oz steak (57 g) and 53 g of *reference protein* isn't the same, because cooked steak contains only 27% of protein[4], or less than 15 g. You need to consume at least an 8 oz steak to satisfy daily requirements, assuming you have perfect digestion and the meat wasn't burned.

Also keep in mind that, relative to an individual's age and weight, fat and protein requirements are higher for growing children, for the elderly to compensate for diminishing digestion, for women during pregnancy and lactation, for body builders and physical laborers, for people recovering from disease, or who are under stress, and similar circumstances.

The rest is really, really simple. Just note one key distinction—I am using the terms "losing fat" or "fat loss" rather then "losing weight" or "weight loss," because that's what you are after—real *fat* loss rather than phantom *weight* loss.

- If you consume more than the 200 g glucose needed daily, the body will convert the excess into body fat. That's how you gain fat. The rate of conversion is approximately 1 g of fat for 3 g of glucose. That's 9 "fat" calories divided by 4 "carbs" calories plus a liberal allotment for the energy required for consumption, digestion, and conversion.
- If you consume less than 200 g glucose, the body will "burn" fat to compensate for the shortage at a rate of about 1 gram of fat for every 2 grams of glucose. That's how you lose fat. Dr. Atkins incorrectly called this process *ketosis,* because the *ketones* are the intermediary product of the biochemical reactions which convert fatty acids into cellular energy. The correct name is *lipolysis.*
- Before converting body fat into glucose, the body utilizes fatty acids derived from food. Thus, if you have too much fat in the diet, the body will not "burn" its own fat until disposing of all fat from food. That means consuming above 75 g of dietary fat stops

the loss of body fat dead in its tracks.

- If you consume less than 75 g of fat, the body will "draw" its own fat to produce enzymes, hormones, vitamins, cell membranes, and other essential substances. That's how you are losing fat.
- If you consume more than 75 g of fat, the body will dispatch the excess right under your skin. That's how you gain fat.
- If you consume less than 53 g of protein, the body will break muscle tissue into the amino acids needed for building cells, neurotransmitters, hormones, digestive enzymes, and other essential structures and substances. The process is called "muscle wasting." You certainly can lose weight this way, but, for obvious reasons, it isn't a desirable weight loss, and it isn't a loss of fat.
- If you consume more than 53 g proteins, the body will convert certain excesses into muscle tissue. The stronger the muscles, the more protein they will take. You gain weight that way, but this isn't from fat, and it is a very desirable weight. However, if you don't have strong muscles (just like most women and children), the excess will get converted into glucose, and the excess glucose will get converted into body fat. And that's how you gain body fat from overeating protein.

Of course, these processes are much more elaborate and complex, the numbers are approximate, and you can easily pick up the specifics from any decent medical biochemistry textbook. But that's enough for us to figure out and conclude that to consistently lose fat, you need to take the following steps:

- Consume far fewer carbohydrates (the source of glucose) than the body's daily needs. That's the only way to enable lipolysis (fat loss).
- Consume little or no fat to make sure that lipolysis "burns" body fat, not fat from food. (On a zero-fat diet it is still critical to obtain essential fatty acids that the body can't synthesize. Liquid cod liver oil is the best source, and two teaspoons daily is all you need.)
- Do not consume more protein than your body needs for plastic purposes, otherwise it will be converted into glucose, and will stop lipolysis.

And, conversely:

- You aren't going to lose any fat as long as you consume carbo-hydrates in excess of your daily needs;
- You aren't going to lose any fat as long as you are consuming more fat than is needed for plastic needs;
- You aren't going to lose any fat as long as you are consuming significantly more protein than is needed for plastic needs.

The South Beach diet performs somewhat better than Atkins, because, much to his credit, Dr. Agatston urges moderation in everything—carbs, fat, and protein. But this is still not enough for the sustained and permanent weight loss that readers desire. As long as excess carbs, fat, and protein are still present in the diet, the loss of body fat is a physiological impossibility, period.

To summarize: in order to consistently lose fat on a low-carb diet, you must keep your body in a perpetual state of *lipolysis*. To accomplish this feat you must consume: (a) ZERO carbs; (b) under 60 grams of protein to prevent muscle wasting, and (c) under 70–80 grams of fat to enjoy some level of satiety, enhance the digestion of proteins, maintain the integrity of intestinal mucosa, and prevent the formation of gallstones. (Please adjust these figures to your own weight and levels of activity!)

Alas, nothing even remotely close is recommended by either the Atkins or South Beach diets. Why, then, do so many people report losing between 5 to 15 lbs (2.2- 6.8 kg) during the induction stage? Are they all lying? What, then, explains the weight loss during the induction stage (phase one) anyway?

They're not lying. As I said before, they're simply observing phantom weight loss, meaning the loss of (1) fat, (2) body water, (3) foods in transit, and (4) accumulated stools.

A moderate *loss of fat* (1) is possible, but not likely. Here is why:
- At best, on a ZERO CARBS diet it is possible to lose between 80 to 100 g (2.8–3.5 oz) of body fat daily, based on the fact that one gram of fat provides the equivalent of 2.25 g of glucose (9 cal / 4 cal = 2.25) And that's assuming a moderate—under 60–80 g (2.1–2.8 oz) each—consumption of fat and protein.
- Losing more body fat than the above calculation suggests is physiologically impossible, unless you speed metabolism with in-

tense exercise or stimulants such as ephedra. But that's not what most dieters are willing, capable, or permitted to do, and it isn't what was required by either the Atkins or South Beach diets.

Thus, a realistically attainable loss of fat during the induction stage (phase one) is under 1.4 kg (3 lbs); (14 days * 100 g). Obviously, even this minor fat loss wouldn't happen if you followed Atkins' advice and consumed unlimited amounts of fat and protein. And you can lose only half that much fat on the South Beach diet, if you followed Dr. Agatston's menu and consumed around 100 g (3.5 oz) of carbohydrates.

For comparison's sake, the total daily weight loss during complete starvation ranges—depending on starting weight and activity level—from 200 to 400 g (7–10.4 oz), which is the physiological weight loss ceiling. This, of course, includes the loss of fat and protein used for the body's plastic needs.

Here's a real-life example: David Blaine, who spent 44 days without food, emerged from his glass cage 55 lbs (25 kg) lighter.[5] Assuming 20 of those pounds were phantom weight loss (he'd been stuffing himself with loads of food just before going in), the magician was losing 0.79 lb (358 g) per day. And that was definitely at the high-end of the scale—hanging in a transparent box in the center of London under the 24/7 scrutiny of gawking crowds requires a great deal more energy than a simple, straightforward fast.

Now the *water loss* (2). Since 45 to 65% of an adult's body weight is composed of water, a person may drop 5% of that volume before dehydration sets in. For a 176 lbs (80 kg) person, a 5% loss represents between 5.7 and 6.2 lbs (2.6–2.8 kg). And here is what's happening during the induction (phase one) stage of either diet:

- *Reduced water consumption.* After cutting out carbohydrate-heavy foods, such as fruits and vegetables, the amount of "hidden" water consumed with them is greatly reduced, too. With less water in the diet, the rate of water loss via urine, perspiration, and exhaled air is faster than the rate of replacement. This, incidentally, is why there are so many complaints about dehydration among Atkins dieters.

- *Reduction of potassium.* A diet rich in grains, cereals, fruits, and vegetables is lopsided toward a significant excess of dietary potassium. The excess potassium causes water retention (edema), particularly when the diet is also low in sodium (table salt). Edema is common in vegetarian and high-carb diets, and it's apparent from swollen feet, bags under the eyes, and migraine headaches (related to cerebral edema). Because low-carb diets contain very low levels of potassium, the body may shed excess water quickly. The amount of weight loss related to "potassium overload," as this condition is called, is hard to estimate, but it may also be considerable.
- *Reduction of edema.* For some overweight individuals, a preceding low-protein diet may have caused water retention because of acute albumin deficiency—a blood protein that is synthesized from a dietary protein. The drop of albumin affects plasma osmotic pressure, and excess electrolytes are moved into intercellular space, causing edema. As soon as adequate protein intake is resumed, the edema subsides. The amount of weight loss related to protein malnutrition is hard to estimate, but it may also be considerable.

To summarize: If water loss is all you want, drink less, keep your regular diet, reduce potassium-rich products, consume at least 1 g of protein per kg of body weight, and visit the sauna often.

Now, moving on to the melting "crap" part. First, there are *foods in transit* (3):
- At any given time, the body contains two to three day's worth of what you ate and drank. Depending on your particular appetite, it adds up to 6 to 9 lbs (2.7–4 kg) worth of "stuff" even after accounting for urination, perspiration, and breathing.
- Once you shift to a low-carb diet, the weight of *foods in transit* goes down because you are now consuming considerably less food (by gross weight).

To summarize: The actual difference of consumed food before and during the induction phase varies greatly from person to person, so I'll assume this weight reduction at a modest 3 lbs (1.4 kg), less than the weight of a single dinner of most adult Americans.

Finally, there are *accumulated stools* (4):

- The large intestine may easily hold 10 to 15 lbs (4.5–6.8 kg) of compacted feces without causing noticeable distress.
- When you begin the induction (phase one) stage, the stools are still voluminous, and the large intestine continues eliminating them regularly until the onset of constipation, in about one week's time.

To summarize: At the rate of 300 to 500 g per day (average weight of stool on a high-fiber diet), elimination accounts for the loss of 5 to 7 lbs (2—3 kg) in the first week alone. After adding up all these losses—improbable loss of fat, minor loss of water, tiny reduction of food still transiting through the intestines, and reasonable elimination of stools—here is what you end up with:

**The components of weight loss during the induction stage of the Atkins or South Beach diets:**

| Weight loss from | Daily Weight loss | Duration of loss | Total loss |
|---|---|---|---|
| 1. Loss of fat | 100 g (3.5 oz) | 14 | 3 lbs (1.4 kg) |
| 2. Intestinal content in transit | Varies | 2–3 days | 3 lbs (1.4 kg) |
| 3. Endogenous (body) water | Varies | 3–5 days | 5.7 lbs (2.6 kg) |
| 4. Accumulated stools | Varies | 4–6 days | 5.0 lbs (2.2 kg) |
| **Total weight loss** | | | **16.7 lbs (7.6 kg)** |

As you can see, the total estimated weight loss comes to a substantial 16.7 lbs (7.6 kg) while using the most conservative estimates. From this, 13.7 lbs is a phantom weight loss made of water, foods that are still being digested, and stools.

Even then, this considerable weight loss can be accomplished only by someone who follows a very strict, literal form of induction: zero carbs and under 80 grams of fat and protein each for 14 days; almost a starvation protocol for most people. That's why both Dr. Atkins and Dr. Agatston hedged their claims of 14-day weight loss at, respectively, 2 to 16 lbs and 8 to 13 lbs, knowing well that very few people can diet exactly "by the book." To hedge even more, Dr. Atkins invented the fictional term *metabolic resistance,* so he could disown failing dieters:

*– Blame yourself, lady. You aren't losing weight because your metabolic resistance is to-o-o high!*

It gets even worse if you continue to the next stage—the *ongoing weight loss* (OWL) on Atkins, or *phase two* on South Beach. The fat loss stops on both diets for all but the most physically active and dedicated dieters. And those on Atkins would begin gaining back real fat even faster, because now they are permitted unrestricted fat and protein consumption along with carbohydrates. In other words, Three-Card Monte is over.

Luckily, there's still a consolation prize: relieving one's body of excess water and "crap" is actually a great deed. Not exactly what was set out to be accomplished in the first place, but still good for the health, body, and mind. That said, as soon as the induction stage is over, so is the loss of weight. There simply isn't any more food, water, and "crap" left inside, and in most cases, that's a moment when constipation sets in. The "honeymoon" is over for good. People reach the dreaded *plateau* of the Atkins or South Beach diets.

The loss of "foods in transit," water, and stools also explains the precipitous reduction of the waistline (clothing size) during induction. The reduction happens because the four conditions typically related to a high-fiber diet are now gone: edema, intestinal bloating, flatulence, and impacted stools. Serendipitously, the "shrinking" intestines happen to be right under the waistline.

You can easily accomplish a similar feat by taking a massive dose of laxatives and spending several hours in a hot sauna. That's what some jockeys do before races to reduce their weight, or some women to squeeze into tight-fitting gowns. Not really much fun and bad for the health, but it may easily bring a size 12 body down to an 8—good enough to crash a party. Just don't crash yourself from severe dehydration.

Was Dr. Atkins aware of all this? At some point he probably was. But it must be hard to admit that one's empire was built, literally, on crap, and that all this time one's readers and patients had been "dumping" water and stools, not fat. And if Dr. Atkins didn't know it, all things considered, he's darn lucky not to have lived long enough to get embarrassed by the "revelations" in this book.

Does Dr. Agatston, the author of the South Beach Diet, know this? It's hard to say. If he did, his book should have described the phantom weight loss phenomenon, and it wouldn't mislead people into believing that they are losing real fat, as opposed to just phantom weight. Well, his book doesn't even have an index entry for *constipation,* so what do you expect?

It's also worth noting that the "fit and fabulous" inhabitants of South Beach, Florida represent a cross-section of overweight Americans in the same way the Victoria Secret's catalogue represents the average American woman. And I can also assure you that the carefree diets of the young jocks and beach bunnies who populate South Beach are as close to Dr. Agatston's diet as New York is to Miami.

*– So would you say the Atkins and South Beach diets are frauds?*

Well, I wouldn't go that far, but there's an incredible amount of naiveté and ineptness associated with them, that's for sure. You expect this kind of crudeness from quack "dieticians," but not from bona-fide medical doctors. At the very least, both deserve credit for turning back the onslaught of the high-carb menace.

### Misfortune loves company

Besides indigestible fiber, other factors, conditions, and considerations may contribute to diet-related constipation, or cause it directly. The majority of them are amply described in this book, but here's a brief reprise:

- *Disbacteriosis.* A healthy large intestine depends on abundant intestinal flora to keep stools soft, small, and moist. If the stools become hard and dry without fiber, it means that the bacteria aren't there to perform their magic. *Solution:* Restore intestinal flora, following recommendations in Chapter 11, *Avoiding the Perils of Transition* (see page 211).

- *Absence of soluble fiber.* Intestinal flora needs something to gorge on to keep procreating. Its favorite food is complex carbohydrates in the form of soluble fiber, which reaches the large intestine undigested. *Solution:* Provide supplemental soluble fiber when all other sources of carbohydrates are absent. It will not affect your weight loss as severely as other forms of carbohydrates.

- *Potassium deficiency.* Restrictive low-carb diets are commonly deficient in potassium—a mineral responsible for retaining water inside cellular structures that hold stool's moisture. *Solution:* Maintain adequate intake of dietary potassium.

- *Loss of rectal sensitivity.* When the volume of fiber-free stools is greatly reduced, the body no longer senses the urge that precedes physiologically-normal defecation. *Solution:* Follow recommendations in Chapter 11, *Avoiding the Perils of Transition.*

- *Anorectal disorders.* Small, hard stools and intense straining may cause or exacerbate preexisting conditions, such as hemorrhoidal disease or anal fissures. *Solution:* Do not begin a low-carb diet without adequate preparation. It means implementing all of the above steps and reconditioning your body to eliminate small stools regularly. Follow the related recommendations provided in this book.

If you aren't up to the task, by all means heed Dr. Atkins' advice and take fiber laxatives. It's always better to replace one evil with another to save yourself from an even greater evil—namely, severe constipation and irreversible damage of anorectal organs. Since by now you already know the perils of too much indigestible fiber, you can't say I didn't warn you.

And, by the way, keep in mind that dietary fiber in any form— either from laxatives or food—is a major stimulant of a ravenous appetite. What else do you expect from a substance called *INDIGESTIBLE?* The fact is, the body can't differentiate between the things you swallow, so it dutifully keeps trying to digest whatever is inside. And it keeps trying, and trying, and trying...

And while it keeps trying, the stomach and intestines keep o-o-o-ozing digestive juices and enzymes to complete this senseless task. And the more these juices and enzymes are splashing around inside you, the more they stimulate more appetite, especially a few hours after the last meal. And if you don't "feed the burner" with foods that neutralize these potent acidic juices and flesh-eating proteolysis enzymes, they eventually cause all kinds of problems, from ubiquitous heartburn to deadly ulcerative colitis, and everything in between.

Well, you get the picture. Besides a torn anus, increased appetite is the last thing you want to deal with, right?


### Don't be sorry, be ready!

There are more troubles with the Atkins and South Beach diets than just fiber. I identified at least thirty by studying the respective books, analyzing medical literature, and reviewing dieters' feedback on Internet forums. You can review a complete list at www.FixingUpAtkins.com.

Should you decide to attempt a low-carb diet again, these key points should help you to prevent constipation from ruining an already meager meal plan:

- *Don't rush.* If you suffer from constipation, have a history of constipation, or suspect that you may have latent constipation, study this book first.
- *Take it easy.* Analyze your present diet, and start reducing fiber content gradually. This is essential to prevent fecal impaction, which is probable after an abrupt withdrawal of all fiber.
- *Watch your toilet bowl.* Do not commence a low-carb diet without attaining small, soft, and regular stools first (Bristol Stool Form Scale type 4 to 6, see page 117). Only after accomplishing this objective may you safely start dieting.
- *Face the hard truth.* If you already have colorectal disorders that impede painless and regular defecation, realize that you will need to replace the fiber (either dietary, or medicinal, or both) with safer means described in this book, and on a permanent basis.
- *Be realistic.* It took you ten, twenty, thirty, or more years to gain all that weight, and to rack up the conditions that are contributing to constipation and fiber dependence. It takes time, patience, and perseverance to plod along, a few ounces at a time.
- *Expect to stumble.* Even with the best palliative means to "enable" regular stools, you may still get constipated occasionally. Fortunately, the tools and methods to overcome any mishap are described in this book.
- *Keep an eye on the prize.* The goal of any weight-loss diet isn't just to just look good, but to be healthy. Don't do anything that

can harm your health, otherwise it ain't worth it. No matter how rhetorical it may sound, it's still true.

For desert, nurture this thought—just by following the suggestions in this chapter and this book, you may easily drop 10–15 lbs of weight without even trying, and, in the process, shave a few inches off your waistline. And all this without getting constipated.

## Summary

- The overall reduction of carbohydrates in low-carb diets also reduces the amount of intrinsic dietary fiber. The sudden absence of fiber may cause constipation, especially during the induction stage.
- Constipation, which follows the withdrawal of fiber, indicates chronic dependence on the laxative effect of dietary fiber and the presence of latent constipation.
- The considerable weight loss experienced during the induction stage of a low-carb diet isn't the loss of fat, but mainly body water, intestinal content in transit, and accumulated stools.
- An effective, long-term, low-carb diet requires careful preparation and gradual transition. Small and soft (BFS type 4 to 6, see page 117) stools must be attained with minimal amounts of dietary fiber in the diet prior to transition to the induction diet.
- The effect both the Atkins and South Beach diets have on constipation is comparable. Neither diet provides adequate directions and precautions to overcome constipation. Dr. Atkins' advice to use supplemental fiber laxatives is outright harmful, because it stimulates continuous appetite, causes intestinal distress, and may harm colorectal organs.
- Although the South Beach diet is less permissive, it possesses all of the same shortcomings as the Atkins Diet—namely, it can't facilitate sustained loss of fat (vs. phantom weight loss) because it contains too many carbohydrates to facilitate *lipolysis* (the utilization of body fat for energy).
- The factors that may cause diet-related constipation are addressed in relevant chapters of this book, and should be considered before committing to any kind of diet.

- The implementation of the recommendations in this chapter—namely, the reduction of dietary fiber and elimination of latent constipation—may result in considerable weight loss and size reduction in most individuals, unrelated to the loss of body fat.
- A sustained and permanent weight loss requires a diet with a near zero amount of carbohydrates, and a moderate consumption of quality fats and proteins, not exceeding 1 g per kg of body weight each.
- Digestible (i.e. soluble) fiber is essential for large intestine ecology and is harmless when consumed in moderation. Small amounts of supplemental soluble fiber, such as pectin, inulin, FOS, and others, are needed to sustain intestinal flora throughout the diet.
- Even without intensive physical exercise, a daily loss of 80 to 100 g (2.8–3.5 oz) of body fat is attainable. This translates to the loss of 2.4 to 3 kg (5.3–6.6 lbs) each month.

\*\*\*

# Footnotes

[1] Glucose Homeostasis and Fuel Metabolism; Medical Biochemistry, John Baynes and Marek Dominiczak; p. 243.

[2] Lipids. Recommended Dietary Allowances. National Academy Press. 10th Edition, p. 49.

[3] Ibid., p. 59.

[4] Beef, short loin, porterhouse steak, separable lean only, trimmed to ¼ fat, USDA select, cooked, broiled; NDB No: 13469; USDA National Nutrient Database for Standard Reference;
http://www.nal.usda.gov/fnic/foodcomp/search/index.html

[5] Magic in a Box; Ripley's Believe it or Not!; 2004 edition, p. 23.

# Part II

# All the Proof You Need

*The reasonable man adapts himself to the world;*
*the unreasonable man persists in trying to adapt*
*the world to himself. Therefore all progress*
*depends on the unreasonable man.*

George Bernard Shaw (1856—1950)

# PART II. INTRODUCTION

## THE FIBER MENACE GETS REAL

Conceivably, an experienced medical writer can write about anything related to health and medicine. The amount of information—textbooks, physicians' references, academic research, clinical and epidemiological data—is infinite, and it's yours for the taking in the libraries and on the Internet.

Predictably, a book about dietary fiber based on all of those sources would recommend *more fiber, more water,* and *more exercise,* because that's what the consensus is among the top clinical, academic, and public health researchers. Why, then, would someone write a book that calls fiber a menace and declares it a threat to public health—the complete opposite of mainstream opinion?

The answer is: because it is! And I have the first-hand knowledge of it not from studying medical publications, but from years of pain and suffering caused by progressively worsening irritable bowel syndrome, constipation, hemorrhoidal disease, and anal fissures. None of them came from poor health, lack of medical care, or misfortune, but from a high-fiber diet, recommended by well-intentioned physicians.

So I knew from the get-go that fiber-related complications would be a tough nut to crack. But it was only after I began researching and writing about it that I came to realize just how complicated, multifaceted, and challenging this problem really is, especially when all of the "aggravating" aspects are factored in—age, health, gender, occupation, medications, ethnicity, even one's character. In a nutshell, what I learned during the years of hardship, recovery, and research into this subject, is this:

- At one point or another, anyone may experience costiveness (large, hard stools) or constipation (irregular stools). There are many reasons behind these conditions, ranging from bad parenting to bad poisoning, from too much fiber to too little fat, and everything in between. Whenever external factors compromise bowel movement, the normal bacteria inside the large intestine are the first to suffer. Because these bacteria make up the bulk of normal stools, once they're gone, stools become harder and irregular. Chapter 4, *Disbacteriosis*, describes the sorry travails of these hard-working little bugs, deciphers the events that precede their demise, and explains their connection to health, longevity, and disease.

- After the bacteria are gone, fiber enters the picture to replace their function. For a while, it works as advertised. Fiber makes stools larger and not as hard, and the problems appear to be gone. Unfortunately, this is merely calm before calamity: "normality" comes not from restoring the body's natural clockwork, but from replacing it with an outside bulking agent; essentially, a laxative. For a while, the problems are hidden because you don't yet feel them. Chapter 5, *Constipation*, describes the transition through the three phases of fiber-dependence that accompanies the functional (reversible), latent (hidden), and organic (irreversible, only manageable) stages of constipation.

- Here comes the reckoning: large stools and the straining needed to expel them wear out and damage the small, taut and extremely delicate anal canal. Enlarged hemorrhoids are the first signs of trouble. As hemorrhoids get larger, the anal canal opening gets smaller, and constipation gets worse. When that happens, most people add more fiber to their diets. Naturally, the stools get even larger, the anal canal opening even smaller, and the constipation more severe than ever. Chapter 6, *Hemorrhoidal Disease*, describes the role of fiber in the pathogenesis and evolution of this disorder, which afflicts up to half of all adult Americans. That's about the same number of people who became overweight on high-carb, high-fiber diets. What goes around, comes around.

- As we get older, the muscles, bones, eyes, and hearing all grow weaker. The large intestine is no exception. If, by the age of 50, up to half of Americans are affected by hemorrhoidal disease, by the age of 60 up to half are affected by diverticular disease, which is an irreversible bulging of the large intestine. There is only one force that can make the intestinal walls bulge out: large stools. There is only one food component that can cause them: dietary fiber. Chapter 7, *Diverticular Disease*, explains why this happens, what you can do to prevent it, or how to make the condition benign if you already have it. Trust me, you don't want to experience the complications.

- The combined impact of disbacteriosis, a fiber-rich diet, laxatives, constipation, and hemorrhoids (not necessarily all of them or in that order), brings along yet another torment—irritable bowel syndrome. It is a functional condition, which means that it's completely reversible. The problem is that everyone tries to reverse it with more fiber and more drugs, rather than with less fiber and bacterial supplements. Chapter 8, *Irritable Bowel Syndrome*, explains why up to 60 million Americans "can't get no relief," and how many of them set themselves up for what's addressed in Chapter 9.

- Ulcerative colitis and Crohn's disease are considered irreversible conditions, points of no return. Sure they are, as long as they're treated with even more fiber, even more antibiotics, even more immunodepressants, even more antispasmodics, and even more laxatives. After you finish reading Chapter 9, *Ulcerative Colitis and Crohn's Disease*, you, too, will be scratching your head in disbelief. If, God forbid, you suffer from one of these conditions, you'll know what to do to turn back the tide. If you do nothing, ulcerative colitis increases the chances of your getting colorectal cancer by 3,200%.[1]

- Think about it: according to this book, dietary fiber is the primary cause of ulcerative colitis. Ulcerative colitis increases the chances of getting colon cancer a great many times over. To prevent colon cancer, you're being told to consume more fiber. Well, hope springs eternal, as they say. Chapter 10, *Colon Cancer*, reviews recent research data that tells the unwelcome truth: fiber does little or nothing to prevent colon cancer, and may actually contribute to colon cancer. This research doesn't come from the bowels of the Internet, but from some of the most distinguished medical publications and establishments out there, such as *The Lancet, The New England Journal of Medicine,* Centers for Disease Control and Prevention, The National Cancer Institute, The World Health Organization, and the like.

It simply can't be so, right? Well, keep reading!

## Footnotes

[1] Ulcerative Colitis; NIH Publication No. 03–1597 April 2003; http://digestive.niddk.nih.gov/ddiseases/pubs/colitis/

*There are over 400 species of bacteria in the colon; bacteria*
*make up 30–50% of the total dry matter in the feces,*
*or even 75% according to other calculation.*

R.F. Schmidt, G. Thews
Human Physiology, 2nd edition

# CHAPTER FOUR

## DISBACTERIOSIS

How do you debunk popular ideas about fiber's role in digestion and elimination without being accused of committing a sacrilege, when it has already became a gold-standard treatment for "regularity," a miracle laxative, and a concept so embedded in the minds of doctors and patients alike that it's no longer even questioned by anyone?

Well, there are "sacred truths," and then there are long-established, indisputable facts of human physiology:

- Breast milk has zero fiber, yet healthy babies produce abundant (relative to their weight and size) stools several times daily.
- People who fast for weeks at a time have regular stools, even though they consume nothing but water.
- Some people (the lucky ones) who attempted the Atkins Diet, had no problem with constipation, even though their diet contained zero or minor amounts of fiber.
- Indigenous Inuit (Eskimo) people, who inhabit the Arctic coast of North America, some parts of Greenland, and northern Siberia, consume a fiber-free diet, and aren't affected by constipation.

None of the above makes any sense, conventionally speaking. People can't have regular stools without consuming any fiber, right?

Wrong! The reason you're stumped is simple: you've been conditioned to believe that normal stools are made mainly from food, and that fiber is required to make them. Inevitably, the next logical inference forms a familiar logic:

## IF FIBER MAKES GOOD STOOLS, LET'S FIX BAD ONES WITH MORE FIBER

It seems perfectly logical, right?

Wrong again! Actually, normal stools shouldn't contain any remnants of undigested food. Dietary proteins, fats, carbohydrates, and even fiber must digest completely. If something you ate exits your body *as is,* it means it wasn't digested or couldn't get digested to begin with, such as denatured protein (burnt meat). Technically, even *indigestible* fiber should be fermented by intestinal bacteria.

That's why a stool exam that shows any visible remnants of undigested fats, proteins, or carbohydrates, or even specks of undigested fiber (any at all), points to impaired digestion, and one disease or another that affects the organ(s) responsible for digestion and the absorption of a specific nutrient. That much is written in any medical reference book, and the observation of stools is widely used as an effective diagnostic tool for disorders of digestion and the digestive organs.

So what, then, are stools made from, if not food and fiber? Primarily water, intestinal bacteria (single cell, free-living microorganisms), dead bacteria and cells shed by the body, mineral salts, coloring pigments, and traces of fat. Intestinal bacteria are by far the largest component of stools. Let's repeat again the quotation that opens this chapter:

---

*Human Physiology:* There are over 400 species of bacteria in the colon; bacteria make up 30%–50% of the total dry matter in the feces, or even 75% according to other calculation.[1]

Besides other important tasks, these abundant bacteria make normal stools, unless they are completely or partially decimated by the vestiges of civilized living, or even—harder to believe—by dietary fiber.

## Bacterial functions: Welcomed everywhere but in the West

When babies are born, their digestive organs are sterile. Their large intestines get "cultured" after the first few sips of *colostrum,* a thin yellowish fluid "infested" with the mother's bacteria and rich in essential nutrients. Colostrum precedes the flow of fat- and protein-rich breast milk. The process continues with breast milk, and the intestinal flora of newborns matures to "adult" status by the sixth month.

Placing newborns on formula without first letting them taste colostrum and breast milk is a serious mistake. It may hound young parents for years to come as they grapple with their offspring's food allergies, diarrhea, constipation, and poor general health. But for many breastfed babies, even the breast milk may lack essential bacteria because of their mothers' prior exposure to environmental pollutants, antibiotics, and mercury in dental amalgams. That's why nowadays, many newborns develop gastrointestinal and auto-immune disorders as often as their formula-fed brethrens: their mothers suffer from acute *disbacteriosis,* a change of composition and/or volume of normal intestinal flora.

The presence of bacteria in dairy milk—good ones from the inside of the cow, bad ones from a dirty udder, contaminated hands, or unsanitary utensils—explains why, by law, raw milk must be pasteurized. This is true not so much to prevent human infections (humans drank raw milk for ages), but to prevent spoilage from bacterial fermentation.

Before the statutory pasteurization of dairy milk, lactose intolerance to milk protein wasn't as big an issue as it's become today, because milk's innate bacteria would assist in fermenting lactose and breaking down protein while the milk was still in the stomach or upper intestine—a process similar to yogurt-making. That's why fermented dairy products, such as yogurt, buttermilk, kefir, and others don't cause lactose intolerance or allergies as much (or at all) as regular pasteurized milk does.

In special circumstances, such as allergies, malnutrition, impaired immunity, severe burns, and others, doctors may prescribe a donor's breast milk to babies or even adults. Unfortunately, human donor milk also must be pasteurized, and is useless for its primary functions: proper digestion thanks to the innate flora, and restoration of intestinal flora.

Intestinal flora—the sum of all indigenous bacteria that reside inside the intestinal tract (the host)—is considered an organ in itself, just like the liver or bone marrow, because the bacteria perform a range of essential, health-critical functions that can't be reliably duplicated by any other means. Researchers determined those functions by comparing sterile lab animals (without any intestinal flora) with control animals that had normal flora. All of these findings have been confirmed in people as well. Here's a brief listing of the intestinal flora's most important functions:

- *Water retention in stools.* Single cell organisms, such as bacteria, contain mostly water, encircled by impenetrable membranes. In large quantities, they provide normal stools with its amorphous qualities. That's why dry stools reliably point to disbacteriosis.

- *Formation of normal stools.* Since bacteria represent the most dominant component of normal stools, their absence may cause persistent chronic diarrhea.

- *Manufacturing of essential vitamins.* Bacteria synthesize a whole range of substances, including certain B-complex vitamins, vitamin $B_{12}$, and vitamin K, which is essential for proper blood coagulation.

- *Protecting intestinal epithelium (mucosa) from pathogens.* Normal intestinal flora controls the population of undesirable bacteria, such as *Candida albicans* (yeast) or the infective strains of *E. coli.* The mechanisms of protection are numerous—competition for food supply, adhesion to intestinal mucosa, maintenance of desired pH balance, and production of peroxides and enzymes, which kill foreign bacteria.

- *Tissue development and regeneration.* The intestinal mucosal membrane (epithelium) and lymphatic tissues (Peyer's patches) of sterilized lab animals are poorly developed vis-à-vis healthy animals. The shortcomings of weak mucosal membrane for intestinal health and underdeveloped lymphatic tissues for immunity are self-evident.

- *Immunity.* Normal intestinal bacteria are responsible for enabling *phagocytosis*—the body-wide destruction of pathogenic bacteria, viruses, allergens, and other foreign objects by *phagocytes,* which are specialized blood cells responsible for non-specific (before antibodies) immune system defenses.

Besides the obvious conditions (constipation, diarrhea, and disorders related to B- and K-vitamin deficiencies) other common conditions that have been associated with disbacteriosis are irritable bowel syndrome, ulcerative colitis, Crohn's disease, fatigue, diabetes, colon and breast cancers, acne, eczema, psoriasis, asthma, allergies, joint diseases (rheumatoid arthritis, gout, osteoarthritis), and others.

Despite all this, *disbacteriosis (a.k.a. dysbiosis)*—literally, a *sterile gut*—isn't recognized by mainstream Western medicine as a disorder, even though it's a bona fide medical condition in the rest of the world, particularly in Eastern Europe.

You won't find a single reference to this condition on the Web sites of either The American Gastroenterological Association or The American Medical Association,[2] while in fact the 1908 Nobel Prize in Medicine[3] was awarded to Paul Ehrlich (Goettingen University, Goettingen, Germany) and Ilya Mechnikov (Institute Pasteur, Paris, France) "in recognition of their work on immunity," specifically the discovery of phagocytosis.

*The Merck Manual of Diagnosis and Therapy* indirectly acknowledges the "possibility" of disbacteriosis (but not the condition) while discussing *antibiotic-associated colitis,* a condition that occurs when "various antibiotics may alter the balance of normal colonic flora and allow overgrowth of C. difficile, an anaerobic gram-positive bacillus."[4] Much to the *Merck's* credit, it states "...lactobacillus or rectally instilled bacteroides may be required in patients who have multiple relapses"; doctor-speak for the restoration of intestinal flora with oral supplements or enemas, a subject discussed in Chapter 11, *Avoiding the Perils of Transition.*

When I was growing up in the late nineteen-fifties, pediatric clinics in Ukraine routinely dispensed specially prepared "Acidophilus milk" for children affected by diarrhea, constipation, or any other digestive disorder. It was a fermented dairy drink made daily from cow's raw milk, specifically inoculated with live bacterial cultures essential for intestinal health. Today, you can find somewhat similar (sans raw milk) "live" preparations in food health stores, but not in pharmacies, which dispense antibiotics.

Besides the GI tract functions, non-pathogenic bacteria maintain a healthy bioecology of the epithelium, the upper layer of skin and mucosa. Indigenous bacteria prevent colonization by pathogens of the entire skin surface, the epithelium of eyes (conjunctiva), nose, oral cavity, pharynx, urethra, penis, and vagina.

Antibacterial drugs, soaps, shampoos, creams, gargles, and vaginal douches destroy normal flora, and cause a rapid proliferation of pathogens, expressed in conditions such as conjunctivitis, cellulitis (a bacterial skin infection, not to be confused with cellulite), seborrhea, acne, sinusitis, mouth sores, gingivitis, periodontal disease, vaginal yeast infection, chronic inflammation of urethra and bladder, and many others.

Restoring normal flora becomes exceedingly difficult, if not impossible, if a person becomes dependent on antibacterial means of infectious control. That's why anything with the words "antibacterial" on it should be avoided like the plague, unless specifically prescribed by a physician for a confirmed life-threatening infectious disease.

### Common causes of disbacteriosis

What causes disbacteriosis? Well, anything that kills *bad* bacteria also kills *good* bacteria, which are identical single-cell living organisms, albeit better behaving. Here's just a brief list of the most egregious villains. You will not find any particular recommendations here, because they're self-evident: *don't use fiber, avoid antibiotics, remove amalgam fillings, use natural soaps,* etc. Here we go:

- *Protein deficiency.* Intestinal flora derives its energy and plastic nutrients not from food, but from mucin, which is secreted by healthy mucous membranes. Mucin is a glycoprotein—a molecule that bonds glucose with amino acids. Gastric and intestinal mucus is formed by combining mucin and water. Mucus protects the lining of the stomach and intestines from mechanical damage, enzymes, gastric acid, astringent bile, and food-born pathogens. The deficiency of the essential amino acid threonine, for example, curbs the body's ability to produce mucin, and, correspondingly, bacteria's ability to function and procreate.

- *Excess dietary fiber.* (Yes, you're reading it right.) The by-products of fiber's bacterial fermentation (short chain fatty acids, ethanol, and lactic acid) destroy bacteria for the same reason acids and alcohols are routinely used to sterilize surgical instruments—they burst bacterial membranes on contact. And that's how fiber addiction develops: as the fermentation destroys bacteria, you need more and more fiber to form stools. If you suddenly drop all fiber, and no longer have many bacteria left, constipation sets in as soon as the large intestine clears itself of the remaining bulk.

- *Intestinal acidity.* Besides fermentation, excess acidity may occur when the pancreas fails to neutralize the stomach's content because of pancreatic disorders or obstruction. In this instance, acidic digestive juices spill into the large intestine and destroy bacteria. Interestingly enough, the most likely cause of obstruction in an otherwise healthy person is the blockage of the pancreatic ducts by—you guessed it—too much indigestible fiber in the duodenum. Normal acidity (i.e. safe for bacteria) for stools is within the 6 to 7.2 pH range.

- *Diarrhea.* Acute intestinal infection, food poisoning, laxatives, medical intervention, and other conditions may cause prolonged diarrhea, which will literally wash out all of the bacteria from your gut. An appendectomy (the removal of the appendix) also increases the risk of disbacteriosis, because the appendix preserves the "starter" culture when diarrhea occurs.

- *Antibiotics and antibacterial medication* (such as sulfanilamide, sulpha derivatives, Dynapen, Urex, Nydrazid, Macrodantin, Rifadin, and many others). Antibiotics and antibacterial drugs play an important, life-saving role in many circumstances. However, these drugs are widely and indiscriminately overprescribed to children and adults alike. One such prescription is often sufficient to wipe out the entire bacterial population of your gut.

- *Antibiotic residue in fowl, fish, livestock, and milk.* Industrial farming necessitates the use of continuous, large doses of antibiotics to keep crowded, confined animals alive. Inevitably, some of these antibiotics transfer to the food supply, and affect humans.

- *Heavy metals.* Mercury, lead, arsenic, cadmium, nickel, silver, and other metals are extremely toxic, even in trace amounts. The sources of contamination vary from industrial pollutants to household chemicals, batteries to electronic components, measuring devices, and other sources. Children are the most vulnerable.

- *Silverware.* Silver is traditionally used for kitchen utensils, goblets, plates, and pitchers for its strong antibacterial properties. Silver flatware isn't such a good idea after all, especially for babies.

- *Mercury from dental amalgam.* This pollutant is omnipresent in the United States. Amalgam fillings are placed indiscriminately into cavities, because amalgam is cheap and easy to work with. The American Dental Association insists that dental amalgam is safe,[5] while the Occupational Safety Health Administration (OSHA) and Environmental Protection Agency (EPA) classify amalgam as a toxic and hazardous substance: "Another source of exposure to low levels of elemental mercury in the general population is elemental mercury released in the mouth from dental amalgam fillings"[6] (Transportation, storage, and disposal of mercury is regulated by the Code of Federal Regulations, 29 CFR 1910.1000, and its willful violation is a criminal offense, except when mercury is "stored" in your mouth by a licensed dentist.) It isn't surprising that dentists in the United States have the highest rate of depression, suicide, and drug and alcohol addiction, and the lowest life expectancy among all medical professionals. This could likely be the result of long-term exposure to mercury, which, as already mentioned, is a potent poison, neurotoxin, and carcinogen; one that gradually destroys nervous systems, causes cancers, kills off friendly bacteria, and brings about... an addiction to fiber.

- *Artificial food coloring.* Years ago, a color pigment called *crystal violet* (also known as *crystal gentian*) was widely used as a topical antiseptic. There are good reasons to believe that long-term exposure to artificial food coloring may affect intestinal bacteria in the same way crystal violet affected (killed) topical bacteria.

- *Medical treatments and environmental pollutants.* Chemo- and radiotherapy kill bacteria for the same reason they kill cancerous cells. There are other factors that negatively affect the intestinal flora, such as industrial pollutants, household chemicals, antibacterial soaps, and toxic substances found in toothpaste, shampoo, and detergents.
- *Quackery.* If stools aren't "clean," then the colon must be "dirty." This apparently logical inference is the base for "miracle cures" of constipation, migraine, halitosis, yeast infection, indigestion, and an endless array of other ills. While most of these conditions are indeed connected to the dysfunction of the large intestine, "cleaning" the colon isn't a solution, but a sure formula for creating even more problems by causing even more severe forms of disbacteriosis.

Then there are things most city dwellers *don't do* that may cause harm. In the past several years, popular media and medical journals widely reported that children who attend day care,[7] live on farms, or grow up cuddling pets or livestock don't suffer from asthma or other respiratory disease as often as children who don't.

What's going on in the kindergartens and on the farms that makes these kids cold- and asthma-resistant? Well, they sneeze at each other, don't wash their hands as often, play with domesticated animals, and eat unwashed produce from manured land, so their little guts "stay current" and their immune systems are continuously challenged. It's a self-vaccination, of a kind.

This phenomenon is called the "hygiene theory," though it should probably be called the "dirt theory." Enlightened English pediatricians are now advising the parents of sickly city kids to take them to play in the sand boxes. If you don't yet know this, sand boxes happen to be the favorite outhouse for neighboring cats. For similar reasons, toddlers, puppies, and even adult dogs, unburdened by a leash and social mores, eat feces *(coprophagia)*, an instinctive survival trait in action.

This book doesn't condone eating feces at any age—it's gross,

dangerous because of stool-born pathogens, worms, and toxoplas-
mosis, and ineffective because bacteria can't survive the strong
acidity of the human stomach. The proper way of inoculating the
large intestine with fecal flora is called *fecal bacteriotherapy.* It's
been employed for ages by natural practitioners of Eastern medicine to ward off diarrhea and constipation. Even some allopathic
(mainstream) doctors, although not in the United States, aren't too
squeamish about it, because it effectively cures otherwise incurable
ulcerative colitis.[8]

## Symptoms of disbacteriosis

Advised by their veterinarians, farmers pay big bucks for bacterial supplements imported from Europe to keep their farm animals
well and productive, because nobody will buy a bloated, underweight, sickly calf who's suffering from chronic diarrhea and digestive distress.

Well, disbacteriosis in humans isn't any more difficult to spot
than it is in livestock. Here are the telltale signs of this condition:

- *Absence of intestinal gases.* When dietary fiber (soluble as well
  as insoluble) is present in the diet, intestinal gases are produced
  by bacterial metabolism. A complete absence of gases (in the
  presence of dietary fiber) suggests an absence of fermentation.
  Small amounts of soluble (digestible) fiber, such as fruit pectin,
  speed up the proliferation of intestinal flora, while avoiding excessive fermentation.

- *Undigested fiber in stool* can be seen as white or dark specs. This
  is best determined by a stool exam performed by a medical lab
  (CDSA, or Comprehensive Digestive Stool Analysis). The same
  exam may superficially determine symbiotic and pathogenic bacterial content and ratio, but only for a minor subset of hundreds
  of innate strains.

- *Constipation.* Constipation is one of the most prominent signs,
  especially when the stools are dry or hard. This means there is
  too little bacteria to loosen up the formed feces and keep them
  moist, because, unlike other stool components, bacterial cells retain moisture.

- *Intermittent or chronic diarrhea, irritable bowel syndrome, ul-*

*cerative colitis, and Crohn's disease.* As you've read above, the introduction of desirable bacteria into the affected large intestine heals these conditions. So it's a no-brainer to assume that, along with fiber, disbacteriosis plays a significant role in their pathogenesis.

- *Frequent respiratory infections, asthma, bronchitis, chronic rhinitis, post-nasal drip, nasal voice, sinus congestions, and allergies.* These primarily chronic conditions indicate a weakened immune system because of disbacteriosis. They usually appear after a routine respiratory infection that was treated with antibiotics, which in turn damaged intestinal flora.

- *Blood-clotting problems.* Hard-to-stop ordinary bleeding and easy bruising (ecchymoses)—dark, blotchy areas of hemorrhages under the skin—may indicate a deficiency of vitamin K, which is a by-product of bacterial metabolism. Before making this determination, rule out vitamin C deficiency (scurvy) and anticlotting medications such as *aspirin, ibuprofen, naproxen* (NSAIDs), *warfarin,* and others.

- *Neurological problems and anemia.* Vitamin $B_{12}$ is essential for the normal functioning of the nervous system and production of red blood cells. Since red meat and eggs were almost eliminated from the "healthy" Western diet until the Atkins-style diet came into vogue, the intestinal flora was the only remaining "natural" source of vitamin $B_{12}$. Numbness and tingling of the hands and feet, paleness, shortness of breath, chronic fatigue, a sore mouth and tongue, and mental confusion are the most common symptoms of a vitamin $B_{12}$ deficiency. At this stage, supplements are the only viable option to quickly treat and reverse these symptoms.

Keep in mind that any one of these signs may indicate other conditions. It's always best to consult a caring, competent physician and ask him or her to arrange for a comprehensive digestive stool analysis (CDSA) at a medical lab.

As you can see, when the bacteria are suffering, everything else suffers too: your immune system doesn't protect you as well as it used to, your blood doesn't coagulate, your stool lacks moisture, and your colon gets irritable and inflamed from a multitude of factors. Once the bacteria are gone, something must take their place and restore some of their functions. That's how and why dietary fiber entered the picture:

- First, to stimulate the growth of intestinal flora by feeding remaining bacteria with abundant fiber. It kind of works initially, but it's a bad idea, really, because the excess acidity from fermenting too much fiber kills off an already dwindling population of hard-working microbes.

- Secondly, fiber was introduced to bulk up stools after the bacteria were completely demolished, and when constipation or diarrhea set in. The result of this action, unfortunately, is even worse than the remedy—irritable bowel syndrome, diarrhea, inflammation, and reduced immunity (all outcomes of disbacteriosis-related diarrhea or constipation).

- Finally, as colorectal disorders, caused by coarse, bulky stools, grow worse, a person requires more and more fiber to "plunge" out ever-larger stools.

Naturally, the enlightened way to prevent and treat disbacteriosis isn't with fiber, more fiber, and even more fiber, but with... intestinal bacteria. This concept is discussed in Chapter 11, *Avoiding the Perils of Transition* (see page 211). Why such a simple, elegant, practical, inexpensive, and foolproof idea escaped Western medicine still escapes me.

## Summary

- Normal intestinal flora is comprised from hundreds of varieties of bacteria, which are specific to the human body. Humans obtain indigenous bacteria from mother's milk.

- Children who do not receive breast milk are likely to develop digestive and immune disorders related to the absence of beneficial flora.

- Intestinal flora is essential for the normal functioning of the human body. Despite its role, function, and importance, its utility isn't fully recognized by Western medicine.

- The deficiency or absence of intestinal flora is called *disbacteri-*

*osis.* This bona fide medical condition isn't recognized by Western allopathic medicine either, even though its ill effects (antibiotic-associated colitis) are well known.

- Indiscriminate use of antibiotics in medicine and agriculture is one of the major causes of disbacteriosis. The restoration of intestinal flora should always follow a treatment with antibiotics.

- Digestive disorders of the upper GI tract can damage intestinal flora by allowing reactive substances such as hydrochloric acid, bile, digestive enzymes, alcohols, and fatty acids into the large intestine.

- The fermentation of dietary fiber may damage intestinal flora by producing excessive acidity and alcohol.

- Intestinal flora is vulnerable to environmental, household, and medicinal agents, which have a pronounced antibacterial effect.

- Intestinal flora comprises the largest organic part of stools. The absence or deficiency of intestinal flora causes a reduction in stools and constipation.

- Instead of restoring intestinal flora, Western medicine relies on its replacement with fiber to alleviate constipation, because undigested fiber increases the volume of stools.

- Treatment of constipation related to disbacteriosis was the primary rational for the relatively recent (first part of the nineteenth century) and purposeful introduction of fiber ("bulk," "roughage") into the human diet.

- The decimation of intestinal flora exposes the internal organs to colonization with undesirable bacteria, weakens the immune system, and causes a shortage of essential vitamins.

- People who live in natural habitats do not experience disbacteriosis because they aren't exposed to factors that can damage intestinal flora. Certain intrinsic factors of natural living ("hygiene theory," untreated water and raw dairy products) help enhance the natural flora's viability.

- Diarrhea, constipation, infectious diseases, severe colorectal disorders, and vitamin deficiencies are the primary symptoms of disbacteriosis.

- Disbacteriosis and resulting diseases can be effectively treated with the restoration of intestinal flora and with dietary supplements. (See Chapter 11, *Avoiding the Perils of Transition.*)

# Footnotes

[1] R.F. Schmidt, G. Thews. Colonic Motility. *Human Physiology, 2nd edition.* 29.7:733.

[2] Search on keywords "disbacteriosis" and "dysbiosis": www.ama-assn.org, www.gastro.org, on 6/19/2004.

[3] The Nobel Prize in Physiology or Medicine 1908. *Nobel e-Museum.* http://www.nobel.se/medicine/laureates/1908/index.html

[4] Antibiotic-Associated Colitis; 3:29; The Merck Manual Of Diagnosis and Therapy; http://www.merck.com/mrkshared/mmanual/section3/chapter29/29a.jsp

[5] American Dental Association. "ADA continues to believe that amalgam is a valuable, viable and safe choice for dental patients and concurs with the findings of the U.S. Public Health Service that amalgam has 'continuing value in maintaining oral health.'» *ADA Statement on Dental Amalgam,* Revised January 8, 2002; http://www.ada.org/prof/resources/positions/statements/amalgam.asp

[6] Mercury Compounds. *U.S. Environmental Protection Agency.* http://www.epa.gov/ttn/atw/hlthef/mercury.html

[7] Thomas M. Ball, M.D., M.P.H, et al. Siblings, Day-Care Attendance, and the Risk of Asthma and Wheezing during Childhood, New England Journal of Medicine, 2000 Aug;343:538–543.

[8] Borody TJ, Warren EF, Leis S, Surace R, Ashman O.; Treatment of ulcerative colitis using fecal bacteriotherapy; *Journal of Clinical Gastroenterology.* 2003 Jul;37(1):42–7. PMID: 12811208.

*Constipation was [sic] the most common digestive
complaint in the United States, outnumbering
all other chronic digestive conditions.*
Epidemiology of constipation in the United States[1]

*Constipation may have other serious consequences; an
increased risk of colon cancer has been reported...*
The Review of Gastroenterological Disorders[2]

*Although it may be extremely bothersome,
constipation itself usually is not serious.*
American Gastroenterological Association[3]

# CHAPTER FIVE

# CONSTIPATION

## Constipation epidemiology: One case of crappy bookkeeping

A reliable, accurate statistic on the prevalence of constipation isn't available, because (ironically), it isn't considered a condition serious enough to merit thorough research and analysis. According to an article in *The Review of Gastroenterological Disorders,* "the exact prevalence of constipation depends on the definition used; prevalence estimates range from 2% to 28%."[4] The implications of such a considerable spread are obvious:

- There are no clear-cut diagnostic criteria for constipation, hence the majority of patients who suffer from constipation are undiagnosed. You should use the guidelines suggested in this book to evaluate your own condition.
- Constipation isn't recognized as a health-threatening condition

until it's too late. In the words of the article cited above, "constipation is not of clinical importance until it causes physical risks or impairs quality of life." It shouldn't get to that point. Once "quality of life" is affected, the side effects of constipation, such as enlarged hemorrhoids, are no longer reversible.

- The "seriousness" of constipation depends on who you ask. For some doctors it's just a nuisance, for others it's (it's) the precursor of colorectal cancer. Obviously, you're better off choosing a doctor who believes the latter.

- If constipation isn't considered serious by your doctor, it means it's not going to be treated as promptly and properly as it should be, and it's more likely causing or worsening colorectal complications. Ask you doctors to reconsider their approach, and refer them to the sources referenced in this book.

- If constipation is considered a serious condition (as it should be), reading this book may literally "save your ass," even though you or your doctor may believe that, thanks to fiber, you don't have any problems, and, therefore, that fiber is safe and working for you. Study this book to understand the multifaceted perils of fiber.

According to a 1989 National Health Interview Survey,[5] about 5.3 million Americans (approximately 2.5%) complained about frequent constipation. A later report from the same survey (the last time the question was asked), conducted by the Centers for Disease Control and Prevention (CDC), indicated that just 3 million people experienced chronic constipation in 1996 (over 1%), even though the overall population and the number of aging baby boomers increased substantially between those years.

Obviously, these numbers don't add up. If, indeed, constipation outnumbers "all other chronic digestive conditions," then the number of complainers should have been in the tens of millions, considering that over 21.3 million[6] Americans had been diagnosed with stomach ulcers, or that up to 20% of adult Americans suffer from irritable bowel syndrome, which is customarily accompanied by constipation.

There are several reasons for such a huge disparity between the actual numbers and the erroneous results of the National Health Interview Survey:

- First, assessing the disease by asking people to self-diagnose isn't objective. That's what is taking place during the surveys conducted via verbal interviews, like the ones mentioned above.
- Secondly, constipation isn't technically a disease, hence it isn't being tracked in the same way as, for example, billable conditions diagnosable by doctors, such as IBS or ulcers.
- Third, the majority of people don't bother complaining about intermittent constipation because they rely on a variety of over-the-counter and home-brewed remedies to manage it.
- Fourth, ongoing constipation treatment doesn't get reimbursed by most medical insurance policies, hence it doesn't get tracked as reliably as those diseases reimbursed by state, federal, and private insurers.
- Fifth, constipation related to weight-loss diets, such as Atkins or South Beach, doesn't get reported either, because most people simply abandon their diets, and return to regular high-fiber, high-carb fare.
- Sixth, a great number of people are embarrassed to talk to their doctors, or even spouses, about constipation.
- Finally, when dietary means such as fiber-fortified cereals, herbal teas, or prune juice are used as laxatives, people may have "regular" stools, and not consider themselves constipated. This paradox is discussed in greater depth in the *Latent Constipation* section later in this chapter.

When a reliable, direct statistic isn't available, it can be determined indirectly. There is, for example, nothing uncertain about the prevalence of hemorrhoidal and diverticular diseases, two "can't miss" side effects of chronic constipation:

---

*National Institutes of Health:* Hemorrhoids may result from straining to move stool. [...] About half of the population have hemorrhoids by age 50.[7]

---

The reverse analysis of this statistic is rather straightforward: If half of the adults have enlarged hemorrhoids by the age of 50, it means that most of them are straining while moving their bowels. Since only people with constipation or anorectal disorders caused by constipation (including hemorrhoids) need to strain, we can then conclude that about half of the population, by the age of 50, suffers from chronic or intermittent constipation.

According to actual "hands-on" data collected by anorectal surgeons at the Hemorrhoid Care Medical Clinic[8] in San Diego, California, enlarged hemorrhoids are detected in over two-thirds of patients during a routine physical exam. In other words, the actual occurrence of hemorrhoidal disease is even more prevalent than the NIH statistical estimate, but we'll stay with the most conservative figures.

To corroborate the "hemorrhoidal" conclusions, let's take a look at diverticular disease, which also results from constipation-related straining. Its equally alarming "proliferation" reconfirms the statistic on hemorrhoidal disease. According to the same NIH source:

---

About half of all people over the age of 60 have diverticulosis. [...] Constipation makes the muscles strain to move stool that is too hard. It is the main cause of increased pressure in the colon. This excess pressure might cause the weak spots in the colon to bulge out and become diverticula.[9]

---

As you can see, the causes and the numbers correspond: half the adults over 60 suffer from diverticular disease related to straining, which in turn only happens among people who are constipated. Obviously, constipation, whether chronic or intermittent, commences long before these people reach 60.

At this moment some readers may ask a reasonable and perfectly appropriate question:

– *I often strain to move my bowels too, but I am not constipated. Why?*

The answer depends on how you define the term "constipation." If it is just "not having stool at regular intervals," as most people believe, then indeed you aren't constipated. But the classic definition of constipation is "*difficult, incomplete, or infrequent evacuation of dry hardened feces from the bowels,*"[10] exactly the kind of stool that not only necessitates straining, but meets the criteria for

"constipation," and eventually causes hemorrhoidal and diverticular diseases.

The term "constipation" is derived from Latin's' *constipatio*—
literally, a crowding together. The "crowded together" stools become large and hard. The outcome is succinctly described by The
International Foundation for Functional Gastrointestinal Disorders:

---

In constipation, stools become large and hard and become in-
creasingly more difficult and uncomfortable to expel. This can
lead to an enlarged rectum and colon and lead to decreased sensation. This leads to increasing difficulty in having a bowel movement.[11]

---

As you can see, the original meaning of the term "constipation"
isn't "lack of regularity" or "absence of stools," as most people
think, but "difficult," "uncomfortable," "hard," and "large." In
other words:

### YOU'RE CONSTIPATED WHEN YOU ARE NOT EXPERIENCING EASY AND COMPLETE STOOLS WITHOUT STRAINING

There's only one way to enjoy this kind of bathroom nirvana—a
low-fiber diet and daily, or even better, twice-daily stools. But
that's the complete opposite of what countless medical authorities
have been preaching all along, namely that if you *eat more fiber,
frequency of stools doesn't matter,* as long as it's no less than three
times a week.

Wrong! Ignoring the frequency of stools shifts the emphasis from
eliminating the causes of constipation to the management of infrequent stools. And, at first glance, what can be a better remedy to
accomplish this task than honest-to-goodness "natural fiber?" At
"first glance," yes, but not at second—the more fiber you add to
bulk up the stools, the more damage you'll cause to yourself, because along with more fiber, the stools are becoming *larger* and
*harder* as well.

And this brings us back to the perils of dietary fiber on one's
plate, inside one's large intestine, and, finally, inside one's stool.

To understand why fiber harms the large intestine, why fiber makes constipation more severe, and why fiber isn't an effective treatment for constipation, you must first understand the functionality of the large intestine. Considering all the hoopla surrounding the "health" benefits of fiber, asking you to take this book's "fiber menace" claims on faith alone wouldn't be fair either to you or to the advocates of fiber.

## The large intestine: Understand the guts, enjoy the glory

The digestive functions inside the large intestine are as essential as those inside the stomach and small intestine, because bacterial fermentation—a function exclusive to the large intestine—produces a number of vital micronutrients and immune co-factors. The large intestine completes the digestion cycle by performing these four critical functions:

- *Recovery of nutrients.* Water, electrolytes, and micronutrients are absorbed from chyme through the mucous membrane (mucosa). When absorption fails, the person experiences diarrhea.
- *Bacterial fermentation.* Chyme is mixed with colonic bacteria (intestinal flora), which ferment the remaining carbohydrates and produce a broad range of essential micronutrients, including vitamin K and certain B-complex vitamins. When the fermentation fails, the person experiences disbacteriosis—a complex, slow-evolving syndrome of hard-to-pin down ailments related to the vitamins' deficiencies.
- *Temporary storage.* Dehydrated, fermented chyme is mixed with bacteria and mucus, and formed into feces. Exemplary feces contain about 70–75% water, and traces of fat. The rest is organic solids—bacteria, dead cells, coloring pigments, and some undigested components. The feces' cellular components (mainly bacteria) retain water and maintain the stool's pliability. Dried out, hard stool, which is one of the symptoms of disbacteriosis, doesn't point to dehydration (a mistaken view), but to the lack of synergistic bacteria needed to retain water.
- *Elimination.* The frequency of elimination is primarily the function of diet content and physical shape—fiber and youth speeds it up. Ideally, healthy adults should move the bowels once or twice

a day. The widely held view that *moving the bowels from three times daily to three times weekly* is normal, is incorrect.

The logic behind the large intestine's arch-like architecture is apparent from those functions: it is inverted to keep the liquid chyme inside for as long as it takes to ferment, dehydrate and assimilate essential nutrients, and to convert them into feces. The chyme becomes "stools" by the time it reaches the descending colon. From this point on it is brownish, shaped slightly, smelly, and ready to be expelled.

The size and shape of the large intestine is determined by the species' need to ferment fiber—the more fiber in the diet, the larger the size. Finicky carnivores, like cats, have a gut similar to humans, but much smaller; herbivores, such as sheep, goats, or cows, have a straight, large one; omnivores, like we humans, are in-between, size-wise. Not surprisingly, if we eat like cows, our gut will grow enlarged (distended) to accommodate all that fiber bulk, so even normal-weight humans may look, from the side, like chimps and monkeys, whose guts are habitually distended from chewing and fermenting fibrous leaves around the clock.

On a diet relatively free of indigestible fiber, the journey of chyme from cecum to sewer takes, give or take, 72 hours in test subjects.[12] When indigestible fiber is generously added to the diet, the transit time drops down to just 24 hours because the large intestine rushes to expel the excess fiber, in order to avoid mechanical (from too much bulk) and chemical (from too much acidity) damage to its delicate mucous lining.

If evolution intended that 72 hours are what's needed for feces to travel to the sewer, then that's what it takes. If you force the refuse out in 24 hours, the essential by-products of intestinal metabolism—electrolytes, vitamins, immune co-factors, and God knows what else—don't get assimilated back into the body, and, at the very least, you experience abdominal cramps from too much peristalsis.

However, if you are chronically constipated, even when you add fiber, the trip down may take much longer than 72 hours. When this occurs, the stools are no longer small, soft, and pliable. Instead, they're impacted—large, hard, and compressed, and not ex-

actly in the shape desirable for the delicate anal canal, or for the
even more delicate mucous layer of rectum and colon.

Lo and behold, the recommendation to use fiber in order to
stimulate *colonic motility*—the peristaltic and mechanical movement of fecal masses through the colon—was based on experiments conducted with carefully screened healthy individuals, who
were young and constipation-free. To determine transit time, participants were ingesting small metal pellets, and their stool was x-
rayed to locate them.

But if you are no longer young, already have a history of constipation and colorectal disorders, such as hemorrhoids, the journey
of fiber to the toilet bowl may take weeks, especially when the colon is already packed with large stools waiting for their turn to be
eliminated. In this case, the newly arriving fiber acts just like a
plunger, and then patiently waits itself to be plunged. When there
is no fiber "plunger" in the diet, constipation quickly sets in. And
that, of course, describes the addiction that results from a dependence on fiber to move the bowels.


### The colon: An epilogue to a meal

As chyme travels up the colon, water, electrolytes, and remaining
nutrients are slowly absorbed through the *epithelium,* a mucous
membrane that lines the insides of the intestines. In turn, the epithelium—more specifically, its abundant *goblet cells*—secretes
mucus to lubricate and protect the epithelium from damage, and to
bind dehydrated chyme into feces. These two actions lead to two
important observations:

- First, it isn't water that binds and forms feces, but colonic mucus.
  In fact, the colon does everything it can to remove the free-
  floating water that isn't bound inside the cellular structure of
  dead cells, bacteria, and undigested fiber.
- Second, if the formed, voluminous, dried-out stool is often strong
  enough to tear apart the skin inside the anal canal, imagine the
  kind of damage it can do to the featherweight lining inside the
  colon. It opens up the pathway for ulcers and precancerous polyps to take hold there.

The movement of fecal mass through the colon (motility) is governed by *propulsive contraction.* The motility is slow, and it's controlled by the *teniae*—thin, ribbon-like muscles equally spaced throughout the length of the colon, giving it the appearance of a string-tied roast with bulges of meat protruding between the coils. These pouch-like bulges in the colon are called *haustrum.*

Meal composition (not volume, and not fiber) influences motility more than any other factor:

---

*Human Physiology:* Motility is influenced by the energy content and composition of the meal, but not by its volume or pH. Energy-rich meals with a high fat content increase motility; carbohydrates and proteins have no effect.[13]

---

This little-known fact is important for the understanding and prevention of constipation, especially age-related constipation. Low-fat or fat-free diets are more likely to cause impaction among older adults, whose colonic motility is too slow to begin with because of weak intestinal muscles—a condition known as *atonic* or *lazy colon.*

The alternating contractions and relaxation of two adjoining *teniae ribbons* propel stools along their way, but most often they contract in different regions in order to mix fecal mass, not move it. Several times daily a coordinated *mass peristaltic movement* occurs, which propels stools from the transverse to sigmoid colon. This particular movement is hard to miss, because it usually happens ten to fifteen minutes after a meal or drink. This effect of food on colonic peristalsis is called the *gastrocolic reflex.*

The combination of these two actions—gastrocolic reflex and mass peristaltic movement—precedes the urge to defecate. The urge diminishes in people who are accustomed to suppressing it, those who are dependant on fiber and laxatives, have a long history of constipation, or are old and infirm. Nerve damage related to colorectal distention (from large stools), surgery (to fix damage caused by large stools), medication, diabetes, or a deficiency of certain vitamins may also reduce or eliminate the urge that sends healthy people running to the bathroom.

One reliable way to prevent the gastrocolic reflex from happen-

ing in the wrong place and at the wrong time is to not eat or drink
if the appropriate bathroom facilities aren't readily available, especially if you failed to relieve yourself before leaving home.

The other "reliable" way to suppress the gastrocolic reflex and
cause constipation are extended low-level stress and anxiety.
That's why following the adage "don't worry, be happy" will protect you from constipation better than fiber will. According to researchers, personality "accounted for about as much variance in
stool output as did dietary fiber." [14] And from what we already
know about fiber, that's saying a lot.

Special events, such as a honeymoon for couples who didn't experience living together before becoming married, may represent a
particular hazard to the large intestine. Sharing the same bed and
bath 24/7 for the first time isn't exactly a stress-free situation for
many newlyweds. Some couples, women particularly, are likely to
return from a honeymoon constipated and disappointed, rather than
satisfied and happy.

Don't contain the defecation urge for too long—the "tight ass"
personality trait isn't, at least initially, a function of character, but
of a bad diet, unusual circumstances, and equally bad toilet habits.

The opposite is true in extremely stressful situations, such as an
accident, tragic news, a crucial exam, or winning the lottery. Instead of constipation, these events may cause vomiting and/or diarrhea. The mechanism here is altogether different, and the main
culprit behind either vomiting or diarrhea is abruptly elevated
blood pressure:

- First, in response to extreme stress, the metabolic hormones (insulin and glucagon) and the stress hormones (adrenalin,
  noradrenalin, and cortisol) cause an almost instantaneous constriction of the blood vessels and a rapid release of glucose from
  the liver and muscles, where it is stored.
- Second, the combined action of constricted blood vessels and
  high blood sugar (glucose) causes an instant spike in blood pressure. The spike may be high enough to jam a blood pressure
  monitor, just like the spikes that cause strokes and heart attacks.
- Third, to prevent damage to the brain, heart, kidney, liver, and
  blood vessels, the body instantly takes a corrective action and literally unloads the excess blood plasma from the closed vascular

loop by dumping it into the stomach and/or intestines via the cells and glands that ooze digestive juices.

- Fourth, an almost instantaneous release of so much fluid into the stomach can cause vomiting (from overloading), especially if food and digestive juices are already present there.
- Fifth, a substantial drop in blood pressure follows the release of plasma into the stomach and/or intestines. This condition (falling blood pressure and blood sugar) is made perceptible by a weakness in the knees and a relaxation of the rectal muscles that control the sphincters.
- Finally, a rapidly increasing volume of fluid in the large intestine, combined with relaxed rectal and anal sphincters, literally flushes out the entire content of the large intestine, often in profuse quantities.

So if you want someone to instantly lose lots of weight (water and feces) and relieve constipation at once, take them to a horror movie, steal their car, hire someone to simulate a hold-up, or do any other stupid thing that will scare the hell out of them.

Incidentally, abdominal cramps during critical exams, job interviews, blind dates, public performances, and similar events are all from the same causes—increased muscle tone, fear-induced elevated blood pressure, and a surge of excess electrolytes into the intestines. And the sudden lapse of memory that often accompanies the cramps results from insufficient circulation of blood in the brain because of a narrowing of cerebral blood vessels and capillaries.

I know of only a few proven recipes to combat fear—preparedness, practice, and visualization. Also, it wouldn't hurt on these occasions to make sure that you are well rested, your digestive organs aren't stuffed with fiber, and your large intestine isn't packed with fiber-laden large stools.

### The rectum: All's well that ends well

The rectum is very much like an exit dock in a space station—it separates the rest of the "ship" from the perils of harsh outer space. Hence, the rectum of a healthy person is empty at all times. Its brief contact with stools and gases happens only on their final journey out to the sewer.

Unlike the colon's circular musculature, the rectum's is longitudinal, with strands of muscles running from top to bottom, very much like the drawings of biceps that hang in medical offices. The rectum's muscles stretch out to accommodate the feces as they move down from the colon, and they contract back to initiate defecation. The rectum's contraction completes an elaborate sequence of preceding events:

- The gastrocolic reflex, stimulated by eating and/or drinking, is a perceptible prologue of this process. Alas, it's an easy reflex to suppress directly (consciously), or indirectly, through stress, lack of attention, habit, and similar factors. The more often you suppress it, the greater your chances of developing a life-long dependence on fiber to move your bowels. The gastrocolic reflex actuates the next step.

- The colonic mass peristaltic movement occurs without conscious control. It's impossible to suppress by will, but stress, age, laxatives, and systemic muscular relaxants (such as narcoleptics, antidepressants, blood pressure and cholesterol-lowering medication) can diminish it significantly, and bring on fiber dependence. (This particular side effect is always stated on the prescription information circular for each medication.) The mass peristaltic movement propels feces into the rectum.

- The stretching of the rectum by incoming stools is, by far, the most important condition for regularity. Not surprisingly, the long-term stretching of the rectum, common among individuals who consume a great deal of fiber, eventually leads to the loss of rectal sensitivity, and inhibits natural defecation. The stretching of the rectum stimulates contraction, and…

- At the very end of this process, following your explicit instruction to relax the external sphincter, the rectum contracts to begin the elimination of stools that are now inside the rectal ampoule. Again, the rectum's ability to contract diminishes with age, from medication, from nerve damage related to diabetes and inadequate nutrition, muscular disorders, and also from extended periods of stretching by stool enlarged (bulked up) by fiber.

- A final, and most crucial participant in this process is the *nerve plexus* along the anorectal line—the juncture of rectum and anal canal. When the stools reach this intersection, the final signal is sent to the autonomous nervous system to complete elimination. All of the same factors that compromise the rectum's ability to react and contract, desensitize the anal nerve plexus: large stools, nerve damage, hemorrhoids, anal fissures, medication, and others. Alas, as we age, these factors grow more and more pronounced.

The rectum can stretch to accommodate up to 2 liters (2 qt) of stools. This is essential to avoid incontinence, but when the stored feces becomes hard and dry, this particular ability becomes a negative, as it allows stools to accumulate into one large impacted lump that at some point may grow too big to get out.

There are three horizontal dividers that separate sigmoid colon from rectum, aptly named *horizontal folds*. These folds help retain stools inside the colon while allowing gases to pass through. Amazingly, evolution took into account even this anti-social contingency.

So how come Mother Nature didn't account for fiber dependence and its prominent side effects? Because the savages didn't depend on fiber and bathrooms the way city dwellers do:

- Just like animals in the wild, humans, until urbanization, had no shame associated with defecation, and relieved themselves as soon as they sensed the urge. (Lesson to us: avoid suppressing the defecation urge when restroom facilities are readily available.)
- Their natural world, which included pristine water and abundant meats (especially internal organs), kept their intestines continuously recharged with essential bacteria. (Lesson to us: continue to wash hands, boil water, and cook meats, but eliminate disbacteriosis using more enlightened methods.)
- They defecated in the most natural and strain-free way—a squatting position—rather than sitting straight up on a high toilet bowl. (Lesson to us: watch out for little kids. A traditional chamber pot, not a child seat over the toilet, is the best choice for their undeveloped bodies, and will help to prevent constipation and dependence on laxatives and fiber for the rest of their lives.)
- And, of course, until very recently humans didn't consume prodigious amounts of processed dietary fiber year round, and they didn't have anyone to tell them otherwise. (Lesson to us: use intelligent ways to navigate the sea of conflicting advice.)

Normally the rectum is empty, with stools kept out by the first of those horizontal folds inside the sigmoid and descending colons. You can verify it by adorning a preferred hand with a surgical glove, and slowly inserting a heavily lubricated forefinger (use pure petroleum jelly) inside the anal canal. If the rectum is empty, you'll feel nothing. If it isn't, you finger will feel the hardened stools, the kind that is usually referred to as "formed." And that's not normal.

If you move a small volume of loose stool regularly, there's no point poking around inside. But if you are dependent on fiber, suffer from constipation, or your stools are hard and large, you don't need a doctor's license to check out the content of your own rectum. It isn't any more gross than wiping your behind. Doctors routinely perform anal exams while checking out hemorrhoids, the male prostate gland, or the female uterus through the anus.

### The Anal Canal: The weakest link in the long chain

The anal canal is shorter than Panama's, but as treacherous to navigate, and the most prone to jams and bottlenecks. A precise coordination of the rectum and anal sphincters is required to complete defecation. The other participants are the internal obturator and levator muscles of the anus, pelvic muscles, and diaphragm, but they all play second fiddle.

The ideal act of defecation shouldn't take any more effort than that of urination. This may be hard to believe, but it's true nevertheless. Just ask any healthy, constipation-free child on a low-fiber diet about his or her happy experience.

You should barely feel the movement of a stool of normal form and consistency. If you have enlarged hemorrhoids, you may feel them protruding, but this is an entirely different sensation from that of hardened feces chafing and scraping against the delicate tissues of the anal canal.

If you need to strain, it means your stool has already become enlarged and hardened, and that the rectum's muscle tone isn't sufficient to propel it out through the narrow opening of the anal canal. Hence the need to apply additional straining pressure on the colon and rectum to expel the large feces, bulked up by indigestible fiber. We are back again to the perils of fiber and its role in constipation.

## No fiber, no stool vs. no fiber, normal stool

Without fiber, remnants of food in the stool of a healthy person aren't detectable. Even the word *feces* is derived from Latin *faex,* or *dregs*—a small amount, a residue. Apparently, the ancient Romans hadn't yet tasted bran cereal when naming it.

This profound point—that normal stools aren't composed of food, but of *physiological waste*—is a mental challenge even for medical professionals, because most Westerners are accustomed to seeing primarily large, voluminous stools—the term derived from the Anglo-Saxon *stol*—seat.[15]

Nonetheless, the point shines through when I highlight this undeniable fact again and again: fit, healthy people without a history of colorectal disease, constipation, and disbacteriosis, who are placed on a liquid diet or who are starved, continue to HAVE REGULAR STOOLS the entire time. And if their preceding diet was low in fiber, the changes in stool volume are negligible. If you're still in doubt, here's an illuminating excerpt from a classic European medical reference:

The sparing Schmidt's Diet consists of 1–1.5 liters of milk, 2–3 soft-boiled eggs, white bread with butter, 125 g of ground meat, 200 g of mashed potatoes, and oatmeal with caloric value of 2250 calories. **The feces of a healthy person on this diet doesn't contain any food residue**.

[...] The Pevsner's Diet represents a heavy digestive load for a healthy person. It includes 200 g of white and 200 g of black [rye] bread, 250 g of grilled meat, 100 g of butter, 40 g of sugar, fried potatoes, carrots, salads, coleslaw, buckwheat, rice, and fresh fruits. Its caloric value is 3250 calories. **The feces of healthy persons on this diet contains large amounts of undigested fiber and some muscle tissue**.[16]

As you can see, on the Schmidt's diet, which is rather generous, permissive, and varied, the feces of a healthy person "*doesn't contain any food residue.*" But as soon as we turn to the more typical Western fare—breads, cereals, fruits, and vegetables—represented by the Pevsner's diet, the stool of an even healthy person "*contains large amounts of undigested fiber*" and "*muscle tissue*" from burned (grilled) meat.

Unfortunately, the *no fiber/no stool* connection is so insidiously prevalent that it's difficult to remove even from the minds of experienced gastroenterologists and proctologists. The correct cause and effect connection is, of course, *no fiber/less stool*. And that's exactly what happens when you switch from a high-fiber diet to a low-fiber one, such as the Atkins diet:

- Without fiber in the diet, the volume of feces in the colon drops five to ten times from its preceding volume. The receptors in the rectum, which respond to the stretching of its walls, no longer detect such a small volume of stool, and it remains unexpelled until its volume either reaches the stimulation threshold, or the person takes laxatives.

- As the fecal mass accumulates in the colon, it becomes dehydrated, compressed, and hardened. When the increased fecal volume finally stimulates elimination reflexes, its hardness requires straining in order to expel it. While passing, the hard stools damage the delicate tissues and blood vessels that surround the anal canal.

And when an accumulation of hardened fecal mass occurs, the grossest error one can make is to follow the prevailing advice (including Atkins'), which is to ingest "therapeutic" fiber to dislodge and expel it. In this case, the probability of injury to the colon, rectum, and anal canal is practically unavoidable, because the extra fiber behaves just like a proverbial bull in a china shop.

## Constipation treatment: Riskier than the disease

Whoever came up with the notion that undigested fiber is a health food was thinking about "dirty colons" and constipation:

*Problem:*   The colon is dirty with stools, microbes, worms, rotten food, etc. If I can get rid of "dirt" faster, I am going to be healthier.

*Solution:*   Consume more indigestible fiber to cleanse the colon of "dirt." Helps with constipation, too.

To simple-minded quack nutritionists, the stinky stuff that comes out of the body is indeed "dirt." So they followed an obvious cause and effect approach to problem solving:

*Cause:*  Indigestible fiber causes larger stools, which stimulates and speeds up elimination.
*Effect:*  Large, speedy stools keep the colon clean.

It sounds great on paper, and, just as with most drugs, it even works for a while in healthy people who don't have any anorectal damage. But this approach isn't addressing several important questions:

– Is the colon indeed "dirty" with bad microbes, worms, and rotten food? (A: No, it isn't. In fact, the colon becomes dysfunctional when the bacteria are wiped out. Worms are extremely rare among adults, particularly in cities. Healthy people don't have "rotten" food in the colon, unless they consume fiber.)
– What causes constipation in the first place? (A: Literally, the absence of "dirt" (i.e. bacteria), and the presence of undigested fiber.)
– What can be done to eliminate those causes? (A: Restoration of the bacteria population, elimination of fiber, reduction of stool sizes.)

But when these questions aren't answered at all, or the answers are wrong, or the real causes of intestinal disorders aren't addressed, then fiber, just like most drugs, becomes a quick fix. And drugs, no matter how innocent they may act or seem at first, have side effects, and so does fiber.

The fiber-based treatment recommendations for constipation, as proposed by the American Gastroenterological Association, serve as the basic guidelines for the *gatekeepers*[17]—the family physicians who hear about constipation-related problems from their patients before they can grant them a referral to the more expensive specialists (the gastroenterologists themselves). And here is what they may recommend:

**What Is The Treatment For Constipation?**
A well-balanced diet that includes fiber-rich foods, such as unprocessed bran, whole-grain bread, and fresh fruits and vegetables, is recommended. Drinking plenty of fluids and exercising
regularly will help to stimulate intestinal activity. Special exercises may be necessary to tone up abdominal muscles after pregnancy or whenever abdominal muscles are lax.[18]

Unfortunately, *more* fiber to bulk up the stool and *more* exercise
to strengthen abdominal muscles are the principal reasons behind
straining, even though the same document bluntly warns that
*"Constipation can lead to complications, such as hemorrhoids
caused by extreme straining"*[19] without first telling the readers that
only large stools, created by fiber, require "extreme straining."

That's unfortunate, but easy to understand. Gastroenterologists—
the principal members of the American Gastroenterological Association—are surgeons, not nutritionists. They are trained to operate
on the endless complications of "extreme straining," such as prolapsed hemorrhoids, lacerated anuses, rotting diverticula, perfo-
rated colons, and hemorrhaging ulcers. Constipation isn't their
"thing," hence they rely on a quick and simple fiber solution for
patients who don't require surgery yet.

That fiber and straining eventually make constipation even more
severe, and can cause irreversible side effects, is beside the point,
because, as long as you are "regular," all parties are happy. You're
happy because fiber delivers "regular" stools, your doctor, because
you're quickly "healed," and your insurer, because the fiber solution is dirt cheap. and your pharmacist, because you're hooked for
life.

And that's the reason why a recent search[20] of the well-stocked
Internet pharmacy for "fiber" revealed a whopping 65 fiber-based
laxatives. Why so many? Because natural fiber from the diet alone
doesn't work. Just consider these conclusions from one of the most
authoritative books about functional digestive disorders published
in the United States, but authored by the international consortium
of the world's leading gastroenterologists—*Rome II Diagnostic
Criteria For Functional Gastrointestinal Disorders.*

First, about the merits of consuming a fiber-rich diet for people already affected by chronic constipation:

---

*Rome II:* ...there is little or no relationship between dietary fiber intake and whole gut transit time; (2) constipated patients on the average do not eat less fiber than controls; and (3) patients have lower stool weights and longer transit times than controls whether treated with wheat bran or not.[21]

---

In other words, everything you've heard about fiber hasn't been true: more fiber in the diet doesn't makes stools leave the body any faster, there is no difference in fiber consumption between healthy and constipated people, and adding more fiber doesn't make any difference to either stool weight or transit time. (Please note again that these observations apply to patients with chronic constipation and to dietary fiber from natural foods only. Unlike fiber from the diet, supplemental fiber or fiber-fortified products do increase stool volume and do decrease transit time dramatically, especially in young, healthy subjects without any colorectal damage.) And what about the exercises?

---

*Rome II:* Active or chronic physical exercise has probably no major effect on the functions of healthy colons.[22]

---

As you can see, you can work yourself out into a stupor, but it isn't going to make constipation go away or your colon's health get any better.

And what about water? Here is commentary from an equally respected and credible source, *The Journal of The American Dietetic Association:*

---

It is a common but erroneous belief that the increased weight [of stool] is due primarily to water. The moisture content of human stool is 70% to 75% and this does not change when more fiber is consumed. In other words, fiber in the colon is not more effective at holding water in the lumen [intestinal cavity] than the other components of stool.[23]

---

Please give me a glass of water. I'm fainting...

You must be asking yourself the same question I once asked my-self: how come so many experts managed to err so badly on all three counts—fiber, water, and exercise? How could these well-educated doctors, scientists, and researchers be so wrong, and wrong for so long?

Well, there are many reasons, but none of them are malicious. In an ideal world, when anyone develops constipation, doctors would investigate and quickly remedy the dysfunction(s) that caused it. But investigating the numerous causes of constipation requires an individual approach to each patient. That means an investment of time and effort and expertise on the part of family doctors, inter-nists, and pediatricians, and that's not what usually happens be-cause they don't have the time, they aren't paid enough to devote the effort, and they lack the specialized expertise. Hence, they re-vert to a simple solution—more supplemental fiber, more water, more exercise.

Not surprisingly, for anyone but the very old and frail who al-ready lack the strength to strain, adding supplemental fiber actually works for a while, because it makes stools larger, and stronger ab-dominal muscles indeed help to expel these large stools out. While you're still relatively young and healthy, supplemental fiber works "as advertised" for a period of time.

But as time goes by, enlarged hemorrhoids become the most prominent result of large stools and straining. Enlarged hemor-rhoids reduce the aperture of the anal canal from the already small to the very small. To overcome the resistance of a smaller opening, more fiber and straining are needed. At one point the colorectal damage becomes so severe that adding any more fiber, or straining harder, no longer works.

So how can you determine on your own that the constipation treatment isn't causing you more damage? This is really simple. The treatment is wrong when:

- You can't achieve defecation without a laxative, or specific foods that have laxative properties, such as prunes, herbal teas, agar-agar, and others;
- Your diet includes added fiber from supplements or fiber-fortified foods, such as cereals, crackers, muffins, etc.;
- You are consuming 400–500 grams of carbohydrates daily from

the products that belong to the grain, fruit, and vegetable groups in order to ingest more natural fiber;

- You don't have normal stools at least daily or twice daily;
- Bowel movements, even minor ones, require straining, and your stools are large.

This last characteristic—*large stools*—is relative. How do you determine what's large, and what's not? Fortunately, there is a rational method for establishing benchmarks that will help you to objectively evaluate your stools.

### The Bristol Stool Form Scale: Form follows dysfunction

The British take their stools much more seriously than the Americans. Researchers at the Bristol Royal Infirmary—a hospital in Bristol, England—developed a visual guide for stools. This guide is called the Bristol Stool Form Scale,[24] *BSF scale* for short. It is a self-diagnostic tool that helps skittish patients and doctors alike discuss this delicate subject without getting embarrassed. You just look at a simple chart, point to what approximates the content of your toilet bowl, and your doctor (or this book) tells you whether the form is right or wrong.

There are seven types of stools in the chart, each with a brief annotation (in italics below). The publication that features the BSF scale doesn't provide any substantive comments beyond the brief: "*The ideal stools are types 3* [wrong!] *and 4, especially type 4* [correct], *as they are most likely to glide out without any fuss whatsoever.*"[25] The original definitions are in italics. The expanded commentaries are mine:

Type 1: *Separate hard lumps, like nuts*—Typical for acute disbacteriosis. These stools lack a normal amorphous quality, because bacteria are missing and there is nothing to retain water. The lumps are hard and abrasive, the typical diameter ranges from 1 to 2 cm (0.4–0.8"), and they're painful to pass, because the lumps are hard and scratchy. There is a high likelihood of anorectal bleeding from mechanical laceration of the anal canal. Typical for post-antibiotic treatments and for people attempting fiber-free (low-carb) diets. Flatulence isn't likely, because fermentation of fiber isn't taking place.

Type 2: *Sausage-like but lumpy*—Represents a combination of Type 1 stools impacted into a single mass and lumped together by fiber components and some bacteria. Typical for organic constipation. The diameter is 3 to 4 cm (1.2–1.6"). This type is the most destructive by far because its size is near or exceeds the maximum opening of the anal canal's aperture (3.5 cm). It's bound to cause extreme straining during elimination, and most likely to cause anal canal laceration, hemorrhoidal prolapse, or diverticulosis. To attain this form, the stools must be in the colon for at least several weeks instead of the normal 72 hours. Anorectal pain, hemorrhoidal disease, anal fissures, withholding or delaying of defecation, and a history of chronic constipation are the most likely causes. Minor flatulence is probable. A person experiencing these stools is most likely to suffer from irritable bowel syndrome because of continuous pressure of large stools on the intestinal walls. The possibility of obstruction of the small intestine is high, because the large intestine is filled to capacity with stools. Adding supplemental fiber to expel these stools is dangerous, because the expanded fiber has no place to go, and may cause hernia, obstruction, or perforation of the small and large intestine alike.

Type 3: *Like a sausage but with cracks in the surface*—This form has all of the characteristics of Type 2 stools, but the transit time is faster, between one and two weeks. Typical for latent constipation. The diameter is 2 to 3.5 cm (0.8–1.4"). Irritable bowel syndrome is likely. Flatulence is minor, because of disbacteriosis. The fact that it hasn't became as enlarged as Type 2 suggests that the defecations are regular. Straining is required. All of the adverse effects typical for Type 2 stools are likely for type 3, especially the rapid deterioration of hemorrhoidal disease.

Type 4: *Like a sausage or snake, smooth and soft*—This form is normal for someone defecating once daily. The diameter is 1 to 2 cm (0.4–0.8"). The larger diameter suggests a longer transit time or a large amount of dietary fiber in the diet.

Type 5: *Soft blobs with clear-cut edges*—I consider this form ideal. It is typical for a person who has stools twice or three times daily, after major meals. The diameter is 1 to 1.5 cm (0.4–0.6").

Type 6: *Fluffy pieces with ragged edges, a mushy stool*—This form is close to the margins of comfort in several respects. First, it may be difficult to control the urge, especially when you don't have immediate access to a bathroom. Second, it is a rather messy affair to manage with toilet paper alone, unless you have access to a flexible shower or bidet. Otherwise, I consider it borderline normal. These kind of stools may suggest a slightly hyperactive colon (fast motility), excess dietary potassium, or sudden dehydration or spike in blood pressure related to stress (both cause the rapid release of water and potassium from blood plasma into the intestinal cavity). It can also indicate a hypersensitive personality prone to stress, too many spices, drinking water with a high mineral content, or the use of osmotic (mineral salts) laxatives.

Type 7: *Watery, no solid pieces*—This, of course, is diarrhea, a subject outside the scope of this chapter with just one important and notable exception—so-called *paradoxical* diarrhea. It's typical for people (especially young children and infirm or convalescing adults) affected by fecal impaction—a condition that follows or accompanies type 1 stools. During paradoxical diarrhea the liquid contents of the small intestine (up to 1.5–2 liters/quarts daily) have no place to go but down, because the large intestine is stuffed with impacted stools throughout its entire length. Some water gets absorbed, the rest accumulates in the rectum. The reason this type of diarrhea is called *paradoxical* is not because its nature isn't known or understood, but because being severely constipated and experiencing diarrhea all at once, is, indeed, a paradoxical situation. Unfortunately, it's all too common.

To avoid problems later on, check the content of the toilet bowl at every opportunity to make sure that your stool's type is close to optimal. Here are several additional points:

- *Weight.* About 80 to 100 grams (2.5–3.2 oz) per defecation is considered the norm on a low-fiber diet. Normal stools are heavier than water. Floating stools indicate an overabundance of undigested fiber and gases from fermentation. Many sources indicate that floating stool is normal. It isn't!
- *Consistency.* A stool of normal consistency and frequency should be amorphous, slightly formed. This morphology assures easy, straining-free passing, and a consistent triggering of urge.
- *Form.* A formed stool between types 4 and 3 is bound to cause problems for people who already have colorectal disorders, such as hemorrhoids, fissures, ulcers, fistulas, abrasions, cuts, and tears, all caused by excessive mechanical pressure on the anal canal walls, and amplified by straining.
- *Shape.* A soft, loose stool may not be perfectly round, because it assumes the geometry of your anal canal, which in turn may be affected by internal hemorrhoids. Many people may have enlarged internal hemorrhoids without actually knowing it.
- *Misconceptions.* The popular scare—*when the stool isn't perfectly round, it may mean a tumor*—may have validity only when the stools are large and hard (the tumor shapes the form), but not so much when they are small, thin, and pliable (the anal canal geometry shapes the form). If in doubt, it's best to consult a physician.
- *Warning signs.* If the stool is formed, long, uninterrupted, and over 2 cm (0.8") in diameter, it means that regular elimination is incomplete, and the formed stools may be extending all the way back past the descending colon.
- *Danger zone.* The most telltale sign of fecal impaction is that the formed stool looks just like the anatomical drawings of the colon: evenly spaced bulges on the outside repeat the anatomical pattern of *haustrum* inside the large intestine.

- *Complications.* The mechanical properties of large stools—dryness, hardness, abrasiveness, and bulk—are the primary causes of irritable bowel syndrome, ulcerative colitis, and diverticular disease.

By now, you should understand why voluminous, round, well-formed stools (BSF 3)—the type most medical authorities, including the Bristol Stool Form Scale authors, would like you to have—are destructive for your colon's health, for the normal functioning of your rectum, and for your anal canal's structural integrity.

Unfortunately, whenever you don't have stools like these, most Western doctors, nutritionists, and dietitians are likely to recommend more fiber, more water, and more exercise, which is the exact opposite of what you should do to protect yourself from colorectal damage related to large stools and straining. And that's how once benign *functional* constipation turns into *latent,* and, eventually, into irreversible *organic.*

## The three stages of constipation

To better comprehend the connection between fiber dependence, constipation, and related colorectal disorders, you must first understand its progression through the functional, latent, and organic stages.

### Functional constipation: Easy comes, rarely goes (away, that is)

In general, a condition is considered *functional* when there are no changes in the normal physiology of a particular organ. In the case of constipation it means that nothing specific, such as enlarged hemorrhoids or tumors, impedes defecation.

For otherwise healthy people, functional constipation is the initial stage of constipation. It may happen for a variety of reasons, such as a sudden change of diet, embarrassment with "toilet duties" while on a honeymoon, a shift in regular schedule while on vacation or a business trip, side effects of medication, a bout with diarrhea, extended stress, major trauma or surgery unrelated to colorectal organs, and similar circumstances.

The mainstream diagnostic criteria (by Rome II) for functional constipation are (1) straining, (2) hard or lumpy stools, (3) sensation of incomplete evacuation, (4) sensation of blockage, (5) the need for manual disimpaction, and (6) less than three defecations per week.[26] Actually, when a person experiences all of these symptoms, the constipation is way past the functional stage.

Irregular defecation is the most prominent characteristic of functional constipation. The stool's size may increase, remain unchanged, or become smaller.

- Reduced stool size and hardness (BSF type 1) indicate an insufficiency of intestinal flora, which may be caused by preceding diarrhea, ongoing medications, or various environmental and food-born toxins.
- The increased stool size (BSF type 2 and 3) indicates an impaction of stool, and may be related to non-physiological factors, such as change of diet, business trip, vacation, and others.
- If the stool, regardless of size, becomes hard and dry, it may indicate potassium deficiency—a mineral that is responsible for moisture retention.

At this point most individuals will either visit a doctor or take matters into their own hands. What happens next depends on the remedy:

- If you address and eliminate the primary cause(s) behind functional constipation, and restore daily stools that match BSF type 4 to 6, you are back to normal. That's what this book teaches. End of story.
- If you begin taking over-the-counter laxatives to maintain "regularity," you'll gradually transition to latent constipation. That's what many people decide to do on their own, and the constipation never goes away; only "irregularity" gets chased away.
- If you add more fiber to your diet in order to increase the stool's size and volume, you'll also gradually transition to latent constipation. Unfortunately, that's what most medical authorities urge people to do, and the story goes on.

As you can see, becoming "regular" doesn't mean becoming "healthy" or "recovered." Your goal must always be *small, soft, and moist stool* (BSF 4 to 6) at regular (at least daily) intervals, not just *any stool regularly.* When you fail to accomplish that goal, the next stage is...

## Latent constipation: The hidden menace

If you have regular stools now because your diet contains lots of fiber or you're dependent on laxatives, whether natural or synthetic, your constipation is *latent*—concealed, without apparent symptoms, because either your current diet *is* the laxative or your diet is supplemented *by* a laxative.

When fiber, especially supplemental, becomes a laxative, it works by increasing stools' size. That's why doctors refer to fiber as *bulk, bulking agents,* or *roughage.* Not surprisingly, large stool size and volume (type 2 to 3) are the most prominent characteristics of latent constipation.

The following table illustrates this connection between fiber and the resulting volume of stool. The ash content—what remains after the test sample is burned—is a reliable approximation of post-digestion remnants of fiber-free food. Here are the examples:

**Indigestible content of selected food (per 100 g, ash + fiber)[27]**

| Food | Dietary fiber (g) | Ash (g) | Indigestible content (g) | Ratio (%%) |
|---|---|---|---|---|
| Kellogg's All-Bran With Extra Fiber | 51.1 | 5.30 | 56.40 | 56.40% |
| Fiber One (cereal) | 47.5 | 4.09 | 51.59 | 51.59% |
| Wheat bran, crude | 42.8 | 5.79 | 48.59 | 48.59% |
| Rice bran, crude | 21.0 | 9.98 | 30.98 | 30.98% |
| Split peas | 22.5 | 2.66 | 25.16 | 25.16% |
| Almonds | 11.8 | 3.11 | 14.91 | 14.9% |
| Quaker oatmeal | 9.0 | 3.50 | 12.50 | 12.50% |
| Raisin Nut Bran (cereal) | 9.2 | 2.66 | 11.86 | 11.86% |
| Pecans | 9.6 | 1.49 | 11.09 | 11.09% |
| Peanuts | 8.5 | 2.33 | 10.83 | 10.83% |
| Whole wheat bread | 6.6 | 2.30 | 8.90 | 8.90% |
| Rye bread | 5.8 | 2.50 | 8.30 | 8.30% |
| Spinach | 2.7 | 1.70 | 4.40 | 4.40% |

| Bread (bleached wheat) | 2.3 | 1.90 | 4.20 | 4.20% |
|---|---|---|---|---|
| Broccoli | 3.0 | 0.92 | 3.92 | 3.92% |
| Carrots | 3.0 | 0.87 | 3.87 | 3.87% |
| Cabbage | 2.3 | 0.72 | 3.02 | 3.02% |
| Apples | 2.7 | 0.26 | 2.96 | 2.96% |
| Salmon | 0 | 1.53 | 1.53 | 1.53% |
| Eggs | 0 | 1.36 | 1.36 | 1.36% |
| Pork | 0 | 1.29 | 1.29 | 1.29% |
| Beef | 0 | 0.90 | 0.90 | 0.90% |
| Whole milk | 0 | 0.72 | 0.72 | 0.72% |
| Breast milk | 0 | 0.20 | 0.20 | 0.20% |

As you can see, legumes, nuts, peanuts, and processed, man-made foods, particularly cereals and breads, are the largest offenders in terms of indigestible fiber content. Natural, unprocessed vegetables in moderation are fine as long as they are themselves "low-carb"—tomatoes (4.6%), cucumbers (3.6%), squash (3.3%), cabbage (5.6%), and similar vegetables containing under 6% of carbohydrates, including fiber content.

Eventually, thanks to the ongoing impact of larger stools on the colon, rectum, and anus, latent constipation transforms into *organic*. Hemorrhoidal disease—the irreversible enlargement of hemorrhoids—is the hallmark of encroaching organic constipation.

While the functional stage is relatively short-lived and often intermittent, latent constipation may last for decades. The actual length depends on a person's age and treatment:

- If latent constipation starts at a relatively young age (while the internal organs are still strong and flexible) it may continue relatively unnoticed into the mid- to late thirties.
- If it starts in the late twenties or early thirties, you'll start noticing its impact by the early forties.
- Finally, if it starts in the late thirties or early forties, you'll see its impact in just a few years.

Obviously, the more fiber you take to treat constipation, the faster you transition to the organic stage. That's unfortunate, but true.

You may have been led to believe that constipation is a symptom of irritable bowel syndrome, Crohn's disease, and ulcerative colitis. This isn't so. In fact, these conditions are the symptoms or the results of latent constipation, and the ever-increasing fiber content of your diet.

This fact—that the major disorders of the large intestine are caused by dietary fiber consumed to manage hidden constipation (not a theory, not a hypothesis, not a concept, but a hard, irrefutable fact)—represents the core of this book and its central thesis: to prevent and eliminate chronic colorectal disorders, you must eliminate *latent* constipation first.

You may have also been led to believe that constipation is one of the "side effects" of low-carb diets such as the Atkins and South Beach diets. This isn't true, either. Diet-related constipation is a symptom of *latent* constipation, too. If low-carb diets suddenly make you constipated, it simply means that your current diet is no longer providing enough bulk from fiber to stimulate defecation. If you suddenly dropped a laxative, the situation would be identical, because the fiber in your preceding diet was the laxative.

Again, this fact, that low-carb diet-related constipation is a symptom of *latent* constipation caused by the withdrawal of fiber (not a theory, not a hypothesis, not a concept, but a hard, irrefutable fact) also represents the core of this book and its key thesis: to enjoy a low-carb, low-fiber diet, you must first eliminate *latent* constipation.

And if you don't eliminate *latent* constipation, it turns into the next phase as inevitably as winter follows autumn.

### Organic constipation: No turning back, but not entirely hopeless

If *functional* constipation is distinguished by irregularity and *latent* by large stools, *organic* is distinguished by all of the above plus the ongoing difficulty to attain not just "regular" stool, but any stool. And the reasons are:

- *Permanent organ changes.* The stool gets stalled because of enlarged hemorrhoids, because of a stretching of the colon and rectum, because of anal fissures, because of nerve damage to the anal receptors and loss of sensitivity, and similar factors.

- *Irreversible loss of natural function.* It means there is slow go or no go even when the circumstances are ideal and the stool morphology is perfect.
- *Continuing dependence on laxatives.* It means that you can no longer "get regular" by just fixing up circumstances and the stool's shape and form, and may require some form of external assistance to move your bowels for the rest of your life.

Organic constipation speeds up aging and chronic disease, unless luck intervenes and you get the chance to read this or a similar book in time to manage it by means safer than adding an ever-increasing amount of fiber, or ever harsher and more addictive laxatives.

Fortunately, there are natural ways of managing organic constipation without the use of fiber or stimulant laxatives, and ways to make sure the side effects won't get worse, and will remain nothing more than a manageable nuisance. Considering all the other indignities of aging—reading glasses, enlarged prostate, sagging breasts, receding gums—a few more minor nuisances here and there isn't such a big deal, especially when visiting the bathroom is no longer such a dreaded event.

So, as you can see, the operative word for organic constipation is "manage," not "fully recover." That's why reading this book is imperative while you can still "fully recover," because functional constipation is preventable, avoidable, and reversible. It will not turn into latent if it's handled right and early. Latent constipation is completely or partially reversible, meaning it will not cause further damage to the colon, rectum, and anus, or become chronic.

There is, however, some "icing on the cake" even for organic constipation. While it may be too late to undo the existing damage, you can always halt further erosion and complications, which are discussed in greater depth throughout this book.

### Colorectal disorders: The domino effect of fiber

Nature prescribes a gradual decline and eventual death for us, but it doesn't presume that hemorrhoidal disease, diverticulosis, irritable bowel syndrome, ulcerative colitis or Crohn's disease will inevitably accompany normal aging. Those "lucky" ones who die from old age without experiencing any of these disorders are the proof of God's intent to keep our large intestines fit and sound until our last breath.

Thus, it isn't God's will to make you suffer from constipation, hemorrhoidal disease, or ulcerative colitis, but it's the actions of your parents (first), and, later, your own actions (or lack thereof), that bring the punishment. The next five chapters continue to investigate the connection between fiber, constipation, and major colorectal disorders.

## Summary

- Constipation is a poorly recognized medical condition. It isn't considered serious by most medical authorities, and is mostly noted after it's already caused irreversible colorectal disorders.
- The prevalence of constipation in the population is significantly underreported, because different research venues use different criteria to define constipation.
- Constipation is a primary causative factor behind major colorectal disorders, such as irritable bowel syndrome, hemorrhoidal and diverticular diseases, ulcerative colitis, Crohn's disease, colon cancer, and others.
- Chronic, late-stage constipation seriously affects the quality of life, and is difficult to treat because of irreversible changes in the anatomy and physiology of the large intestine.
- There are three types of constipation—functional, latent, and organic. The length of transition from one type to another is determined by age, constipation severity, and form of treatment.
- Dietary and supplemental fiber has become the primary form of constipation treatment because it produces large stools and, presumably, speeds up elimination (motility).
- Dietary (natural) fiber doesn't materially affect the progression of constipation, stool size, and motility in healthy individuals. (Supplemental fiber does!)
- Physical exercise doesn't improve the outcome of constipation treatment, while the development of strong abdominal muscles to enable straining is likely to cause significant anorectal damage.

- Additional water consumption doesn't improve the constipation outcome regardless of the amount of added fiber.
- The treatment of constipation by encouraging "large stools" is the primary reason behind its worsening and progression to the organic stage.
- Latent constipation is difficult to recognize because a fiber-rich diet is a de facto laxative, and regular stools obscure the underlining problem.
- The straining required to move large stools is the primary reason behind colorectal disorders related to constipation. Small normal stools don't require any effort to eliminate.
- The Bristol Stool Form Scale classifies stools by form, size, and consistency into seven types. Each particular type of stool helps determine the health and integrity of the colorectal organs.
- The stools that match the Bristol Stool Form Scale type 4 to 6 are considered normal, while type 4 to 5 are ideal.
- Fiber, whether dietary or supplemental, is clearly not a proper preventive or solution for constipation treatment, because it causes stools to be larger and more voluminous, than the optimal (BSF type 4 or 5).
- Specific recommendations to treat constipation, fiber dependence, and related colorectal disorders are presented in Part III.

***

# Footnotes

---

[1] Epidemiology of constipation in the United States. Sonnenberg A. Koch TR., Dis Colon Rectum. 1989 Jan;32(1):1–8.

[2] Definitions, epidemiology, and impact of chronic constipation; Rev Gastroenterol Disord. 2004;4 Suppl 2:S3-S10. PMID: 15184814.

[3] Constipation; American Gastroenterological Association; on-line brochure; www.gastro.org/clinicalRes/brochures/constipation.html

[4] Definitions, epidemiology, and impact of chronic constipation; Rev Gastroenterol Disord. 2004;4 Suppl 2:S3-S10. PMID: 15184814.

[5] Prevalence of Major Digestive Disorders and Bowel Symptoms, 1989; National Center for Health Statistics, #212, March 24, 1992.

[6] Digestive Disorders, Fast Stats A-to-Z; National Center for Health Statistics; http://www.cdc.gov/nchs/fastats/digestiv.htm

[7] Hemorrhoids; NIH Publication No. 02–3021; February 2002; http://digestive.niddk.nih.gov/ddiseases/pubs/hemorrhoids/index.htm

[8] What are hemorrhoids? Hemorrhoid.net, a web site of Hemorrhoid Care Medical Clinic; http://www.hemorrhoid.net/hemorrhoids.php#introhem

[9] Diverticulosis and Diverticulitis; NIH Publication No. 04–1163; April 2004; http://digestive.niddk.nih.gov/ddiseases/pubs/diverticulosis/

[10] Constipation; The American Heritage® Dictionary of the English Language, Fourth Edition Copyright © 2000 by Houghton Mifflin Company; on-line edition: http://dictionary.reference.com/search?q=constipation

[11] About Kids GI Health; Constipation; International Foundation for Functional Gastrointestinal Disorders; http://www.aboutkidsgi.org/characteristics.html#constipation

[12] R.F. Schmidt, G. Thews. Colonic Motility. *Human Physiology, 2nd edition.* 29.7:730.

[13] Ibid. 29.7:731.

[14] Tucker DM, et al; Dietary fiber and personality factors as determinants of stool output; Gastroenterology. 1981 Nov;81(5):879–83.

[15] A commode is a piece of furniture with a compartment for a chamber pot. Depending on the owner's social status, upscale commodes—the progenies of contemporary bathrooms—had a seat concealed by the flip-up cover. The less fortunate had to rely on the outhouse or ditch. Most of the underdeveloped world still does, and, actually, this is to their advantage, as the squatting position over a ditch is far more natural and superior to the higher-up toilet bowl, and less likely to cause constipation and hemorrhoids.

[16] Concise Medical Encyclopedia in six volumes, Volume 2, page 364, article "Feces." (Russian language, 1991, Publishing House Soviet Encyclopedia.)

[17] *Gatekeeper* is the term used in the managed medical care industry (HMO). It describes the role of primary care physicians to limit patients' access to expensive specialists. The gatekeepers, on average, allot less than 10 minutes to each patient.

[18] Constipation; American Gastroenterological Association; on-line brochure; www.gastro.org/clinicalRes/brochures/constipation.html

[19] Ibid.

[20] Site search on keyword "Fiber." July 2, 2004. www.riteaid.com

[21] Functional Constipation; Rome II: The Functional Gastrointestinal Disorders by Douglas A. Drossman (editor); 3:386.

[22] Ibid.

[23] Health implications of dietary fiber; J Am Diet Assoc 2002;102:993–1000; http://www.eatright.org/Public/GovernmentAffairs/92_adar2_0702.cfm

[24] Information about the Bristol Stool Form Scale is available on the Family Doctor Books' web site (http://www.familydoctor.co.uk), which "are published by Family Doctor Publications in association with the British Medical Association." Information is excerpted from the book entitled "Understanding your Bowels" by Dr. Ken Heaton. The actual preview chapter contains a number of egregious errors, particularly in the *Passage times through the gut* chart. While the rest of the information is mostly accurate and useful, some of the information will differ from this book in similar ways as most medical and popular literature related to this subject. The suggestion that Type 3 stool is "ideal" is incorrect, because this form is typical of latent constipation. http://www.familydoctor.co.uk/htdocs/bowels/bowels_specimen.html

[25] Ibid.

[26] Functional Constipation; Rome II: The Functional Gastrointestinal Disorders by Douglas A. Drossman (editor); 3:384;

[27] USDA Nutrient Database for Standard Reference; www.nal.usda.gov/fnic/cgi-bin/nut_search.pl

*Hemorrhoids are very common in both men
and women. About half of the population
have hemorrhoids by age 50.*

National Institutes of Health[1]

# CHAPTER SIX

---

# HEMORRHOIDAL DISEASE

---

### What nature giveth, Newton's law taketh

From what we already know concerning the impact lifestyle, nutrition, and medicine have on stools, it isn't hard to comprehend the forces behind the pandemic of hemorrhoidal disease, which actually starts with a little "defect" in human anatomy. Here's what I mean by this:

Besides pain, discomfort, and embarrassment, the most unpleasant thing about hemorrhoidal disease is its negative impact on the aperture of the anal canal, which maxes out in healthy adults at 3.5 cm (1.37") or about this much:

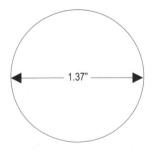

As you can see, it's not that wide. So when the anus is stretched out this much, you'll certainly feel discomfort, or even pain, just as with any other body orifice when it's expanded to the max. Just try to swallow a small apple whole. Sure, you can shoehorn it in, but oh, will it hurt.

The anal canal, too, can pass large stools through. It doesn't have a choice, does it? But it wasn't intended to do so regularly, in the same way your teeth weren't intended to open beer bottles, even though they can. Not surprisingly, when the anal canal is over-stretched by large stools, the forces needed to pass them—pressure from the inside, straining from the outside—cause hemorrhoids to enlarge, and this brief passage to the sewer gradually becomes one long tortuous journey.

How torturous? Based on the U.S. Census 2000, "half of the population" by age fifty translates into 38 million victims of he-morrhoidal disease. Once you factor in people under fifty and the undiagnosed, the actual number is much greater.

Fiber-related constipation and straining (a telltale sign of latent constipation and disbacteriosis) are the two principal causes of hemorrhoidal disease. The number of affected individuals illu-strates just how widespread those two problems are.

What giveth? Newton's third law, of course: *for every action there is an equal and opposite reaction.* Here's what I mean:

- As hemorrhoids get larger, the anal canal aperture gets smaller, and the stools become harder to pass;
- As the difficulty of passing stools intensifies, the need to strain grows more pronounced, and the hemorrhoidal pathologies grow worse;
- As the first two problems evolve, people keep increasing the amount of dietary and/or supplemental fiber to counteract defe-cation difficulties;
- As people increase the amount of fiber in their diet, their stool keep getting larger, causing further enlargement of hemorrhoids, while the anal aperture becomes smaller and smaller;
- As the anal aperture becomes smaller and the stools larger, peo-ple experience more constipation, strain harder, feel more pain, and begin experiencing other complications described elsewhere in this book.

If not interrupted by luck, education, or God's will, this vicious cycle continues unabated until patients may need surgery to fix rectal prolapse, anal fissures, fistulas, abscesses, fecal incontinence, or other related ailments.

Because most surgeries leave scars, damage nerves, and affect surrounding tissues, recovery is rarely one hundred percent. The muscle damage alone may place you in pampers for the rest of your life because of fecal incontinence. The residual pain may cause incomplete or delayed stools—the culprits behind chronic fecal impaction with its own compliment of nasty ills, such as diverticular disease, irritable bowel syndrome, ulcerative colitis, precancerous polyps, and, to top it off, colorectal cancer itself.

No, I'm not making all this up. Here is what proctologists—the physicians who specialize in mending hemorrhoids—have to say about the unfolding of hemorrhoidal disease:

---

*Hemorrhoid.net:* Unfortunately, a hemorrhoidal condition only tends to get worse over the years, NEVER better [original emphasis—ed.].[2]

---

That is certainly true if you continue treating constipation and hemorrhoidal disease with evermore fiber, water, and exercise. Otherwise, *never say never!*


### A case of mistaken identity

It may surprise you to learn that every individual on planet Earth possesses hemorrhoids since birth. It's true, because hemorrhoids aren't what you think they are. What you think they are, is, in fact, *hemorrhoidal disease,* not *hemorrhoids.* What's the difference?

Well, hemorrhoids (plural) are the internal bundles of vascular, muscular, and connective soft tissue that lines the anal canal and the region around the anus. The three main bundles (also referred to as anal cushions) encircle the anal canal, and some minor ones are situated in between. A ligament connects each sponge-like bundle to the underlying muscle, and the mucous membrane protects them from above.

Just like all other organs, hemorrhoids develop while still in the womb. They are part and parcel of human anatomy, not a pathology or disease. Their function is to protect (cushion) the internal structures of the anal canal from the passing stools. They are almost like the bearings on which the stools ride.

To some degree the function (and dysfunction) of hemorrhoids is similar to calluses that protect joints from friction damage. And, just as calluses on your palms can bulge, blister, and bleed as the result of too much hard labor, so can hemorrhoids from large stools and straining. No surprise there.

The term *hemorrhoid* (singular) means the condition, the sum of symptoms related to the inflammation, enlargement, thrombosis, and/or prolapse of hemorrhoids (tissue bundles). Doctors and patients alike universally refer to hemorrhoidal disease as *hemorrhoids*, which is technically incorrect. That's why this chapter refers to *hemorrhoidal disease* throughout, rather than *hemorrhoids*.

The two types of hemorrhoids are distinguished anatomically— internal and external. While the external hemorrhoids are innervated by the same nerves that supply the skin in the perianal region, the internal hemorrhoids aren't innervated at all and do not cause pain, even when enlarged. Let us be grateful to Mother Nature for small mercies!

Enlarged internal hemorrhoids are detected in two-thirds of all patients during routine anorectal examinations.[3] The absence of innervation explains why many people with a history of constipation may not realize that they have hemorrhoidal disease, until suddenly confronted with hemorrhoidal bleeding or prolapse.

In the case of external hemorrhoidal disease, the pain emanates from the area protruded by dilated hemorrhoidal veins. The dilation is caused by venal thrombosis. The thrombosis is caused by blood clots. Usually, the clotting happens from a specific event that can cause venal obstruction. It may be the passing of large stools, intense straining, the lifting of heavy objects, hard labor, diarrhea, childbearing, anal intercourse, and similar actions.

The pain goes away after the blood clot dissolves and the affected vein shrinks, though never completely. The vein's new shape causes skin folds (tags) which may protrude temporarily (after defecation) or permanently. That's when secondary conditions, such as prolonged sitting or standing, an alcoholic binge, smoking, a hot bath, sauna or the like, trigger events that may cause a recurrence of another clot and protrusion.

Unlike external hemorrhoids, internal hemorrhoids cause pain indirectly. The pain is precipitated by *rectal prolapse*—the protrusion of internal hemorrhoids outside the anus, while the following conditions cause actual pain:

- The spasm of the anal sphincter complex caused by the prolapsed hemorrhoids.
- The strangulation of the prolapsed hemorrhoidal tissue.
- The inflammation of the perianal skin caused by the residue of mucus and fecal matter, supplied by prolapsed tissue.
- The spasm of the anal sphincter may cause the thrombosis of underlining hemorrhoidal veins, which in turn may cause new external hemorrhoids, or aggravate existing ones.

To prevent a possible necrosis of strangulated hemorrhoidal tissue, an affected individual must seek medical attention immediately. When it isn't available, the prolapsed hemorrhoids should be returned back into the anal canal in order to relieve pain and prevent possible necrosis and infection. The affected area must be cleansed with warm water, which also helps to relax the anal sphincter. Petroleum jelly or non-medicated hemorrhoidal cream should be used to lubricate prolapsed hemorrhoids and the surrounding area before maneuvering them back inside.

### Taking care of bloody business

Bleeding specific to hemorrhoidal disease isn't from the thrombosed veins (another popular misconception), but from the abrasions, cuts, fissures, fistulas, or ulcerations of the mucosal membrane that lines the anal canal. The bright red color of the blood indicates its arterial, rather than venous, nature.

Hemorrhoidal bleedings are distinguished by crimson streaks of fresh blood on the passing stools. The stool itself doesn't change color, because there was no prior contact between it and the wound. At times, the bleeding may be profuse, but it usually stops when defecation is completed. In any event, it is best to see a doctor, and get checked out for this or any other source of bleeding.

The mucosal membrane that lines the anal canal is quite resilient and infection-proof. It quickly heals, and will not bleed again as long as stools remain soft and small (BSF type 5 or 6). If the stools remain type 1 to 4 (lumpy, large, hard), or you strain while relieving yourself, the bleeding may continue and get worse. In those instances, an initial small abrasion may turn into a fissure (split that won't heal), a fistula (duct from anus into perianal region), or an abscess (encapsulated pus)—conditions which, considering the location and "traffic," are extremely painful, infection-prone, and hard to treat and heal.

If the stool's appearance is tar-like, it may mean that there is internal bleeding at some point upstream, beginning from the esophagus. The color changes to tar after coagulated blood mixes with feces.

Keep this important point in mind: if blood emanates from upper intestinal tract organs (esophagus, stomach, duodenum, small intestine), the bleeding may have started at least three to four days before you see first signs of it. That's how long it normally takes for chyme to turn into stool and reach the toilet bowl. For people who are severely constipated it may take even longer. This means that by the time the blood in stools is detected, its loss may be considerable.

Certain food (beets, blueberries, black licorice), supplements (dietary iron), antacids (Pepto-Bismol), or a sudden release of conjugated billiary salts[4] may also give stools a tar-like appearance. Instead of panicking, don't flush the toilet, and run to the nearest drugstore to purchase a *Fecal Occult Blood Test* (FOBT) kit. To regain your piece of mind, follow the instructions provided with the kit—usually a strip of paper that you'll drop into the toilet—to observe changes. (The *occult* in the test name means *hidden,* not *mystic.*)

If the test is positive, and your pulse rate happens to be high, your blood pressure low, your appearance pale, and you find that you're short of breath, fatigued, or dizzy, these are the symptoms of serious blood loss and you should call 911 at once. If you still feel fine, get to the nearest emergency room ASAP, and advise the triage nurse that you've just had a positive FOBT. They'll know what to look for next. And don't waste precious time seeing your local doctor, because you'll be sent to the nearest hospital anyway, and in the meantime could be losing equally precious blood.

I'm assuming you recognize the importance of inspecting your stools at every opportunity. Besides saving yourself a lot of grief, it may actually save your life. In many cases, the toilet bowl predicts your future with more certainty than a crystal ball.

### Good treatment or good grief?

Hemorrhoidal disease is grouped into four categories—from the 1st degree, which is the least serious, to the 4th degree, which usually requires surgery. Repeatedly prolapsing internal hemorrhoids are commonly treated by nonoperative methods, such as rubber band ligation, sclerotherapy, cryoterapy, photocoagulation, laser ablation, and others.

Surgical treatments are reserved for the more complex cases (usually 4th degree). Recurring external hemorrhoids are treated by surgical excision of the overlying skin folds and underlying veins. The procedure is performed under local anesthetic, and usually on an outpatient basis.

The consensus among surgeons who specialize in treating anorectal disorders is that asymptomatic enlarged hemorrhoids are better off left alone, and that the conservative treatment—thorough hygiene, prevention of diarrhea and constipation, avoidance of known triggers, and soft, small, and regular stools that don't require straining to expel—is the safest, most reliable approach.

The medical profession is also in universal agreement that straining (related either to diarrhea or constipation) and large stools (type 2 and 3) are the primary reasons behind recurring prolapses of internal and/or external hemorrhoids.

Where this book digresses from mainstream medical opinion is on how to prevent diarrhea, avoid straining, eliminate constipation, and achieve small stools.

- *This book advises*: That fiber, commonly referred to as "roughage" or a "bulking agent" is the progeny of rough, bulky stools, and the overriding cause behind the emergence (etiology) and worsening (regression) of hemorrhoidal disease. Do not use fiber to prevent and treat hemorrhoidal disease.

- *Mainstream medicine advises*: Use abundant dietary fiber to prevent and treat hemorrhoidal disease. The more fiber, the merrier.
Don't forger the water and exercise, so you can strain harder.

Here's an example of this reckless advice, excerpted from the on-
line patient brochure put out by the American Gastroenterological
Association:

---

**What is the Treatment?**

Often all that is needed to reduce symptoms [of hemorrhoids—
ed] is to include more fiber in your diet to soften the stool. Eat
more fresh fruits, leafy vegetables, whole grain breads and cereals (especially bran). Drinking six to eight glasses of fluid (not
alcohol) each day will also help. Softer stools make it easier to
empty the bowels and lessen pressure on the veins.[5]

---

Here's another example, this time from the National Institutes of
Health. I underlined two of the most striking contradictions—
namely, if you want to relieve pressure and straining, you need to
*reduce* stool's bulk, not *increase* it:

---

**What is the treatment?**

Preventing the recurrence of hemorrhoids will require relieving
the pressure and straining of constipation. Doctors will often recommend increasing fiber and fluids in the diet. Eating the right
amount of fiber and drinking six to eight glasses of fluid (not alcohol) results in softer, <u>bulkier</u> stools. A softer stool makes emptying the bowels easier and lessens the pressure on hemorrhoids
caused by straining. Eliminating straining also helps prevent the
hemorrhoids from protruding. Good sources of fiber are fruits,
vegetables, and whole grains. In addition, doctors may suggest a
<u>bulk</u> stool softener or a fiber supplement such as psyllium
(Metamucil) or methylcellulose (Citrucel).[6]

---

Oh, and they didn't forget about exercise. That's in another para-
graph:

**How are hemorrhoids prevented?**
Exercise, including walking, and increased fiber in the diet help reduce constipation and straining by producing stools that are softer and easier to pass.[7]

Let's forgive the authors for stating that "exercise, including walking," produces softer stool. You can walk yourself to death, and your stool isn't going to get any softer. The "real" value of exercise isn't in softer stools, but in stronger abdominal muscles, which are required for the extra straining necessary to squeeze out all the bulk that comes with fiber.

The surgeons, whose "NEVER better" opinion about the outcome of hemorrhoidal disease I cited earlier, don't diverge from the party line either, and provide equally contradictory advice:

**How Are Hemorrhoids Prevented?**
The best way to prevent hemorrhoids is to keep stools soft so they pass easily, thus decreasing pressure, and to empty bowels without undue straining as soon as possible after the urge occurs. Exercise, including walking, and eating a high fiber diet, help reduce constipation and straining by producing stools that are softer and easier to pass.[8]

Good grief! The same old story: more fiber, more water, more walking. With advice like this you may as well sell your gut to devil!

But we all agree on one point: to prevent and treat hemorrhoidal disease you must have small, soft, regular stools and you must not strain. We just differ on the approach: theirs, with bran; mine, with brain. Take care of the colon's health, and hemorrhoids will take care of themselves. By the time you're through with this book, you should be through with fiber dependence, constipation, and, by extension, with aggravated hemorrhoids.

Unfortunately, you can't undo the damage already caused by large stools and straining—the dilated hemorrhoidal veins, the enlarged internal hemorrhoids, and the skin folds around the anus. But you can prevent veins from getting dilated further, and hemorrhoids from becoming larger and protruding even more. In most

cases that's enough to stop pain, inflammation, bleeding, or prolapse, as long as you guard your anus with the same vigilance you
guard your credit rating.

## Summary: Mind over fecal matter

To prevent hemorrhoidal disease from disfiguring your anus,
consider the following key points:

- Hemorrhoids are an intrinsic part of human anatomy. They protect the internal structures of the anal canal (muscles, vessels, tissues) from passing stools.
- There are two type of hemorrhoids—external and internal. They
  are distinguished by their location and innervation.
- Hemorrhoids enlarge from internal pressure caused by large
  stools, and external pressure caused by straining.
- Internal hemorrhoids do not cause pain, unless they prolapse outside the anus.
- The prolapse of internal hemorrhoids is caused primarily by
  large stools and extreme straining specific to late stage latent and
  organic constipation.
- The prolapse of external hemorrhoids is caused by the dilation
  and thrombosis of hemorrhoidal veins.
- External hemorrhoids cause pain, the sensation of which is related to inflammation of the skin that surrounds the thrombosed
  venal prolapse.
- Other conditions cause hemorrhoidal disease indirectly, by either
  applying pressure similar to the passing of large stools—such as
  during anal intercourse, or straining during pregnancy and bouts
  of diarrhea—or through the lifting of heavy objects.
- Enlarged hemorrhoids are a chronic but benign condition. Hemorrhoidal disease is an acute recurring condition, characterized
  by inflammation, pain, and/or bleeding of affected tissues.
- The enlargement of hemorrhoids narrows the aperture of the anal
  canal. This contributes to the development of constipation, larger
  stools, and further damage.
- Type 1, 2 or 3 stools (hard and/or large) on the BSF scale cause
  hemorrhoidal disease because their dimensions exceed the ana-

tomical "specification" of the anal canal.

- Any stools above 2.5 cm (1") in width are likely to cause the enlargement of hemorrhoids. To prevent hemorrhoids from enlarging, stools must match type 4 to 6 on the BSF scale.
- Dietary fiber is an indirect cause of hemorrhoidal disease, because it causes large stools.
- The elimination of dietary fiber (to reduce stool size and density) from the diet is a principal strategy for the treatment and prevention of hemorrhoidal disease and related complications.
- The commonly accepted recommendation to use dietary fiber for the treatment and prevention of hemorrhoidal disease is incorrect. Dietary fiber will aggravate enlarged hemorrhoids, because increased stool size causes additional pressure inside the anal canal.
- The appearance of blood on passing stools indicates a laceration of the anal mucosa that covers internal hemorrhoids. The blood may appear without any visible symptoms of hemorrhoidal disease. Consult your doctor at once to diagnose the source of bleeding, and to eliminate all other probable causes.
- Asymptomatic enlarged hemorrhoids do not require any treatment except dietary modification (exclusion of fiber), and the maintenance of small, soft stools, which don't require straining.
- If or when hemorrhoidal disease impacts your quality of life, or prevents you from having timely, regular stools because of pain, fear, or other factors, discuss more proactive treatment options with a specialist.
- Most doctors are qualified to perform outpatient surgeries related to hemorrhoidal diseases. For best results choose a physician who specializes exclusively in anorectal surgeries. There is no substitute for experience when dealing with this delicate area.
- There are many surgical and non-surgical methods to treat hemorrhoidal disease. Some are safer than others. Always ask your doctor about his or her approach, and investigate its pros and cons to avoid common complications such as chronic pain or fecal incontinence.
- If hemorrhoidal disease is left untreated, and its causes aren't eliminated, there is a distinct possibility of further anorectal complications such as anal fissures, fistulas, and abscesses, which in most cases require surgical intervention.

- If you are experiencing an acute stage of hemorrhoidal disease, follow your doctor's directions until the symptoms subside. Do not drop prescribed medication. Do not drop supplemental fiber laxatives (to prevent even more severe constipation), unless you replace it by the safer methods described in this book.

\*\*\*

# Footnotes

[1] Hemorrhoids; NIH Publication No. 02–3021; February 2002;
http://digestive.niddk.nih.gov/ddiseases/pubs/hemorrhoids/index.htm

[2] What are hemorrhoids? Hemorrhoid.net, a web site of Hemorrhoid Care Medical Clinic;
http://www.hemorrhoid.net/hemorrhoids.php#introhem

[3] Ibid.

[4] The conjugated billiary salts form in the gallbladder from bile, and are the precursors of gallbladder stones. Fat-free or low-fat diets and obstruction of the duct that connects the gallbladder to the duodenum contribute to formation of gallstones. The obstruction itself may be caused by salts, stones, inflammation, or a combination of all three. The actual release of salts may be sudden, without any apparent reason, or preceded by a specific event, such as an airplane flight, certain foods, or medication. Apparently, the changes in atmospheric pressure or some other factors may cause the release of billiary salts during or after the flight. When the released salts reach the large intestine, they cause profuse stools or diarrhea because of their strong laxative effect. People may often confuse this condition with "travelers" diarrhea, since it isn't described in medial literature.

[5] Clinical Resources (Patient Brochures). *The American Gastroenterological Association.*
http://www.gastro.org/clinicalRes/brochures/hemorrhoids.html

[6] Hemorrhoids; NIH Publication No. 02–3021; February 2002;
http://digestive.niddk.nih.gov/ddiseases/pubs/hemorrhoids/index.htm

[7] Ibid.

[8] What are hemorrhoids? Hemorrhoid.net, a web site of Hemorrhoid Care Medical Clinic;
http://www.hemorrhoid.net/hemorrhoids.php#introhem

*Constipation makes the muscles strain to move stool that is too hard.*
*It is the main cause of increased pressure in the colon.*
*This excess pressure might cause the weak spots in*
*the colon to bulge out and become diverticula.*
Diverticulosis and Diverticulitis; National Institutes of Health[1]

# CHAPTER SEVEN

## DIVERTICULAR DISEASE

If evolution had anticipated today's dietary dogma and lifestyle, it would have designed our large intestines very differently. The colon's pouch-like architecture is the reason behind the existence of *diverticulosis,* a condition where the *haustrum* (colonic bulges) protrudes further outward between the *teniae* (ribbon-like muscles), and forms sacs known as *diverticula* (plural from the Latin "a turn aside").

The colon's original architecture was perfect for hunter-savages, whose lifelong diet was virtually fiber-free. But it's proved disastrous for Westerners, who's diet is loaded with fiber from the moment they start chewing. According to The National Institutes of Health:

About 10 percent of Americans over the age of 40 have diverticulosis. The condition becomes more common as people age. About half of all people over the age of 60 have diverticulosis.[2]

Based on the U.S. Census 2000, "half of all people over the age of 60" translates into 23 million victims of diverticular disease. Once you factor in people under sixty and the undiagnosed, just as with hemorrhoidal disease the actual number is much greater.

Diverticulosis starts developing during the latent stage of fiber-related constipation which, as you may recall, is primarily characterized by straining, hemorrhoids, and type 1–3 large stools on the Bristol Stool Form Scale. The smaller diverticula range in diameter from 3 mm to 3 cm, and are usually multiple. The ones that are really large are most likely single (the singular is diverticulum), and range in diameter from 3 to 15 cm. When fiber-laden feces get "diverted" into diverticula, they tend to get lodged there, and then lump together and harden up.

Diverticulosis can be reliably seen and diagnosed by radiography (X-ray, nuclear scans[3]) or colonoscopy long before most patients experience any symptoms. Overall, smaller diverticula are harmless, as long as feces remain small, soft, and moist, because fecal matter with these properties won't get trapped inside small crevices. But when feces are continuously large, hard, and dense, they may keep even tiny diverticula clogged indefinitely for the same reasons a tight cork keeps liquid inside a vessel turned upside down, even if the neck has multiple crevices on the inside.

As more and more fecal matter gets jam-packed inside each diverticulum, they may enlarge further by the sheer force of outward pressure. Eventually, the epithelium inside one or more diverticulum gets lacerated and infected. The infection may cause inflammation, ulceration, rectal bleeding, excruciating pain, and/or the perforation of the colon wall—collectively called *diverticulitis*.

Besides fiber, other factors and conditions typical for the latent stage of constipation contribute to the development of diverticular disease:

- *Flatulence.* Colonic gasses are a by-product of fiber fermentation in the large intestine. The more fiber in one's diet, the more gas. The pressure, created by gas, is often sufficient to cause a small diverticulum to enlarge and protrude.
- *Straining.* The extra pressure from abdominal and pelvic muscles, especially in the presence of gases and a large volume of feces, is often sufficient to cause protrusions in the *posterior* (back) and *lateral* (side) regions of the colon. The effect is similar to

what happens to an air balloon when you squeeze it—the uncon-strained segments bulge, and the more you squeeze it, the larger the bulges become.

- *Hemorrhoidal disease.* Internal hemorrhoids constrict the anal canal, and prevent the complete elimination of stools. The result-ing fecal impaction causes an enlargement of stools and further protrusion of diverticula.

- *Medication.* Numerous drugs that cause relaxation of the smooth muscles (hypertension, anxiety, antispasmodic) may also inhibit intestinal contractions, propulsion and the timely elimination of feces. This leads to the formation of diverticula, caused by out-ward pressure from enlarged, impacted stools. Ironically, muscu-lar relaxants are the drugs of choice for the ongoing treatment of diverticular disease.

- *Age.* As we get older, the colon walls become less and less elas-tic, and more prone to stretching. Obviously, diverticulosis isn't likely to occur if you avoid its causes, regardless of age. The lucky 50% of still unaffected Americans over the age of sixty are living proof of it.

As you can see, understanding diverticulosis is an easy task: if you blow too much air into a tire, it explodes; if you stuff a casing with too much ground meat, the sausage bursts; if you have gases and bulky stool, the colon wall, unable to resist the pressure, pro-trudes and forms a pouch (diverticulum). And there's just one known nutrient that causes bulky stool and excessive gases at the same time: *indigestible fiber.*

For as long as you use dietary fiber to prevent and/or treat diver-ticular disease, the situation is guaranteed to get worse. Even more problems arise when enlarged, impacted feces finally cause inflam-mation and ulceration of diverticulum: severe pain and rectal bleed-ing at best, and abscesses, colorectal obstruction, perforation of the bowel wall, or peritonitis at worst. 20% to 25% of all people af-fected by diverticulosis develop these conditions, which often re-quires long-term treatment with antibiotics or emergency surgery. To keep this from happening to you, consider the following key points:

## Summary

- Constipation contributes to the progression of diverticular disease, because like fiber, it stimulates straining and the accumulation of stools in the large intestine.
- Most medical authorities in the West, particularly in the United States, advocate the use of fiber for the prevention of diverticular disease.[4,5] This advice is a primary reason behind the dramatic increase in the number of its sufferers.
- The use of dietary fiber for prevention and treatment of diverticular disease is based on unproven theory. In fact, the effective treatment of complications from diverticular disease relies on a fiber-free diet.[6]
- The treatment of diverticular disease with dietary fiber on the one hand, and antispasmodic drugs to counteract fiber's affect on the other, worsens the prognosis and outlook for patients who follow this advice.[7]
- The avoidance of indigestible fiber, the absence of constipation, and maintaining type 4–6 stools on the Bristol Stool Form Scale is the most effective form of prevention and treatment of diverticular disease.
- Men and women over the age of 50 are particularly vulnerable to diverticular disease, and should avoid indigestible fiber more than any other age group.
- The presence of internal and external hemorrhoids predicts a high probability of developing diverticular disease because the pathogenesis of both conditions are similar.
- Early-stage diverticulosis will not turn into diverticulitis if patients maintain a low-fiber diet and avoid constipation.
- Always consult your doctor and pharmacist regarding possible side effects of the medicines you are taking. Do not abandon prescribed medications without consulting a physician.

***

# Footnotes

[1] Diverticulosis and Diverticulitis; NIH Publication No. 04–1163; April 2004; http://digestive.niddk.nih.gov/ddiseases/pubs/diverticulosis/

[2] Ibid.

[3] Diagnostic radiography with specialized gamma camera that detects the distribution of a radioactive compound inside a specific organ or tissue.

[4] Prevention. Diverticular Disease. *Health Guide A-Z.* Jul 2004. http://my.webmd.com/hw/health_guide_atoz/aa41426.asp

[5] Diverticulosis; 3:33; The Merck Manual of Diagnosis and Therapy; http://www.merck.com/mrkshared/mmanual/section3/chapter33/33b.jsp

[6] Ibid.

[7] Prescription Information for DONNATAL EXTENTABS® Rev. 06/04; http://www.donnatal.com/donnatal/prescription_info.asp

*One in five Americans has IBS, making it one of the most common
disorders diagnosed by doctors. It occurs more often in women
than in men, and it usually begins around age 20.*

Irritable Bowel Syndrome;
National Institutes of Health[1]

# CHAPTER EIGHT

## IRRITABLE BOWEL SYNDROME

Irritable bowel syndrome (spastic colon) is a chronic condition characterized by bloating, cramping, persistent abdominal pain or discomfort, frequent bowel movements, and bouts of diarrhea alternating with constipation. Inferring from the opening quote, it afflicts over 60 million Americans.

Left unchecked, irritable bowel syndrome gradually progresses to inflammatory bowel disease (IBD), which is one step away from ulcerative colitis (UC) and Crohn's disease. The fine line that separates IBS from IBD is in the eye of the beholder—if you were to start poking around the bowel of an affected person, you're bound to find some inflammation of the intestinal mucosa. In general, the causes, treatment, and prevention strategies of IBS and IBD are identical, except that in the case of IBD you suffer more, the treatment and healing takes longer, and the urgency is much higher.

Constipation is one of the most common afflictions associated with IBS. When the constipation is *latent,* the underlining conditions are hidden from view by the perception of regularity. That's why ten times as many people complain of having IBS, rather than constipation.

There is an interesting paradox about IBS-related constipation: doctors may not recognize or diagnose IBS because patients may not have constipation at all, or have stools in the prescribed interval of time (at least three times weekly). By "prescribed," I mean the diagnostic criteria set forth in *The Merck Manual of Diagnosis and Therapy*[2] (for general doctors), or the more authoritative source, such as *Rome II Diagnostic Criteria For Functional Gastrointestinal Disorders*[3] (used mainly by the specialists).

The pathologies that cause constipation-related IBS result from an abnormal amount of formed, hardened feces that may accumulate from the rectum all the way back to the cecum. This is a condition typical of latent constipation. The stools correspond to type 1 to 3 on the *Bristol Stool Form Scale*. The extended contact of the formed fecal mass with the intestinal wall causes irritation and mechanical abrasion of the bowel's mucosa, especially during the periodic peristaltic contraction of muscles, and the propulsion of stools toward the rectum. In turn, perennial irritation and abrasion of mucosa cause inflammation and low-level discomfort, while peristalsis causes a more acute pain sensation, ranging from mild to sharp, which is referred to as cramps, or cramping.

Defecation is usually distressing, difficult, and requires intense straining. After defecation, some time passes before the residual abdominal pain subsides. This happens because of the transition of the hardened fecal mass from the upper regions of the large intestine into the lower part, which was just voided by defecation.

The initial accumulation of the hardened fecal mass (that causes IBS) inside the large intestine is the hallmark of *functional* constipation. Fiber by itself doesn't cause IBS. But it does bulk up and harden fecal mass. Fiber creates even more discomfort and pain from the gases and acidity that result from bacterial fermentation. In time, fiber transforms *functional* constipation into *latent,* and, eventually into *organic* because of the colorectal damage incurred from large stools and straining.

Anorectal disorders that result from constipation, such as hemorrhoids and diverticular disease, are the most challenging aspect of IBS to deal with, because they're irreversible. Fortunately, the pain, discomfort, and delayed or incomplete emptying of stools can be overcome, but these problems require a proactive approach, described elsewhere in this book.

Besides constipation, other prominent causes of IBS are:

- *Gastroenteritis.* The large intestine is at the very end of the "food" chain. All of the conditions that adversely affect the stomach (*gastro-*) and small intestine (*-enteritis)* inevitably ricochet in the gut (*-colitis*). Diarrhea, not constipation, is the most likely outcome. Bouts of diarrhea alternate with periods of constipation in the classical IBS pattern, because severe diarrhea washes out the intestinal flora essential for the formation of normal stools. Indigestion, food allergies, dietary irritants, food poisoning, malnutrition, viral and bacterial infections, smoking, chewing tobacco, and other assorted pathologies are the primary causes of *gastroenteritis.*

- *Anorectal disorders.* Anything that causes anal pain during defecation (stimulated by mechanical friction from passing stools or straining) is likely to cause *delayed* or *incomplete emptying* of stools. The pain may emanate from hemorrhoids, anal fissures, diverticular disease, and similar conditions that had previously been caused by chronic constipation or diarrhea. Incomplete emptying of stools leads to fecal impaction, which in turn causes severe IBS-related symptoms.

- *Antibacterial agents* decimate intestinal flora, and cause constipation and related complications, the harbingers of IBS. Among those agents, medicinal antibiotics and dental amalgams (mercury-based fillings) are particularly harmful and omnipresent, especially in the United States, where there are such a huge number of IBS sufferers.

- *Adverse effects of medication.* Numerous prescription and OTC medicines cause IBS-like side effects. This is especially true for "life-style" drugs taken regularly to mitigate the side effects of diets and aging, such as those used to treat heartburn (GERD), hypertension, migraine, diabetes, elevated cholesterol, constipation, bone disease, depression, even IBS itself, and others.

- *Susceptibility to stress.* I avoid saying "personality causes IBS," because individual response to stress is determined, to a large extent, by a person's diet. Actually, this is good news, because it means that you can mitigate the impact of stress by just changing your diet. This aspect of IBS (individual response to stress) is

also the reason behind stress-induced sudden cramping and diarrhea.
- *Bad luck.* For many people, an "introduction" to IBS stems from
  a misfortune—food poisoning, viral or bacterial infection, an allergic reaction to a food, adverse effects of antibiotics intended to
  treat unrelated conditions, or a trauma that leaves one bed-ridden
  for a while.

You can't insure against stress, infections, bad luck, or aging.
You can, however, study this book to "insure" against improper
nutrition and treatments, that makes an already bad situation even
worse.

## Hell of a treatment, or the treatment from hell?

Regardless of the cause of IBS, dietary fiber is a common denominator in the majority of cases. The fiber causes bulk, flatulence, and acidity, which deliver a one-two-three punch that only
the very lucky can resist or deflect.

According to the International Foundation for Functional Gastrointestinal Disorders, we are in the midst of an IBS epidemic:

Irritable bowel syndrome (IBS) is America's hidden health problem—a chronic, recurring disease that racks up in excess of $25
billion in direct and indirect costs each year. IBS affects an estimated 30 [to 60—ed.] million men, women, and children—10 to
20 percent of the U.S. population, yet less than one-half of these
people seek advice from a healthcare professional. IBS occurs in
people of all ages.[4]

The mayhem really starts from getting first-line-of-defense IBS
remedies—more fiber, more water, and more exercise. By the time
you're stuffed with fiber up to your nose, water is pouring out of
your ears, and you're straining to the point of tears with your rein-
vigorated abdominal muscles, you've created more problems for
yourself than you began with because:
- *Constipation-related IBS.* For persons with latent and organic
  constipation, fiber causes stools to become larger, heavier, and

harder, which in turn increase the severity of IBS.

- *Stress-related IBS.* Carbohydrates containing fiber elevate blood sugar and insulin levels, and make a person even more prone to stress.
- *Food allergy-related IBS.* The protein gluten is a potent food allergen. It is abundant in cereals, breads, and pasta made from wheat flour, which are broadly recommended as a major source of dietary fiber.
- *Medicine-related IBS.* Gastrointestinal disorders ranging from indigestion to constipation, from bleeding ulcers to diarrhea, are common side effects of many prescription drugs. If you take fiber to alleviate these side effects, you are adding fiber's own side effects to the mix, and making the whole situation even worse.
- *Colorectal disorder-related IBS.* Conditions such as hemorrhoidal or diverticular disease are caused by large stools and the straining required to expel them. There is only one food component that makes stools larger and heavier—dietary fiber.

Am I blowing everything out of proportion? Well, let's again take another look at the prevailing medical view regarding the best treatment for IBS. According to the National Institutes of Health:

---

**Some foods make IBS better.**
Fiber reduces IBS symptoms—especially constipation—because it makes stool soft, bulky, and easier to pass. Fiber is found in bran, bread, cereal, beans, fruit, and vegetables.[5]

---

But the same document also explains the nature of pain related to irritable bowel syndrome:

---

With IBS, the nerves and muscles in the bowel are extra-sensitive. For example, the muscles may contract too much when you eat. These contractions can cause cramping and diarrhea during or shortly after a meal. Or the nerves can be overly sensitive to the stretching of the bowel (because of gas, for example). Cramping or pain can result.[6]

---

Doesn't this depiction of IBS's action describe exactly what we already know about the damaging properties of fiber and its effect on the large intestine? Yes, it does! The document points out:

- That dietary fiber in the colon stimulates colon contraction (affects muscle activity) in order to evacuate feces in an abnormally short 24 hours instead of the required 72 hours.
- That impacted and expanded dietary fiber contacts the intestinal mucosa, stretches out the bowels, and that fiber's mechanical and volumetric properties are strong irritants (affect nerve sensitivity).
- That the by-products of dietary fiber's bacterial fermentation are highly acidic irritants (again affecting nerve sensitivity), and that the fermentation causes the formation of gases leading to a "stretching of the bowel."
- That all of the above leads to inflammation of the intestinal mucosa, which in turn prevents the absorption of electrolytes and water, leading to diarrhea.
- That "during or shortly after" a meal, the natural gastrocolic reflex stimulates a vigorous contraction of the large intestine, and that this natural action is interpreted as painful "cramping" by victims of IBS.

So what can you do to prevent, treat, and get rid of IBS? Exactly the opposite of what most medical authorities are telling (or not telling) you to do—cut the fiber to reduce the stools' volume, consume water in moderation to prevent gastroenteritis, and exclude drugs that may cause gastrointestinal distress. Here are the details:

- *Eliminate the primary causes of general digestive disorders.* Follow the recommendations throughout this book to gradually rid yourself of conditions affecting the health of the entire alimentary canal.
- *Exclude dietary fiber.* Remove all sources of indigestible and soluble fiber from your diet to reduce stool volume, formation of gases, and the mechanical and chemical irritation that it causes inside the bowel.
- *Reduce water consumption and frequency of meals.* Stop the endless drinking, snacking, and consumption of four or five meals a day to reduce the frequency and severity of the gastrocolic reflex and ensuing perception of "cramping."
- *Restore intestinal microflora.* Maintain proper balance of intesti-

nal microflora to alleviate disbacteriosis, constipation and inflammation.

- *Provide essential nutrients.* Consume adequate quantities of essential protein and fats to restore intestinal mucosa, and eliminate other symptoms and causes of the chronic inflammation of entire alimentary canal (systemic gastroenterocolitis).
- *Eliminate medication side effects.* Phase out all types of medication that affect the large intestine's functionality and/or irritate its mucosal membrane, especially laxatives. Just read the labels!
- *Seek out a competent, caring physician to guide you.* This book, an anatomy primer from a local library, and your unambiguous determination to recover is all that you need to convince a reasonable doctor to help you get rid of IBS. Believe me, the last thing doctors want to deal with are irate patients with irritable bowels.

Ironically, many well-meaning doctors and their families are also victimized by IBS, perhaps even more so than the general population, because they aggressively treat themselves and their families in the way they'd been taught. The scariest claim about IBS, however, is that it's completely risk and damage-free:

---

*National Institutes of Health:* IBS can be painful. But it does not damage the bowel or cause any other diseases.[7]

---

Well, if you disregard diverticulosis, hemorrhoids, anal fissures, ulcerative colitis, precancerous polyps, and colorectal cancer, then I guess there isn't any risk. To keep this from happening to you, consider the following key points:

**Summary:**
- Latent constipation is one of the most common and least recognized causes of IBS.
- IBS-related diarrhea results in functional constipation because diarrhea decimates stool-forming bacteria.
- The treatment of disbacteriosis is essential for effective treatment

of IBS and prevention of IBS-related constipation.

- IBS has many more primary causes than just constipation. Regardless of the causes, functional constipation that results from IBS sets the stage for more severe forms of latent and organic constipation.

- If you have IBS-related constipation, it isn't enough to treat just constipation. You must also treat the causes of IBS to prevent constipation relapse.

- There is no effective medical treatment of IBS. Ironically, leaving IBS untreated may be in some instances safer than undergoing aggressive medical therapy with fiber, antibiotics, and other prescription drugs.

- Conventional treatment of IBS-related constipation with dietary fiber and medication is a principle reason for transforming IBS into Inflammatory Bowel Disease, Crohn's disease, and ulcerative colitis.

- Though the term IBS implies that this is just a bowel-related condition, in fact it commences in the stomach and small intestine, and the treatment must begin there.

- A Western-style diet, especially a diet patterned after the Food Guide Pyramid, predisposes one to the development of IBS, because the core foods in the Pyramid contain hyperallergenic components and known GI irritants, and lack essential, primary amino and fatty acids.

- Diet-related malnutrition is as culpable in the development of IBS as overconsumption in the Western countries.

- Certain lifestyle choices, such as smoking, chewing gum, and consuming alcohol, coffee, carbonated beverages, and artificial sweeteners, may contribute to or directly cause IBS and IBS-related constipation.

- If left untreated, IBS may progress into life-threatening conditions, such as ulcerative colitis and Crohn's disease. Undoubtedly, just as with those conditions, chronic IBS predisposes a person to colorectal cancers.

- Finally, IBS is an eminently avoidable and treatable condition, but not by conventional allopathic means. The information presented in this book is sufficient for overcoming the most stubborn cases of IBS.

- Always consult your doctor and/or pharmacist regarding possible IBS-related side effects of the medicines you are taking. Do not abandon prescribed medications without consulting a physician.

\*\*\*

# Footnotes

[1] Irritable Bowel Syndrome; NIH Publication No. 03–693; April 2003; http://digestive.niddk.nih.gov/ddiseases/pubs/ibs/index.htm

[2] Irritable Bowel Syndrome; 3:32; The Merck Manual of Diagnosis and Therapy; http://www.merck.com/mrkshared/mmanual/section3/chapter32/32a.jsp

[3] Irritable Bowel Syndrome; 7:C1:357; Rome II: The Functional Gastrointestinal Disorders by Douglas A. Drossman (editor); http://www.romecriteria.org/index.html

[4] Irritable Bowel Syndrome; The Burden of Illness; www.IFFGD.org; http://www.aboutibs.org/Publications/IBSBurden.html

[5] What I need to know about Irritable Bowel Syndrome. NIH Publication No. 03–4686, April 2003; http://digestive.niddk.nih.gov/ddiseases/pubs/ibs_ez\

[6] Ibid.

[7] Ibid.

*About 25 percent to 40 percent of ulcerative colitis*
*patients must eventually have their colons removed*
*because of massive bleeding, severe illness,*
*rupture of the colon, or risk of cancer.*
Ulcerative Colitis; National Institutes of Health[1]

# CHAPTER NINE

## ULCERATIVE COLITIS AND CROHN'S DISEASE

### Think outside the box

Ulcerative colitis and Crohn's disease are characterized by inflammation and ulceration of the intestinal mucosa, or the inside upper layer of the intestinal walls (epithelium). In turn, inflammation blocks primary intestinal functions—the absorption of water, electrolytes, and nutrients from the chyme. Naturally, an accumulation of too many unabsorbed fluids in the lumen (the cavity of a tubular organ) causes diarrhea. In turn, the loss of essential fluids and nutrients leads to severe dehydration, malnutrition, loss of electrolytes, and associated complications.

Mainstream medical references classify ulcerative colitis (UC) and Crohn's disease (CD) as Inflammatory Bowel Diseases (IBD). While ulcerative colitis is localized exclusively inside the large intestine, Crohn's disease may extend into both the large and small intestines. According to *The Merck Manual of Diagnosis and Therapy,* the "groupings and subgroupings [of both conditions] are somewhat artificial. Some cases are difficult, if not impossible, to classify."[2]

In other words, the most apparent symptoms (abdominal cramps, pain, diarrhea, bleeding, fever, dehydration, malnutrition, and weight loss) of ulcerative colitis and Crohn's disease appear to be similar, and their respective treatments (diet, medication, rehab, etc.) are also similar. For these reasons, the overview of both conditions is combined into one chapter. For the record, there are significant morphological differences between the two conditions, but they aren't relevant for a treatment and prevention overview. To streamline the narrative, the term "inflammatory bowel diseases" may be used in place of the repetitive "ulcerative colitis and Crohn's disease," unless noted otherwise.

Inflammatory bowel diseases rarely happen out of the blue—they may follow years of Irritable Bowel Syndrome, gastroenteritis, and the other functional disorders of the GI tract described throughout this book. Symptomatically, constipation may or may not be an apparent precursor, because it is often *latent,* i.e., hidden from view, and isn't recognized. But that doesn't mean that it isn't there. In fact, this book's central theme, the critical role of latent constipation in the pathogenesis of intestinal inflammation, is confirmed by the following remarkable fact:

---

*The Merck Manual of Diagnosis and Therapy:* About 1/3 of patients [diagnosed with Crohn's disease] have a history of perianal [around the anus] disease, especially fissures and fistulas, which are sometimes the most prominent or even initial complaint. In children, extraintestinal [perianal] manifestations frequently predominate over GI symptoms.[3]

---

An anal fissure is a laceration of the anal canal mucosa that won't heal. An anal fistula is a duct from the anal canal into the perianal region that was formed from the initial ulceration of the anal mucosa. Let's think outside the box about the connections between fissures, fistulas, constipation, inflammation, and Crohn's disease:

Q. *What causes an anal fissure or fistula?*

A. The extreme straining that's required to expel dry, hard (not necessarily large) stools. Anyone who's ever experienced a fistula or fissure will tell you that they are extremely painful, especially during defecation, and that they bleed often.

Q. *What does this pain do to a person, especially a child?*
A. Pain causes the delaying or withholding of stools to avoid further pain and bleeding. Children may withhold stools for days, even weeks at a time.

Q. *What happens when a person delays or withholds stools?*
A. Formed stools inside the large intestine get impacted from the rectum all the way back to the cecum.

Q. *What happens when the stools get impacted and accumulate throughout the entire length of the large intestine?*
A. They extend all the way back into the small intestine (ileum) and cause intestinal obstruction, which is actually a prominent symptom of Crohn's disease.

Q. *And what happens when this occurs?*
A. The presence of feces in the small intestine causes mucosal inflammation. Inflammation causes profuse diarrhea. Diarrhea is often followed by severe constipation.

After that, it's simple: constipation is either not treated at all or it's treated with fiber. In both cases stools accumulate and impact. Depending on the diet, it may take up to a month to accumulate enough impacted stools to obstruct the small intestine again. At this point diarrhea kicks in again. After this cycle repeats itself several time, a person develops chronic intestinal inflammation or bleeding ulcers, and that's when Crohn's disease or ulcerative colitis are finally diagnosed.

The other probable path to either condition is a matter of just plain bad luck. Accidental food poisoning, travelers' diarrhea, viral infection, or a food allergy may bring along intestinal inflammation, vomiting, and diarrhea. The outcome—a ride to hell or a full recovery—depends on the treatment of the original cause.

- *The prudent approach:* a brief (24 to 48 hours) fast following the attack (you wouldn't have an appetite anyway). Then, a low-density recovery diet for a week or two (no fiber, no known food allergens, and no hard-to-digest foods). After that, the mucosa heals, and you are as good as new.

- *The imprudent approach:* taking drugs to suppress vomiting and/or diarrhea (just recall those happy-go-lucky TV ads), so you can continue eating as if nothing happened. This is, unfortunately, the more typical "protocol," which keeps the intestinal inflammation raging on, and on, and on. Then, at the first sign of diarrhea and blood, the treatment of ulcerative colitis or Crohn's disease starts in earnest, and the ride to hell begins.

You may wonder why two diseases, both culminating with severe diarrhea, are included in this book. The answer is obvious— they may begin with diarrhea, but, actually culminate with equally severe constipation. In other words, as much as constipation may cause ulcerative colitis or Crohn's disease, both of them cause constipation too. Directly, when the recovery is spontaneous, and indirectly as well, after a treatment with prescription drugs and/or fiber.

This book provides ample evidence that the generally accepted treatment of ulcerative colitis and Crohn's disease-related constipation with dietary fiber is THE CAUSE of the next round of diarrhea, and behind the gradual progression (worsening) of both diseases, namely more mucosal inflammation, more ulcerations, more anorectal damage, more blood loss, and more drugs to treat the ensuing diarrhea. This is followed by more fiber to alleviate constipation, and (surprise, surprise) the diarrhea-constipation cycle repeats itself.

The previous chapter (Chapter 8, *Irritable Bowel Syndrome*) provided equally ample evidence that constipation, hidden or not, is one of the leading causes of ulcerative colitis and Crohn's disease.

### The origins of ulcerative colitis and Crohn's disease: Debunking uncommon nonsense

You've probably heard this truism time and again: to cure a disease, you must first eliminate its causes. That's common sense, right? The bad news is: ulcerative colitis is still "incurable," because its causes are still "unknown:"

---

*National Institutes of Health:* Theories abound about what causes ulcerative colitis, but none have been proven. The most popular theory is that the body's immune system reacts to a virus or a bacterium by causing ongoing inflammation in the intestinal wall. [4]

---

Equally bad news: the etiology of Crohn's disease remains as enigmatic as ulcerative colitis:

---

*The Merck Manual of Diagnosis and Therapy:* The fundamental cause of Crohn's disease is unknown. Evidence suggests that a genetic predisposition leads to an unregulated intestinal immune response to an environmental, dietary, or infectious agent. However, no inciting antigen has been identified. [5]

---

The good news is: I don't buy any of that. Let's put aside the theories, and deal with facts. The fact is, there's nothing mysterious or complicated about ulcerative colitis or its causes. The mucosa is the mucosa is the mucosa. The same forces that cause inflammation and ulceration inside one's mouth or stomach may cause similar inflammation and ulceration inside one's intestines, small and large. No difference, except when the stomach is affected, one vomits, and when the intestines are affected, one gets diarrhea.

And there is nothing complicated or mysterious about the treatment of mucosal inflammation or ulcers, either. If, for example, you have bleeding ulcers inside the mouth, you change to a liquid or semi-soft diet to minimize chewing, you exclude spices to avoid contact with hypersensitive tissues, you avoid hot drinks to prevent burns, you don't put anything harsh in your mouth to prevent abrasions, you treat cavities and gum disease to eliminate potential sources of infection, and you don't kiss anyone or engage in oral sex, etc.

And if those ulcers don't heal in few weeks time, you take a doctor-prescribed broad-spectrum antibiotic for a week or two to eliminate probable pathogens. Soon, the ulcers are gone, and hopefully you won't repeat doing the same stupid things that caused inflammation and ulcers in the first place. That's just common sense, right?

It's the same with stomach ulcers. You take a drug or two to inhibit the secretion of hydrochloric acid, you are placed on a low-density diet, you don't smoke or drink alcohol, and, if tests show H.pylori infection, you take antibiotics and antacids to wipe it out. Soon, the ulcers are gone, and hopefully you won't repeat doing the same stupid things that caused them in the first place. That's also common sense, right?

And common sense dictates doing exactly the same things if you have inflammation and bleeding ulcers inside your small intestine (Crohn's disease) and/or large intestine (ulcerative colitis). But that's not what's being done. Quite the opposite. Besides drugs that are supposed to stop diarrhea, patients are advised to take indigestible fiber to prevent the constipation that (surprise, surprise) results from the diarrhea treatment. As in this example by the famous Mayo clinic:

---

Experiment with foods high in fiber (fresh fruits, vegetables and whole grains).[6]

---

If you follow this advice, here is what happens next:
- Indigestible fiber (a.k.a. "bulking agent," "roughage") expands four to five times from its original shape and weight, and enters the intestines.
- While the expanded fiber slowly crawls through the inflamed and ulcerated sections of the small and large intestine, the bacterial fermentation produces fatty acids that are obviously acidic, and gases that are obviously expanding. (To overcome fiber fermentation, many patients are instructed to take potent antibiotics indefinitely instead of eliminating fiber.)
- Expanded fiber remains in permanent contact with inflamed and ulcerated mucosa throughout the entire journey. This fact is meaningless, unless you recall that human intestines were not intended to transport indigested food, only liquid chyme. That, incidentally, is why intestinal obstructions are so common among patients with Crohn's disease.
- Patients who get "treated" with fiber-rich whole grains ingest

profound quantities of dietary gluten, a plant protein and potent food allergen that causes intestinal inflammation known as *celiac disease*. This is one of the precursors (surprise, surprise) of ulcerative colitis and Crohn's disease.

So there we have it: (a) large chunks of bloated fiber are chafing and scraping an inflamed and ulcerated mucosa; (b) profuse gases are pressing on the intestinal walls because they can't escape by the inflamed mucosa; (c) astringent fatty acids are burning the bleeding ulcers because they can't get absorbed past the inflamed mucosa; and (d) the voluminous fiber keeps accumulating inside the intestines, because to relieve the pain from (b) and (c), patients take muscular relaxants, which block intestinal peristalsis altogether, stall the "traffic," and cause the obstruction.

When this situation becomes unbearable, the body responds with violent diarrhea again, and the whole cycle starts anew. Uncommon nonsense, right? So let's now apply common sense to the same problem, namely the inflammation and ulceration of intestinal mucosa.

What's the number one rule of first aid care? Keep inflammation and ulcers (cuts, wounds, abrasions) clean and protected from the elements! So why, then, doesn't this rule apply to intestinal inflammation and ulcers? Why should the insides of the intestines scrape against impacted stools that are full of decaying fibers, nauseating gases, and burning acids? Obviously, one isn't going to earn a PhD or win the Nobel Prize by writing a two-line thesis:

## KEEP INTESTINAL INFLAMMATION AND ULCERS CLEAR OF CONGESTED CRAP!

Of course not! So countless researchers are earnestly struggling to develop fancy theories, harsh treatments, and ever more potent drugs to accomplish the impossible: to heal mucosal inflammation and ulcers inside small and large intestines loaded to the rafters with rotting fiber, large stools, and everything else that comes along.

Impossible! While this "research" continues, hapless patients are still having their colons routinely amputated:

*National Institutes of Health*: About 25 percent to 40 percent of ulcerative colitis patients must eventually have their colons removed because of massive bleeding, severe illness, rupture of the colon, or risk of cancer. Sometimes the doctor will recommend removing the colon if medical treatment fails or if the side effects of corticosteroids or other drugs threaten the patient's health.[7]

Not fun, but still better than dying.

But how about this for first aid: relieve your intestines, both large and small, of congested "crap" and keep them "clean." If done in time (before rupture, or something to this effect) the ulcerative colitis and Crohn's disease will take care of themselves. Or, as they say: no cause—no disease!

Of course, it isn't just fiber, fiber, and fiber. As ulcerative colitis and Crohn's disease advance, other factors, mentioned by the NIH, contribute to their worsening outlook. There are two major theories related to their pathogenesis:

- *Bacterial and viral theory.* Each round of antibiotics decimates intestinal flora, and leaves the large intestine defenseless from endogenous (remaining inside) and exogenous (brought from outside) pathogens. We now know from clinical experience that the restoration of intestinal flora alone cures ulcerative disease in many patients, regardless of the stage.

- *Autoimmune response theory.* When the intestinal mucosa is healthy, it is well protected from the by-products of digestion. When it is inflamed, it is not protected, and may develop antibodies to once-benign components of food, mainly proteins, both plant and animal. The longer the inflammation, the more the antibodies may develop. This means that affected patients may experience strong allergic reactions—histamine release directed by antibodies—to once perfectly acceptable food. These reactions, which may appear just like another relapse of ulcerative colitis or Crohn's disease, are manifested by inflammation and diarrhea. Unfortunately, there is no way to eradicate antibodies, except by suppressing the immune system itself. For obvious reasons, it isn't a wise strategy, although it's commonly employed. A far better strategy is to avoid trigger foods, and these antibodies will eventually wear off just like the antibodies to most vaccines do.

But again, these issues are secondary next to the fundamental rules of treatment and prevention of inflammations and ulcerations: keep the affected organs "clean." I put the clean in quotes here, because in the case of the intestines I mean it figuratively, not literally: let the intestines perform their innate task of transporting fully digested liquid chyme, rather then stuffing them up and down with loads of indigestible, bulky, and rough fiber. Never!

## Mission impossible: The conventional treatment of ulcerative colitis and Crohn's disease

The treatment of both conditions is intended to stabilize patients and suppress the symptoms. Neither the doctors nor the patients really have much choice. The patients are temporarily satisfied because there is less diarrhea, pain, suffering, and bleeding, and the side effects of medications take time to develop. Here are the most popular treatment options:

- *Antibiotics to destroy bacteria.* Broad spectrum antibiotics provide temporary relief because they terminate the fermentation of dietary fiber, formation of gases, and fatty acids by wiping out intestinal flora along with the suspected pathogens. It should, of course, be the other way around—fiber, soluble as well as insoluble, must be excluded to terminate fermentation. It's worth repeating that clinical and practical experience indicates that the restoration of intestinal flora alone is often all that is needed to cure ulcerative colitis for good, and by extension, Crohn's disease. Obviously, antibiotics have their uses, and shouldn't be shunned when prescribed for a real cause, rather than for "just in case."

- *Aminosalicylates to reduce mucosal inflammation.* Unfortunately, these drugs have digestive side effects, such as nausea, vomiting, heartburn, and (surprise, surprise) diarrhea. Not surprisingly, they may work for some patients, but not for long. And the next step is...

- *Corticosteroids to reduce mucosal inflammation.* These hormonal drugs cause typical side effects such as rapid weight gain, elevated blood pressure, depression, anxiety, and risk of infection. Because they impact the body's hormonal balance, they also cause severe acne and rapid growth of facial hair among women. And the next treatment is...

- *Immune system suppressants* to reduce inflammation by literally turning the immune system off. These "killer" drugs are euphemistically called *immunomodulators.* They open the body to a host of other opportunistic infections, from flu to pneumonia, that can easily turn deadly. The immunomodulators may cause permanent damage to the liver, pancreas, and bone marrow. This is especially likely in patients already weakened by ulcerative colitis and Crohn's disease.

- *Anticholinergics to stop peristalsis.* These are systemic (body-wide) muscular relaxants that suppress the effect of acetylcholine, a neurotransmitter that stimulates muscular contractions. These drugs alleviate diarrhea-related muscular cramps and spasms, but unfortunately they also stop the flow of nutrients throughout the entire length of the digestive tract, and cause indigestion, intestinal obstruction, and constipation. Also, these drugs affect other organs that are controlled by muscles, including the heart, salivary and sweat glands, and genitourinary organs.

- *Fiber laxatives to bulk up stools.* Here is a direct quote from *The Merck Manual:* "Hydrophilic mucilloids (eg, methylcellulose or psyllium preparations) sometimes help prevent anal irritation by increasing stool firmness."[8] Of course, we already know what happens with firm stools when they are applied to immobilized, inflamed, and ulcerated intestines.

Inevitably, and for obvious reasons, these drugs fail, or their cumulative side effects overwhelm patients, and radical surgery to remove the colon and/or affected sections of the small intestine is the usual next step:

*National Institutes of Health:* In severe cases, a patient may need surgery to remove the diseased colon. Surgery is the only cure for ulcerative colitis.[9]

And not just to stop the diarrhea and bleeding:

*National Institutes of Health:* About 5 percent of people with ulcerative colitis develop colon cancer. The risk of cancer increases
with the duration and the extent of involvement of the colon. For
example, if only the lower colon and rectum are involved, the
risk of cancer is no higher than normal. However, if the entire colon is involved, the risk of cancer may be as much as 32 times the
normal rate.[10]

Considering the hardship of living without a colon, calling surgery a "cure" is, of course, a euphemism. Unfortunately, for many
people surgery is the only option, because the alternative is death.

Are there alternatives to colon resection (surgical removal)? Absolutely. Ulcerative colitis is an acquired disease, not a congenital
one. Just like with any other disease, the treatment must start from
removing the causes, instead of treating the symptoms. But I am
repeating myself.

The information presented in this book should help you eliminate
some of the preceding conditions—namely, constipation and reliance on dietary fiber to treat it, which contribute to the development of ulcerative colitis and Crohn's disease. Depending on the
stage, these measures may not be enough to arrest these diseases,
and a doctors' involvement is absolutely critical for a patients' recovery. And this means:

### Respect thy doctor

Please note one very important distinction: dietary fiber is just
one of many factors in the etiology of ulcerative colitis and
Crohn's disease. The subject of this chapter is the adverse role of
fiber for persons who are already affected with either disease.

This chapter is not about *the treatment of the ulcerative colitis or
Crohn's disease themselves.* The diarrhea and blood loss alone are
life-threatening conditions, and patients must continue working
with their doctors. I'm confident that no doctors will be hostile to
the suggestions and conclusions made in this book once they've
had a chance to review them.

Furthermore, once their patients begin recovering, doctors will
happily apply similar approaches to their other patients, because

nobody wants to see their patients suffering or dying.

You may ask a reasonable question: why aren't doctors denouncing fiber? The answer is really simple—they simply may not know about its ill effects yet. Just like a decade ago doctors didn't know that calcium deficiency may cause kidney stones, or, most recently, that Vioxx may cause heart attacks, doctors don't yet know that dietary fiber is detrimental in the treatment of ulcerative disease and Crohn's disease.

And the question "You make it so obvious, why can't doctors figure it out?" isn't fair, because of the following considerations:

- *Communication skills.* The ability to express complex concepts and ideas in an accessible format and language is the domain of professional medical writers, not practicing doctors. It takes years to master the art of writing, and, on top of that, a writer must have medical education, life experiences, analytical skills, motivation, time, resources, and the guts to tackle these complex and controversial subjects. That's simply not the domain of doctors, unless, of course, they become medical writers and still possess all of the above.

- *Training and ethics.* Practicing doctors aren't scientists, researchers, or analysts trained to analyze and investigate the causes of diseases. They are confronted with preexisting medical conditions and are trained to take care of them to the best of their abilities. For the same reason you don't expect a policeman to write, or, even worse, decide the laws, you shouldn't expect practicing doctors to be know-it-all scientists or, even worse, conduct experiments and research on unwitting patients.

- *Rules of engagement.* Medical doctors are in one of the most tightly regulated professions. To avoid harm to patients and malpractice suits, they rely on the generally accepted treatment protocols taught in accredited medical schools, and described in blue-chip medical books and references. In general, that's what we all want them to do. And if all of those authoritative sources recommend dietary fiber to treat constipation, they too will recommend this approach to their patients, and will apply it to themselves, and to their family members without the slightest hesitation or doubt in its safety and efficacy. That's the reality.

- *Personal experience.* Doctors may not suspect the connection between dietary fiber and IBD, because they may believe that they themselves benefit from fiber, and, for a while, they don't experience any of its side effects. Indeed, it takes decades for fiber's impact to become apparent in healthy people. But by the time it does, it's hard to determine what hit you—age, bad luck, or fiber. Personal experience and subjective judgment play an important role in medicine. If you don't feel it, you don't pay as much attention to it.

- *Risk aversion.* Independent analysts (such as myself) aren't restricted or limited to any dogma and leave no stone unturned while seeking out better solutions. And, once they believe that they've found better ones, they publish their findings, and stake their reputation and livelihood on the results. That's the kind of risks that doctors don't take, and shouldn't be expected to take.

- *Theory of relativity.* The human body isn't as mysterious as it was once thought to be, but it's still as unpredictable as the weather in early spring. Hence, there is no absolute truth, but many "truths." And reasonable people have the right and obligation to doubt anything that isn't "absolute." And they will. It means that even the best-intentioned doctors may not instantly accept this or that method, regardless of its merits. That's human nature.

- *Inertia.* The field of inflammatory bowel diseases isn't any different from any other field of science or medicine. Not long ago, the top scientists of their day believed that the world was flat. It takes time for old beliefs to wither and die, and new ones to take hold.

When the idea of using fiber for constipation relief was initially advanced in the first half of the 20$^{th}$ century, the average lifespan of Americans was still too short to observe its "global" harm. Besides, it takes decades for symptoms to develop, the diseases to take hold, the statistics to get collected, and for someone to question conventional wisdom.

Well, we know better now. Get on with it, and don't blame doctors for not being clairvoyant. For all I know, doctors are victimized by the fiber scourge even more than the general public, because they start taking 'good' care of their bodies earlier then most of us. And, up to now, that has meant *eating more fiber, drinking more water,* and *exercising the abdominal muscles.* You already know the results all of those activities may cause, and hopefully, because of this book, most doctors will also know about them soon, and will declare a similar loud message:

FIBER ISN'T THE SOLUTION, IT'S THE PROBLEM!

Hence, respect thy doctor! When bloody diarrhea strikes, it isn't the time to read a self-help book. You need a good doctor!

## Summary

- Ulcerative colitis and Crohn's disease are inflammatory diseases of the small and large intestines (IBD). Their causes, symptoms, and treatments are similar.
- Profuse diarrhea and blood loss from localized ulcers are the two primary outcomes of ulcerative colitis and Crohn's disease. Both conditions require intensive medication and treatment to protect patients' lives.
- Certain medicines used to arrest diarrhea cause constipation because they decimate the intestinal flora responsible for forming stools, and because they inhibit intestinal peristalsis, responsible for the propulsion of stools.
- Originally, ulcerative colitis and Crohn's disease may be caused by factors other than constipation. The worsening of their outlook, however, is generally caused by constipation that stems from the treatment of their original causes.
- There is an unambiguous connection between Crohn's disease and latent constipation. Fecal impaction, that causes anal fissures and fistulas, also causes Crohn's disease.
- People with anal fissures and fistulas, particularly children, have the highest risk of Crohn's disease.
- The use of dietary fiber to treat constipation worsens the outlook of inflammatory bowel diseases, because fiber's mechanical and chemical properties aggravate inflammation and ulceration.
- Inflammatory bowel diseases aren't congenital (genetic) conditions. The occurrence of the diseases among family members isn't determined by genes, but by similar styles of nutrition, ex-

posure to similar pathogens, and susceptibility to similar food irritants and allergens.

- People with inflammatory bowel diseases develop allergies to regular food because impaired mucosa may produce antibodies to otherwise benign components of these foods. This doesn't happen when the mucosal membrane is intact.
- The treatment of constipation and other measures suggested in this book should help break the dependence on dietary fiber and medication, and lessen or eliminate the factors that provoke diarrhea.
- In most cases, the restoration of intestinal flora alone may be sufficient to cure ulcerative colitis and Crohn's disease.
- The prevention of inflammatory bowel diseases in children and adults should begin with the elimination and prevention of apparent and/or latent constipation, because both conditions are by far the most dominant causative factors of ulcerated colitis and Crohn's disease.
- Proper recovery from unrelated functional, infectious, viral, and autoimmune diseases of the GI tract is the second (after constipation) most important consideration for the prevention and treatment of inflammatory bowel diseases.
- Medical doctors may not be familiar with the negative role of fiber in the etiology of ulcerative colitis and Crohn's disease because it hasn't been described yet in mainstream medical literature.
- Doctors play an important, if not crucial, role in the treatment of and recovery from inflammatory bowel diseases, particularly during the acute stages of diarrhea and bleeding. In these situations proper diet and the removal of fiber may help, but this isn't sufficient to prevent additional complications or the loss of life.

\*\*\*

# Footnotes

[1] Ulcerative Colitis; NIH Publication No. 03–1597 April 2003;
http://digestive.niddk.nih.gov/ddiseases/pubs/colitis/

[2] Inflammatory Bowel Diseases; 31:3;The Merck Manual of Diagnosis and Therapy;
http://www.merck.com/mrkshared/mmanual/section3/chapter31/31a.jsp

[3] Crohn's Disease; 31:3; The Merck Manual of Diagnosis and Therapy;
http://www.merck.com/mrkshared/mmanual/section3/chapter31/31b.jsp

[4] Ulcerative Colitis; NIH Publication No. 03–1597 April 2003;
http://digestive.niddk.nih.gov/ddiseases/pubs/colitis/

[5] Crohn's Disease; 31:3; The Merck Manual of Diagnosis and Therapy;
http://www.merck.com/mrkshared/mmanual/section3/chapter31/31b.jsp

[6] Diet and Stress; Ulcerative Colitis; Mayo Clinic;
http://www.mayoclinic.org/ulcerative-colitis/diet.html

[7] Ulcerative Colitis; NIH Publication No. 03–1597 April 2003;
http:// digestive.niddk.nih.gov/ddiseases/pubs/colitis/

[8] Crohn's disease; 31:3; The Merck Manual of Diagnosis and Therapy;
http://www.merck.com/mrkshared/mmanual/section3/chapter31/31b.jsp

[9] Ulcerative Colitis; NIH Publication No. 03–1597 April 2003;
http://digestive.niddk.nih.gov/ddiseases/pubs/colitis/

[10] Ibid.

*Adopting a diet that is low in fat and high in fiber,*
*fruits, and vegetables does not influence the risk*
*of recurrence of colorectal adenomas.*

The New England Journal of Medicine[1]

# CHAPTER TEN

## COLON CANCER

### Dietary Fiber: Naturally grown killer

Okay, so fiber isn't good for constipation and it causes all kinds of nasty, but not yet deadly problems. But what about colon cancer? Aren't we getting rid of one plague (fiber), to gain another (cancer)?

That's an excellent and appropriate question. And I'm the last person to encourage you to play Russian roulette. So let's check out the odds.

### Colorectal cancer and dietary fiber

The question whether dietary fiber contributes to colorectal cancer has (at least for me) been answered time and again—yes, it absolutely does. But this isn't what you've probably heard before, or are likely to accept on faith alone. So let's review this issue in greater depth. Undoubtedly, it will come up again and again in your discussions with doctors, relatives, and peers, and you'll need all the armor you can find to deflect the onslaught of ignorance, misinformation, and outright falsehoods.

The term *colorectal cancer* refers to cancers of the colon and the rectum. In general, surgery to remove colon cancer causes less damage than surgery for rectal cancer, because the latter almost always involves removing an entire important organ (the rectum), while with colon cancer, if there's no metastasis, only a section of the colon is removed so that the normal defecation remains functional.

There are also three somewhat confusing terms used in relation to colorectal cancers: colorectal *carcinoma, adenoma,* and *adenocarcinoma.* Technically, *carcinoma* refers to malignant tumors, while adenoma to benign. That said, colorectal adenomas and carcinomas present physicians with similar risk profiles, hence you'll frequently hear the term *colorectal adenocarcinoma.* In either case, surgery is required to remove the intestinal obstruction caused by the tumor, and to halt further spread of the cancer.

The actual nature of the tumor is established by a pathologist from the biopsy sample taken before the surgery, or from a post-surgical tissue sample. In general, when communicating with patients most doctors refer to carcinomas and adenomas interchangeably (colorectal cancer or adenocarcinoma,) because they themselves may not know the distinction until the pathology report.

In medical literature you may encounter yet another, even broader term that specialists use among themselves: a *neoplasm.* It simply means an abnormal growth of tissue mass, which is different from regular tissue, and may be either benign or malignant. Anything abnormal—adenoma, carcinoma, sarcoma (connective tissue malignancy) is therefore a neoplasm. The rest of this chapter uses the term *colorectal cancer,* which for clarity's sake encompasses all other meanings and definitions.

It's a well-established fact that most colorectal cancers are preceded by the formation of precancerous polyps—cellular growths that visibly protrude from the mucous lining of the large intestine. Therefore, anything that can cause temporary or permanent damage to the mucous lining is capable of causing the growth of polyps, that eventually may become tumors.

The terms *polyp* is actually an euphemism for *tumor* and *neoplasm.* Don't kid yourself over the issue of early detection—you should be more concerned about preventing the polyps from developing in the first place, rather than hoping that regular colonoscopies will make you safe. Unless you remove the causes of these polyps, colonoscopies aren't going to save, quite literally, your ass. Thinking otherwise is very profitable for medical sector, but in practical terms, this "prevention" approach is as asinine as putting out fires with gasoline.

So what should you do to prevent polyps?

Protect yourself from harm. The mucosa damage that precedes the appearance of polyps can be (a) mechanical (a cut or abrasion), (b) chemical (caused by an irritant, such as laxatives, fatty acids, bile, etc), (c) viral or bacterial, or (d) a combination of all these factors. Just as with any other organ, the mucosa react with inflammation to superficial injury, or with ulceration and bleeding if the exposure is long-lasting and unrelenting. Can this be from an exposure to fiber? Well, let's think aloud:

- If a substance increases the stool's size and volume five-to-six times and causes permanent stretching, diverticulosis, diverticulitis, hemorrhoids, and anal fissures, then this substance also has the potential to cause mechanical damage to the incomparably more delicate mucosa inside the large intestine, and stimulate the growth of precancerous polyps.
- If a substance causes bacterial fermentation inside the large intestine, leading to the production of highly irritating fatty acids, which may cause diarrhea and ulcerative colitis, or even itching in the anus, then this substance can also cause chemical damage of the mucosa, leading to the formation of polyps.

So what is this substance that can cause both mechanical and chemical damage of the intestinal mucosa? There is only one such substance in the daily diet of most Westerners—dietary fiber that reaches the gut undigested.

- Can it be meat? No, it can't, because meat, any kind of meat, digests completely inside the functioning stomach, and never reaches the large intestine.
- Can it be saturated fat? No, it can't, because saturated fats get digested and absorbed almost completely inside the functional small intestine, and never reach the large intestine.
- Can it be digestible carbohydrates? No, not directly, because digestible carbohydrates too, never reach the large intestine—they

digest completely inside the healthy small intestine, and get absorbed there as well. Indirectly—well, it's a different story.

It's apparent that nothing but indigestible dietary fiber, whatever
the source, can cause mechanical damage either directly or indirectly, by means of the by-products of bacterial fermentation.

But there's a bit more to it. The majority of indigestible fiber
comes in the nice wrapping of digestible carbohydrates—those
proverbial fruits, vegetables, breads, pasta, and cereals, whose ten
to fifteen servings you're supposed to consume daily to stay
healthy:

---

**"Digestible" Carbohydrate May Boost Colorectal Cancer Risk**
Previous studies have not agreed on whether or not eating lots of
carbohydrates is a risk for colon cancer. In a new study, Canadian
researchers set aside the fiber content of carbohydrates, which
may reduce the risk, and examined the remainder, or "digestible"
carbohydrate, namely sugars and starches. The result: their study
showed <u>that people consuming the highest amounts of digestible
carbohydrates had a higher risk for developing colorectal cancer</u>
compared with those eating the lowest amounts.[2]

---

Add to the mix age, stress, medication, dietary and environmental carcinogens, disbacteriosis, and chronic deficiency of essential nutrients—all aggravating factors that impede digestion and
harm the immune system—and we inevitably get what we so
dread:

---

[Colorectal cancer is] the 2nd leading cancer killer in the United
States. In 2004, an estimated 146,940 new cases of colorectal
cancer (cancer of the colon or rectum) will be diagnosed in the
United States, and 56,730 men and women will die of the
disease.[3]

---

From all corners we've been urged to consume a high-fiber diet
to lower the risk of colon cancer. Would this lower it? Not a bit!
Here's an excerpt from an article about fiber from The Harvard
School of Public Health, published in 2004:

For years, Americans have been told to consume a high-fiber diet to lower the risk of colon cancer—mainly on the basis of results from a number of relatively small studies. Unfortunately, this recommendation now seems mistaken, as larger and better-designed studies have failed to show a link between fiber and colon cancer.[4]

Is this something new, or is this book the lone voice of reason? No, it isn't new at all. The wide-open public discourse on the role of fiber started years ago. Here are some excerpts from mainstream sources. Please note the dates and headlines:

**"Study Finds Fiber Ineffective Against Colon Cancer**
BOSTON (Reuters)—The conventional wisdom that a high-fiber diet can protect against colon and rectal cancers may be wrong, a study published in Thursday's New England Journal of Medicine said."; January 21, 1999

**"High-fiber diet may not prevent colon cancer**
NEW YORK (Reuters Health)—A low-fat, high-fiber diet is often recommended as a way of preventing polyps in the lining of the colon—growths associated with an increased risk of colon cancer. But new research casts doubt on this oft-repeated advice. Adopting a low-fat diet rich in fruits, vegetables and other sources of fiber does not prevent the development of intestinal polyps in people who have already had polyps removed, US researchers report."; April 19, 2000

**"Fiber Doesn't Prevent Cancer**
LONDON (Associated Press)—Evidence is mounting that fiber might not prevent colon cancer after all, with a new study suggesting that one type of supplement might even be bad for the colon."; October 12, 2000

**"Fiber May Raise Risk of Colon Polyps**
NEW YORK (Reuters Health)—Last year, a major study reported that dietary fiber had no effect on a person's chances of developing colon cancer. The findings surprised the medical community,

which had been recommending that patients consume more fruits, vegetables and whole grains to lower their risk of the number two cancer killer in America."; October 13, 2000

As you can see, these quotes were collected from news wires years ago. Could our esteemed scientists have missed these stories? Sure they could have. So let's review the articles in the must-read publications such as *Cancer, The Lancet,* or *The New England Journal of Medicine,* that they couldn't miss.

Because the connection between dietary fiber and colorectal cancer is so controversial, I'll cite the following abstracts in close to their original format, except that I shortened the list of co-authors, removed the hard-to-understand discussions of statistical results, and underlined the most pertinent revelations. Here we go:

### Dietary Fiber and the Risk of Colorectal Cancer and Adenoma in Women

New England Journal of Medicine; Jan 21 1999; 340:169–176, Fuchs C. S., [et al]

BACKGROUND: A high intake of dietary fiber has been thought to reduce the risk of colorectal cancer and adenoma.

METHODS: We conducted a prospective study of 88,757 women, who were 34 to 59 years old and had no history of cancer, inflammatory bowel disease, or familial polyposis, who completed a dietary questionnaire in 1980. During a 16-year follow-up period, 787 cases of colorectal cancer were documented. In addition, 1012 patients with adenomas of the distal colon and rectum were found among 27,530 participants who underwent endoscopy during the follow-up period.

RESULTS: After adjustment for age, established risk factors, and total energy intake, we found no association between the intake of dietary fiber and the risk of colorectal cancer; [...] No protective effect of dietary fiber was observed when we omitted adjustment for total energy intake, when events during the first six years of follow-up were excluded, or when we excluded women who altered their fiber intake during the follow-up period. No significant association between fiber intake and the risk of colorectal adenoma was found.

CONCLUSIONS: Our data do not support the existence of an important protective effect of dietary fiber against colorectal cancer or adenoma.

### Carbohydrates and Colorectal Cancer Risk among Chinese in North America

Cancer Epidemiology Biomarkers & Prevention Vol. 11, 187–193, February 2002 Marilyn J. Borugian, [et al]

BACKGROUND: Previous studies have analyzed total carbohydrate as a dietary risk factor for colorectal cancer (CRC) but obtained conflicting results, perhaps attributable in part to the embedded potential confounder, fiber.

METHOD: The aim of this study was to analyze the nonfiber («effective») carbohydrate component (eCarb) separately and to test the hypothesis that effective carbohydrate consumption is directly related to CRC risk.

RESULTS: The data (473 cases and 1192 controls) were from a large, multicenter, case-control study of Chinese residing in North America. [...]

CONCLUSION: These data indicate that increased eCarb and total carbohydrate consumption are both associated with increased risk of CRC in both sexes, and that among women, relative risk appears greatest for the right colon, whereas among men, relative risk appears greatest for the rectum.

## Q&A: The Polyp Prevention Trial and the Wheat Bran Fiber Study by National Cancer Institute
Posted: 04/24/2000, http://cancer.gov/clinicaltrials/developments/qa-polyp-prevention0400#Anchor-Wha-3036

### What is the Polyp Prevention Trial?
The Polyp Prevention Trial was a clinical trial (a research study conducted with volunteers) to determine the effect of a low-fat (20 percent of calories from fat), high-fiber (18 grams per 1,000 calories), high fruit/vegetable (3.5 servings per 1,000 calories) eating plan on the recurrence of precancerous polyps in the colon and rectum.

### What were the results of the Polyp Prevention Trial?
The Polyp Prevention Trial provided no evidence that adopting a low-fat, high-fiber, fruit- and vegetable-enriched eating plan reduces the recurrence of colorectal polyps. Polyp recurrence rates were about the same in the two study groups.

### What is the Wheat Bran Fiber Study?
The Wheat Bran Fiber Study was a clinical trial to assess the role of a wheat bran fiber supplement in the prevention of colorectal polyp recurrence. A group of 1,429 men and women who had had one or more polyps removed at colonoscopy within the previous three months were randomized to a high wheat bran fiber cereal supplement (13.5 grams of fiber in 2/3 cup cereal per day) or low wheat bran fiber cereal supplement (2 grams of fiber in 2/3 cup cereal per day).

### What were the results of the Wheat Bran Fiber Study?
The Wheat Bran Fiber Study provided no evidence that adding a wheat bran fiber cereal supplement to the diet reduces the recurrence of colorectal polyps.

## Calcium and fibre supplementation in prevention of colorectal adenoma recurrence: a randomized intervention trial
Lancet 2000; 356: 1300–06
Claire Bonithon-Kopp, [et al] for the European Cancer Prevention Organisation Study Group.

BACKGROUND: Some epidemiological studies have suggested that high dietary intake of calcium and fibre reduces colorectal carcinogenesis. Available data are not sufficient to serve as a basis for firm dietary advice. We undertook a multicentre randomised trial to test the effect of diet supplementation with calcium and fibre on adenoma recurrence.[...]

INTERPRETATION: Supplementation with fibre as ispaghula husk may have adverse effects on colorectal adenoma recurrence, especially in patients with high dietary calcium intake. Calcium supplementation was associated with a modest but not significant reduction in the risk of adenoma recurrence.

(Author's note: *Ispaghula husk* comes from the crushed seeds of the *Plantago ovata* plant, a native herb from parts of Asia, the Mediterranean, and North Africa. From the same plant family come *Plantago psyllium* seeds[5], the source of psyllium husks used in popular bulking fiber laxatives, such as *Metamucil,* and added to some breakfast cereals to increase their fiber content and decrease blood cholesterol. In the context of the above-cited research, think twice before using these constipation and cholesterol "remedies"— you may be making a deal with the devil.)

### Lack of Effect of a High-Fiber Cereal Supplement on the Recurrence of Colorectal Adenomas

New England Journal of Medicine 2000; 342:1156–1162, Apr 20, 2000; David S. Alberts, M.D., [et al] for The Phoenix Colon Cancer Prevention Physicians' Network; http://content.nejm.org/

BACKGROUND: The risks of colorectal cancer and adenoma, the precursor lesion, are believed to be influenced by dietary factors. Epidemiologic evidence that cereal fiber protects against colorectal cancer is equivocal. We conducted a randomized trial to determine whether dietary supplementation with wheat-bran fiber reduces the rate of recurrence of colorectal adenomas.

METHODS: We randomly assigned 1429 men and women who were 40 to 80 years of age and who had had one or more histologically confirmed colorectal adenomas removed within three months before recruitment to a supervised program of dietary supplementation with either high amounts (13.5 g per day) or low amounts (2 g per day) of wheat-bran fiber. [...]

CONCLUSIONS: As used in this study, a dietary supplement of wheat-bran fiber does not protect against recurrent colorectal adenomas.

As you can plainly see from these top-notch studies by mainstream researchers and institutions, fiber not only doesn't offer any protection from colorectal cancer, but potentially elevates the risks.

And I'm not even touching on the subject of other cancers: deadly mouth cancer, even deadlier esophageal cancer, "curable" stomach cancer (curable because the victims can live for a while without the stomach), the deadliest of all, pancreatic cancer, cancers of the small intestines, you name it—all of the digestive organs that are one way or another overloaded by the overconsumption of dietary carbohydrates and fiber.

And don't get me started on non-digestive cancers. For example, it's a well-established fact that the overweight and diabetic have the highest rates of cancer, and that one can become fat or diabetic only one way: by consuming more carbohydrates than one's body needs or can safely process.

The connection is so obvious here that you don't, *mon ami,* need the dissecting mind of Hercule Poirot to figure this out in less than a minute. The U.S. Center for Disease Control and Prevention, the Ministry of Health of Mexico, and the American Institute for Cancer Research spent a huge amount of money to "prove" the cancer-carbohydrate connection:

---

Results: Carbohydrate intake was positively associated with breast cancer risk. Compared with women in the lowest quartile of total carbohydrate intake, the relative risk of breast cancer for women in the highest quartile was 2.22. [...] No association was observed with total fat intake.[6]

---

Please note that most of the research I cited regarding colon cancer is four to five years old. But none of that changed the minds and opinions of the leading authorities charged with protecting our health. They continue to insist on their enshrined, universal remedy:

TAKE MORE FIBER
AVOID MEAT AND ANIMAL FAT
EAT MORE FRUITS AND VEGETABLES

Here's their most recent and egregious advice as to how to fend off colorectal cancer:

## Colorectal Cancer: Who's at Risk?

*"Diet:* Studies suggest that diets high in fat (especially animal fat) and <u>low in calcium, folate, and fiber may increase the risk of colorectal cancer</u>. Also, some studies suggest that people who eat a diet very low in fruits and vegetables may have a higher risk of colorectal cancer."

> What You Need To Know About™ Cancer of the Colon and Rectum
> National Cancer Institute; NIH Publication No. 03–1552; March 2004
> http://cancer.gov/cancerinfo/wyntk/colon-and-rectum

## Who Is at Risk?

"Other factors that may contribute to the risk for colorectal cancer include <u>low fruit and vegetable intake, a low-fiber and high-fat diet</u>, obesity, alcohol consumption, and tobacco use."

> Colorectal Cancer: The Importance of Prevention and Early Detection
> 2003 Program Fact Sheet
> National Center for Chronic Disease Prevention and Health Promotion
> http://www.cdc.gov/cancer/colorctl/colorect.htm

## What Are the Risk Factors?

"The exact causes of colorectal cancer are not known. However, studies show that the following risk factors increase a person's chances for developing colorectal cancer:

- **Diet.** Diets high in fat and low in fiber seem to be associated with colorectal cancer."

> Colorectal Cancer Detection and Prevention
> The American Gastroenterological Association
> http://www.gastro.org/clinicalRes/brochures/crc.html#Lifestyle (2004)

## Health implications of dietary fiber

**"Go for legumes and whole grains:** <u>A diet high in fiber and low in fat may protect you from colon and rectal cancer.</u> Fiber helps move waste through your digestive tract faster so harmful substances don't have much contact time with your intestinal walls.

Try to consume more complex carbohydrate and fiber-rich foods. Choose fruits with edible skins, legumes, vegetables and whole-grain foods. Your goal should be to consume at least two fruit servings, three vegetable servings and three servings of whole-grain breads and cereals every day.

[...] Despite the inconsistency in the results of fiber and colon cancer studies, the scientific consensus is that there is enough evidence that dietary fiber protects against colon cancer that health professionals should be promoting increased consumption of dietary fiber."

American Dietetic Association
Journal of American Dietetic Association 2002;102:993–1000
http://www.eatright.org/Public/NutritionInformation/index_18836.cfm

As you can see, their attitude is the opposite of what has already been said, studied, and known about the fiber-cancer connection. I am at a loss to explain why. But you still worry about meat and fat, correct? The *Dietary Guidelines for Americans* specifically implies that there's a fat-cancer connection:

---

Choose a diet low in fat, saturated fat, and cholesterol to reduce your risk of heart attack and certain types of cancer.[7]

---

To make sure that this isn't so, I checked out the comparative health (sorry, death) statistics vis-à-vis meat consumption, courtesy of the World Health Organization. Since meat is one of the primary sources of saturated fat and cholesterol in the diet, the countries with the largest meat consumption should have the largest rates of digestive cancers, right? Wrong! In fact, population statistics indicate the complete opposite:

### Meat consumption and the occurrence of digestive cancers[8]

|                             | USA     | France  | Colombia | Cuba   | Armenia |
|-----------------------------|---------|---------|----------|--------|---------|
| Life expectancy             | 79.5    | 82.9    | 74.8     | 79.2   | 73      |
| Healthcare (per capita)     | $4,499  | $2,335  | $616     | $186   | $192    |
| Meat consumption (kg)       | 119     | 90      | 37       | 22     | 16      |
|                             |         |         |          |        |         |
| Digestive cancers (per 1000)|         |         |          |        |         |
| Esophagus (C15)             | 1.1     | 1.1     | 1.9      | 1.2    | 0.6     |
| Stomach (C16)               | 2.1     | 2.7     | 13.1     | 3.2    | 6.7     |
| Colon & Rectum (C19-C21)    | 1.4     | 2.2     | 1.2      | 2.1    | 2.3     |
| Total                       | 4.6     | 6       | 16.2     | 6.5    | 9.6     |

As you can see, the United States—the country with the highest annual consumption of meat (119 kg) had the lowest rate of digestive cancers in general (4.6), and the second lowest of colorectal cancers (1.4). On the other hand, Armenia—a relatively poor country with the lowest annual consumption of meat (16 kg)—had the highest rate of colorectal cancers. Why?

There's no contest here: if the poor people of Armenia can't consume as much meat as the Americans can, they have to replace it with something plentiful and cheap. Invariably, dietary carbohydrates, which also carry along loads of fiber, are the only food that reliably fit into the category of "cheap and plentiful."

And notice the dramatic rate of stomach cancer in Armenia and Columbia—respectively three and six times higher than in the United States. The stomach (the organ designed exclusively for the digestion of meats) is even more adversely affected by carbohydrates and fiber than the better-adapted large intestine.

The colossal rate of stomach cancers in Colombia is likely related to two factors: the high rate of smoking and the even higher rate of ceaseless coffee drinking among Colombians. Both factors—the swallowing of nicotine-laced saliva while smoking and the bitterness of coffee, especially on an empty stomach—stimulate the secretion of potent digestive juices. In the absence of food, this causes high rates of gastritis and stomach ulcers, and chronic inflammation and ulceration of the stomach's mucosa, exactly the same two conditions that precede the development of cancers of the large intestine.

So, if you live in the United States, eat plenty of meat, don't smoke, don't chew gum (again, the saliva factor), and don't abuse coffee, consider yourself lucky. In places where they don't get to eat plenty of meat and fat, and do other stupid things, the risk of digestive cancer is much, much higher.

But again, in terms of cancer, it's the fiber and carbohydrates that are the most damaging. The majority of French men smoke too, and most of them drink plenty of coffee, yet the rate of digestive cancers in fat- and meat-loving France is only slightly higher than in the United States, notwithstanding the Gallic devotion to baguettes and croissants liberally smothered with real butter (82% fat) and triple brie (60% fat).

As France's health statistics prove, the protective properties of meat, saturated fat, and cholesterol are more than skin deep. The French manage to weigh less and live longer than Americans, while spending half as much for health care, and probably twice as much for food. Please note that I am not endorsing all aspects of the French lifestyle, just providing a context for comparative statistics. If the French didn't smoke as much and drank less, perhaps they would live even longer.

Finally, a few words on prevention. When it comes to cancers, we are all in God's hands. That said, digestive cancers are among the easiest to avoid just by letting your digestive organs function the way Mother Nature intended: the mouth, to chew non-fibrous food; the stomach, to digest meats; the small intestine, to absorb nutrients and transport liquid chyme; and the large intestine, to slowly propel the remaining residue along without getting stuffed with pounds and pounds of undigested crap—pardon me, with undigested fiber.

It's simple: do no harm. You don't have to be Hippocrates to understand this. Ignore the hypocrites who continue to insist that to prevent colorectal cancer you should consume more fiber, avoid meat and fat, and eat more fruits, vegetables, grains and legumes. You may as well move to Colombia and enjoy your freshly brewed coffee before, after, and between meals, puff on a fine cigar, and chew sugar-free gum the rest of the time to freshen up your mouth.

Please share this information about the fiber-cancer connection with the avowed vegetarians in your family, social, and business circles—it's never too late to help them reverse their well-intentioned but self-destructive lifestyle.

## Summary

- Colorectal cancers are preceded by polyps. The pathogenesis of polyps is related to the mechanical, chemical, and microbiological damage of the intestinal epithelium (mucosal membrane). Preventing the development of polyps is key to the prevention of colorectal cancer.
- The large stools characteristic of constipation cause mechanical

damage to the epithelium. Dietary fiber is the primary factor behind large stools.

- Disbacteriosis is a primary factor behind fiber dependence. The
  elimination and prevention of disbacteriosis removes the need for
  fiber and minimizes the chances of mechanical damage of the
  epithelium.

- Astringent fatty acids are the by-product of dietary fiber's fermentation inside the large intestine. This acidity is a primary factor behind chemical damage of the intestinal mucosa. Other factors are medication and laxatives. Refraining from the use of
  laxatives, and eradicating excessive fermentation eliminates the
  possibility of chemical damage.

- Normal intestinal bacteria populate the intestinal epithelium and
  protect it from viruses and pathogenic bacteria. Disbacteriosis
  removes these protective properties, and may contribute to
  microbiological damage of the intestinal mucosa. Preventing and
  eliminating disbacteriosis is essential for the prevention of
  microbiological damage.

- Correctly prepared meat can't be a significant factor in pathogenesis of colorectal cancer because it fully digests in the stomach and small intestines and never reaches the large intestine.

- Essential amino acids, found mostly in primary protein (meats),
  are essential for the formation of mucin, a primary component of
  mucus, which is secreted by the intestinal epithelium.

- Processed meats found in cold cuts, charred meat prepared on the
  grill, fried meat, and meat cooked on non-stick surfaces can be a
  source of carcinogenic compounds.

- Broiling, boiling, grilling with natural gas, and pan-frying are the
  safest cooking methods for the prevention of colorectal cancers.

- Saturated fats, such as butter, animal fats, or palm oil, used in
  their natural states or in high-temperature cooking, can't be a
  significant factor in the pathogenesis of colorectal cancers, because they are stable fats that fully digest in the small intestine,
  and they don't reach the large intestine.

- All cellular membranes are built from saturated fat molecules.
  The chronic absence of such fats is likely to compromise cellular
  integrity and metabolism, and can contribute to the development
  of cancers.

- Liquid vegetable fats, including olive and canola oil, especially when used in high-temperature cooking, form carcinogenic trans fatty acids.

- When the molecules of monosaturated and polyunsaturated fats are substituted for saturated fats in cellular membranes, they do not offer the same protective properties, and they may contribute to the development of cancers.

- A low-carb diet is best for the prevention of cancer. An authoritative study concluded that "people consuming the highest amounts of digestible carbohydrates had a higher risk for developing colorectal cancer..."[9] Another study concluded that a high-carbohydrate diet "was positively associated with breast cancer risk."[10] It's a commonly accepted theory that people predisposed to one type of cancer are more likely to develop other cancers.

- Numerous authoritative, long-term studies conclusively prove that dietary fiber doesn't offer any protective properties against colon cancer, or increase the risk of polyp formation.

- In most Western studies, women have a higher risk of developing colorectal cancers than men. It is an established fact that more women than men suffer from constipation, and that women are more likely to consume more carbohydrates and fiber than men (following a "healthy diet"), and less meat and saturated fat.

- Regrettably, public health organizations continue to advocate the increased consumption of fiber for prevention of colorectal cancer. It is likely that the motivation for this can be traced to the commercial interests of companies that profit from the sale of products high in fiber.

- An analysis of mortality data from the countries with the highest and lowest meat consumption indicate that the countries with the lowest levels of meat consumption have the highest rate of gastrointestinal cancers.

- The rate of colorectal cancers in underdeveloped countries would be higher if life expectancy there wasn't 20 to 30 years less than in Western countries. It simply means that people in these countries are dying before reaching the median age of colorectal-cancer mortality.

# Footnotes

[1] Arthur Schatzkin, M.D et al.; Lack of Effect of a Low-Fat, High-Fiber Diet on the Recurrence of Colorectal Adenomas; The New England Journal of Medicine; April 20, 2000; 342:1149-1155.

[2] Joene Hendry; 'Digestible' Carbohydrate May Boost Colorectal Cancer Risk; Reuters Health; June 27, 2002.

[3] National Center for Chronic Disease Prevention and Health; Colorectal Cancer Information;
http://www.cdc.gov/cancer/screenforlife/info.htm

[4] Fiber: Start Rounding It. *Harvard School of Public Health.*
http://www.hsph.harvard.edu/nutritionsource/fiber.html

[5] Psyllium; Alternative Field Crops Manual;
http://www.hort.purdue.edu/newcrop/afcm/psyllium.html

[6] Isabelle Romieu, et al.; Carbohydrates and the Risk of Breast Cancer among Mexican Women; Cancer, Epidemiology, Biomarkers & Prevention 2004 13: 1283–1289.

[7] Federal Citizen Information Center, The Food Guide Pyramid;
http://www.pueblo.gsa.gov/cic_text/food/food-pyramid/main.htm

[8] WHO Cancer Mortality Databank;
http://www-depdb.iarc.fr/who/menu.htm

[9] Joene Hendry; 'Digestible' Carbohydrate May Boost Colorectal Cancer Risk; Reuters Health; June 27, 2002.

[10] Isabelle Romieu, et al.; Carbohydrates and the Risk of Breast Cancer among Mexican Women; Cancer, Epidemiology, Biomarkers & Prevention 2004 13: 1283–1289.

# Part III

# From High To Low Without a Blow

*If I knew I was going to live this long,*
*I'd have taken better care of myself.*

Mickey Mantle (1931–1995)

# PART III. INTRODUCTION

---

## LIVE TO EAT, OR EAT TO LIVE? BOTH!

---

Good news: After reading the preceding chapters, you've de-cided to reduce fiber in your diet. Bad news: It's not going to easy. As this book explains time and again, fiber is an addictive sub-stance.

Good news: An addiction to fiber is easier to break than an addiction to drugs or cigarettes. Bad news: If you've been using fiber as a laxative for some time, or have a history of chronic con-stipation, it's not going to be as simple, because your colorectal or-gans have been irreversibly transformed by large stools and strain-ing.

Good news: Fortunately, it's possible to gradually overcome most of the obstacles presented by colorectal damage. Bad news: Unfortunately, you'll need to make a lifelong effort to manage this situation.

Good news: Your quality of life and overall health will improve a great deal. Your digestive organs will not incur additional dam-age. You may recover some or most of your normal intestinal functions. Bad news: there is no bad news, unless you decide to do nothing. In that case, please return to page one and start read-ing anew; otherwise here is what you'll learn from Part III:

- Imagine the promise of a spectacular and permanent weight loss, and then the disappointment experienced among people who failed on the Atkins or South Beach diets because of constipation, indigestion, hypoglycemia, dehydration, and other "side effects" of reduced fiber diets. This book can malign fiber all it wants, but what good will it do if fiber addiction can't be broken without these debilitating conditions? Chapter 11, *Avoiding the Perils of Transition,* explains the causes behind the fallout of fiber withdrawal, and describes key strategies for a crash-free transition from a high- to low-fiber lifestyle. This brings us to the final chapter.

- Humans are extremely vulnerable to just about anything out of the ordinary: heat, cold, fire, smoke, darkness, slippery surfaces, and so on. The natural, innate fear of trauma and death keeps most of us away from these types of perils. Not so with health—as a rule, most people don't value it until they no longer have it. Inversely, the value of health becomes palpable when we first begin experiencing diseases, especially those that cause pain or defy a quick fix. Chapter 12, *The Low-Fiber Advantage,* enumerates the key benefits of excising fiber from your diet. Those benefits range from weight loss and improved digestion to recovery from diabetes, indigestion, irritable bowel syndrome, Crohn's disease, and ulcerative colitis—disorders that defy conventional treatment because drugs can only sugarcoat their symptoms, but can do nothing to remove their causes. Fiber is the champion of harm among these conditions.

This chapter often refers to a low-fiber lifestyle rather than just to a low-fiber diet for a reason: who can really diet for long? Besides, this book isn't about what to eat. It's about what not to.

*In many cases, the toilet bowl predicts your future
with more certainty than a crystal ball.*

Author

# CHAPTER ELEVEN

# AVOIDING THE PERILS OF TRANSITION

A low-fiber diet isn't exactly chemotherapy. If anyone tells you otherwise and claims that a low-fiber diet isn't safe, or can harm you, or that fiber is an essential nutrient, that person is misinformed.

Consider Japan, for example. It has the highest life expectancy among developed countries,[1] provides free health care to all of its citizens, and yet its health-care costs relative to gross domestic product are among the lowest—7.9% vs. 15% in the United States. This statistic is salient, because it means that the Japanese are much healthier than Americans, and need to spend half as much precious national resources to deliver, according to all accounts, superior medical care.

Anyone who has ever visited Japan, set foot in a Japanese restaurant, read Japanese cookbooks, or is partial to FoodTV, knows that Japanese cuisine—haute and casual alike—is about as low in fiber as it gets. Aside from white rice, which is the main source of carbohydrates for the Japanese, Japanese cooking is dominated by fish, seafood, white and red meats, tofu, and seaweed (0.5% fiber), which is used in salads and wraps.

One cup of cooked rice (186 g) contains just 0.6 g (0.3%) of fiber.[2] Even a prodigious eater, like a sumo wrestler, consumes less fiber from twelve cups of rice than the average five-year-old

American from just one cup (61 g) of relatively benign (fiber-wise) Kellogg's Raisin Bran (7.3 g of fiber, or 11.9%[3]).

Even though white rice is omnipresent, plentiful, and contains 54 g of carbs per one cup serving, the rate of obesity in industrialized, modern Japan is 3.2%, compared to 30.6% in the United States.[4] The exceptionally low fiber content of the Japanese diet is one of the reasons behind this stunning 952% difference.

And if someone tells you that the Japanese are different from Americans, that it's all in the genes—that's not true, either. The genetic difference between an ethnic Japanese and a Caucasian or African-American is just 0.1%—not a big enough difference to attribute the low obesity rate among the native Japanese to genes alone.

Just a few generations ago, before the fiber menace hit Americans full-force, the obesity rate in the United States was almost as low as it is in Japan today. If that's not proof enough for you, modern-day Germany, Ireland, and Italy—the countries that provided the largest gene pool of white Americans—have, respectively, 12.9%, 12.0%, and 8.5% obesity rates.[5] Although these rates are higher than they should or used to be, they're still nowhere near as high as the obesity rate in the United States. So much for genetics.

The obesity rate in Africa is even lower than it is in Japan, except among the very rich, who have adopted Western-style diets. But according to the Centers for Disease Control and Prevention (CDC), 48.8% of adult African-American[6] women are obese, compared to 30.7% of adult white women. This isn't surprising. African-Americans also tend to consume more fiber-rich processed food than do Caucasians.

One diet, highly acclaimed for its high-fiber content from fruits, vegetables, and grains, is the famous Mediterranean diet. But lo and behold, the obesity rate in Greece today stands at 21.9%—not as high as 30.6% in the United States, but it's catching up. Greece also happens to be one of the poorest and least developed countries in the European Union, hence the higher ratio of cheap and plentiful grain crops (a major source of fiber) in the after all not-so-healthy Mediterranean diet.

So pita bread and Greek salad are out, nori (dry seaweed wrap) and kaisou (seaweed salad) are in. But before you snap your chopsticks, your digestive organs must get reacquainted with a low-fiber diet.

### The good, the bad, and the diet-breakers

If a low-fiber diet is safe, healthy, and effective, then why isn't getting off a high-fiber diet a "piece of cake"? Because the consumption of fiber gradually alters the physiology of the digestive organs. And nobody knows the side effects of sudden fiber withdrawal as well as the untold millions of people who failed on the Atkins diet, which, at the very beginning, happens to be not just low-carb, but also fiber-free. Even Dr. Atkins himself failed with his own diet, and he died morbidly obese.[7]

All that being said, a low-fiber diet isn't a low-carb diet, unless you consciously decide to reduce carb intake in order to lose weight, or to prevent and treat carbohydrate-related disorders, such as hypertension, diabetes, or kidney disease.

Let me emphasize this point again: a low-fiber diet has nothing in common with the Atkins diet, except that it is purposefully LOW IN FIBER. If you're healthy and your weight is normal, you may stick with your usual diet, but just cut down on foods high in fiber, such as bran, whole-wheat bread, cereals, or beans. That's really all you need to change. You may not even notice the transition, except that your stools will become noticeably smaller, and you may go down a size or two and lose five to ten pounds of weight, once your intestines expel fiber, water, and any fiber-laden stools "in transit"—the phenomenon already explained in Chapter 3, *Atkins Goes to South Beach.*

Unfortunately, as you may already know from health statistics and personal observation, disease-free and normal-weight people are a shrinking minority, and are more than likely not readers of this book to begin with. So, should you decide to adopt a low-fiber diet for health, weight loss, or any other worthwhile reason, the following information should help you make the transition as trouble-free as possible.

This chapter addresses major conditions that may arise when fiber and carbohydrates are suddenly reduced. The most apparent side effects of fiber withdrawal are constipation and indigestion.

Other challenges come from breaking a dependence on carbohydrates (which customarily accompany high-fiber food) without encountering the usual side effects of their withdrawal, such as hypoglycemia, dehydration, and malnutrition. Let's begin with constipation—the undisputed champion of diet-breakers.

## Constipation

The complete withdrawal of fiber from one's diet reduces the daily volume of stools from the usual 400 to 500 g to under 100 g. As Chapter 5, *Constipation,* explained, 100 g or less of stools daily is considered normal, which makes 400–500 g abnormal, almost freakish. This anomaly isn't just the outcome of consuming fiber, but also a symptom of chronic constipation, which can be either latent (hidden) or organic (from organ damage).

If this is confusing, let's look at it from a different angle: Technically, if you're consuming gobs of fiber, and have three to four comfortable bowel movements daily (each around 100–150 g), your large intestine may be working overtime, but it's perfectly fine. If you have just one bowel movement daily, however, and its volume is three to five times the norm, and it isn't comfortable, it means that your large intestine has already been stretched out and desensitized by large, heavy stools.

And therein lies the problem with fiber withdrawal: when stools suddenly become small and light, most people no longer experience an urge to move their bowels, and inevitably miss bowel movements. When that happens, the smallish stools inside the large intestine quickly become dry, hard, and abrasive (to the anal canal), with physical properties similar to the Bristol Stool Form Scale type 1, described as "separate hard lumps, like nuts." Expelling these stools will obviously drive anyone nuts, from the pain, discomfort, or bleeding associated with a lacerated mucosa.

Nuts or not, the actual perception of constipation differs from person to person. These differences (some subtle, some distinct) are determined by age, gender, health, lifestyle, diet composition, toilet habits, history of colorectal disorders, and other factors discussed earlier in this book.

Regardless of individual perception, the gist of the matter is that stools, when fiber is suddenly withdrawn, can become irregular, dry or hard, cause pain and hemorrhoidal disease, or cause rectal bleeding—all of the usual side effects of severe constipation. These are conditions you'd be better off preventing, rather than giving up halfway and resuming your old diet. Then you'd be back plunging out stools the old-fashioned way—with more and more fiber.

So here is a set of rules to help you along the path of transition. For starters, let's briefly review the obstacles you may encounter while transitioning from a high-fiber diet to low:

- *Colon stretching.* If takes years to stretch out the large intestine to accommodate oversized stools. It's important to understand that "shrinking" it back may take some time. Past a certain age— 50 for some, 60 for others—it may not contract back much or at all. It isn't practical to estimate how long, how fast, or how well the contraction will take place, except by noting the obvious: the younger you are, the faster.
- *Muscular atony.* Unless a person is bedridden, paralyzed from the waist down, suffers from rare endocrine disorders, or is medicated with drugs that impact neuromuscular functions, the colon retains its function to propel stools toward the rectum. What is commonly referred to as an "atonic" or "lazy" colon is really a continuation of the previous problems—a stretched- out, desensitized colon that can't propel much smaller stools because it simply can't "feel" them.
- *Nerve damage.* Large stools, straining, diabetes, anorectal sur- geries, or the habitual suppression of stools can cause irreversible nerve damage to the rectal cavity and the nerve plexus along the juncture of the rectum and anal canal. When the nerve receptors in these areas are damaged or desensitized, the defecation urge sensation is diminished or absent.
- *Disbacteriosis.* Intestinal flora is a major component of normal stools, representing from 50 to 75% of their total weight. When both the fiber and the bacteria are missing, stool volume be- comes even smaller, and more difficult to expel.
- *Hemorrhoidal disease.* Enlarged hemorrhoids constrict the anal canal, and interfere with normal defecation. Although smaller stools help to reduce pain and straining, they may still require a

certain degree of straining to expel them (an action of the abdominal and pelvic muscles). Unfortunately, any straining adversely affects hemorrhoidal disease and its complications.

- *Anorectal pain.* Anal fissures, abrasions, inflammation of the anal mucosa, enlarged hemorrhoids, and similar factors instill a fear of defecation and may cause the withdrawal of stools, which is often unconscious. This condition is especially prevalent among small children, who can't verbalize their feelings. As with hemorrhoidal disease, smaller stools will help to alleviate pain quite a bit, but it's imperative not to miss the opportunity to expel them, otherwise they'll dry out, and become hard, abrasive, and even more painful.

- *Organic disorders.* Certain conditions such as fecal impaction, hypercalcemia, hypothyroidism, Hirschsprung's disease, or colon cancer may cause severe chronic constipation or obstruction, which can't be overcome through toilet discipline, dietary means, or over-the-counter remedies. The screening, diagnosis, and treatment of these conditions require a specialist, and discussing them is outside the scope of this book.

- *Medication.* The list of drugs that contribute to constipation is quite extensive. A recent search for "constipation" of RXList (www.rxlist.com)—a free public access database of over 1,450 prescription drugs—returned 675 matches. Always check the medication you may be taking for constipation-related side effects. If constipation is indeed listed, ask your doctor to prescribe an alternative. Ideally, while transitioning to a low-fiber diet, all external obstacles must be eliminated.

I realize that this is already quite a handful of issues to overcome. Bear in mind that most, if not all of these obstacles, are the outcomes of a high-fiber diet to begin with. In this particular instance, blaming a low fiber-diet for the perils of transition is as sensible as blaming a rape victim for being pretty. Instead of rubbing the victim's face with tar, it's the rapist (fiber in this case) who should be tarred.

Unfortunately, some aspects of managing these conditions may be mutually exclusive: on one hand, you may benefit from retaining a certain bulking agent in your diet while "shrinking" the colon; on the other, the bulk will continue to affect anorectal disorders and cause pain. In these cases you must choose the strategy that's the least harmful.

Below are the rules of constipation prevention while transitioning from high- to low-fiber diet, split into three sections: (1) For people who are free from disorders of the large intestine; (2) For people already affected by constipation and colorectal disorders, such as IBS, hemorrhoidal disease, anal fissures, and nerve damage; (3) Rules that are applicable to both groups.

## Rules of transition for healthy people

For the purpose of this section, "healthy" means the following: (a) you've never experienced chronic constipation; (b) you don't have hemorrhoidal disease; (c) you don't have any colorectal disorders as described in Part II of this book; (d) you don't take any medications that may have constipation listed among its possible side effects; (e) you don't take any laxatives; and (f) your bowel movements are easy (don't require straining), and regular (at least daily). Most children, three-quarters of young adults, close to half of all adults under 50 years of age, and twice as many men as women belong to this fortunate group.

If you "fail" this checklist on any one point, please proceed to the next subsection. Even if you "pass," keep the following points in mind:

- You may have regular stools, and still experience latent constipation. Large stools, moderate straining, and slight discomfort during or after defecation are the symptoms of latent constipation.
- You may have enlarged internal hemorrhoids and not know it. Straining, discomfort during bowel movements, itching in the anal area, and occasional streaks of blood on stools points to the probability of enlarged internal hemorrhoids.

Regardless of your overall health, you may still encounter constipation-like symptoms during the transition, unless you wean yourself from a high-fiber diet gradually. A slow and deliberate transition to a low-fiber diet is the best preventive strategy for healthy people. Here are the required steps:

- Record the approximate fiber intake you get daily from supplements and food sources, including snacks. Keep the tally for several days to average out day-to-day variances. Fiber content per serving is listed on the food labels in grams. Some packages intentionally minimize serving size to camouflage a high carb content. For food without labels, such as fruits, vegetables, or baked goods, consult the USDA National Nutrient Database for Standard Reference at www.nal.usda.gov/fnic/foodcomp/ search/.

- While you're at it, consider tabulating the results in a spreadsheet program like Excel. In addition to fiber, record your daily intake of water, carbohydrates, proteins, and fats. This exercise may be quite an eye opener. Remember, over 50% of raw meat is water, and up to 30% is fat. Don't count the gross weight of uncooked meat as protein. The actual protein content is much, much smaller, usually under 15%. Ditto animal fats: even the "fattiest" butter contains only 82% of fat, heavy cream 37%. After trimming and cooking, most meats contain much less fat, and a good share of the protein becomes useless (denatured) by heat. Vegetable oils are the "fattiest" of fats because they are 100% fat.

- If you're doing these calculations on behalf of your children, divide your own ideal weight by theirs (also ideal). The result tells you just how much smaller their digestive organs are than yours. As this book has already pointed out most young children scorn fiber, because their tiny and sensitive digestive organs feel its ill effects much stronger than the already desensitized stomachs and intestines of most adults. You'll do them and yourself a huge favor by respecting that distinction.

- If your daily consumption of fiber is under 10–15 g, you don't have to change anything. But if your stools are still large and voluminous, it means that you're experiencing a sizable accumulation of stools inside the large intestine—a condition specific to latent constipation. In this case proceed to the next section.

- If your daily consumption of fiber exceeds 15 g, first identify foods that have the highest fiber content. These are usually processed foods, such as cereals, bran, whole-wheat bread, muffins, bagels, and the like. Ideally, you shouldn't eat them anyway, because nutritionally speaking all processed foods are unwholesome. If you aren't inclined to make any changes in your diet, at least replace high-fiber food with low-fiber analogues: corn flakes instead of fiber-fortified cereals, white bread instead of whole wheat, regular muffins instead of bran muffins, green peas instead of lentils, pine nuts instead of peanuts, zucchini instead of broccoli, and so on.

That's really all you need to do. You should see the results (smaller stools) in about three to four days—the amount of time it takes for the large intestine to expel fiber-laden stools. From this point on, keep your fiber intake low, and follow all of the steps outlined below to keep your large intestine healthy, functional, and well-protected from fiber-related carnage.

And if you don't see results—meaning your stools aren't coming out at all, or are dry and hard—it means that your large intestine isn't, after all, in top-notch shape. If this is the case, proceed to the next section.

### Rules of transition for individuals affected by constipation and colorectal disorders

Supplemental fiber must go first. You won't regret this decision because it doesn't relieve constipation anyway, and causes exactly the same problems it purports to relieve and prevent—more constipation, and anorectal damage from large stools.

Fiber from psyllium is probably the most offensive, because it's at once (1) a bulking agent capable of obstructing the esophagus and intestines, (2) an osmotic laxative capable of causing severe diarrhea, (3) a fermentable biomass that causes acidic damage of the intestinal epithelium, and (4) a severe allergen for some people. And all that besides the cramping, bloating, gases, and severe straining required to expel large stools.

According to the 2005 American College of Gastroenterology Functional Gastrointestinal Disorders Task Force,[8] psyllium recommendations are based on several "suboptimally designed" (that's a euphemism for *phony*) clinical trials. Other bulking agents are just as useless:

*Guidelines for the Treatment of Chronic Constipation:* ...poorly designed RCTs [randomly controlled trials] involving fewer than 100 patients do not demonstrate differences between calcium polycarbophil or methylcellulose compared with psyllium.[9]

Supplemental bran didn't perform any better in trials than psyllium (Metamucil), methylcellulose (Citrucel), or calcium polycarbophil (FiberCon) laxatives:

*Guidelines for the Treatment of Chronic Constipation:* Specifically, there are 3 RCTs of wheat bran in patients with chronic constipation, but only 1 is placebo-controlled. This trial did not demonstrate a significant improvement in stool frequency or consistency when compared with a placebo—neither did 2 trials that compared wheat bran with corn biscuits or corn bran.[10]

Next, you should get rid of all natural sources of fiber that contain gluten—a potent plant allergen, especially for people who are already affected by intestinal disorders. That means all kinds of whole wheat cereals, breads, pastas, and baked goods.

Many people who suffer from constipation swear by the stool softening effect of prune and beet juices. These juices contain sorbitol, a sugar alcohol which is also found in bananas, apples, pears, and some berries. Sorbitol is a strong osmotic laxative, hence its stool-softening effect. Unfortunately, sorbitol also tends to accumulate in the cells, causing nerve damage, blindness, deafness, heart attacks, strokes, and kidney damage. Because excess glucose inside the cells gets converted to sorbitol too, consuming those concentrated juices is particularly dangerous for people who are already likely to have elevated blood sugar: the overweight, prediabetic, or diabetic who are still consuming unrestricted carbohydrates.

Finally, watch out for hidden sources of soluble fiber, which is generously added to yogurts, ice creams, milk shakes, snacks, sauces, dressings, condiments, preserves, soups, and so forth. Some of the most common names are: cellulose, methylcellulose, β-glucans, pectin, guar gum, cellulose gum, carrageen, agar-agar, gum acacia (arabic), guarana gum, benzoin, hemicellulose, inulin, lignin, oligofructose, fructooligosaccharides, polydextrose, polylos, resistant dextrin, resistant starch, and many others.[11]

Once you've eliminated all sources of fiber, your now bulk-free diet may not be able to dislodge the stools that are already accumulated in your large intestine. To prevent constipation from taking hold, take the following steps to normalize stools:

- Use saline laxatives[12] such as Milk of Magnesia and Epsom Salts to lavage the large intestine of accumulated large stools. Follow the manufacturer's directions. Milk of Magnesia is an 8% water solution of magnesium hydroxide. It has strong antacid properties, and interferes with gastric digestion if taken with food. Individuals with impaired kidneys may develop toxic levels of magnesium from extended use of Milk of Magnesia. Epsom Salts is a brand name for magnesium sulfate. It's more potent than Milk of Magnesia because it absorbs faster into the bloodstream, and may cause severe diarrhea. Because of their impact on the kidneys, neither Milk of Magnesia nor Epsom Salts are suitable for long-term use. After a thorough lavage you may not have any stools for a day or two. That's normal because it takes about that long for newer stools to reach the rectum. (Please note that magnesium is an essential macromineral, required, among other things, for the proper assimilation of calcium. The above discussion applies only to laxatives which contain high doses of magnesium, but not to elementary magnesium in general.)

- To overcome a diminished urge sensation (because stools are now small), consider using glycerin suppositories. As soon as the suppository contacts the extremely sensitive nerve plexus situated along the anorectal line, the rectum starts contracting. This action imitates normal defecation. The rectal contraction stimulates the mass peristaltic movement, and the colon advances stools into the rectum for immediate expulsion. For adults, it's best to insert two suppositories to assure full contact with the nerve plexus. If you have severe nerve damage, glycerin suppositories aren't effective. It's easy to determine—if suppositories don't cause any reaction a few minutes after insertion, the damage has gone too far. In this case you'll require another long-term approach.

- If you're under 65, your doctor may prescribe Zelnorm (tegaserod)—the only medication approved for long-term use for people who suffer from chronic constipation. Besides being expensive and requiring a prescription, Zelnorm has many side effects, such as headaches, joint pain, severe diarrhea, abdominal cramping, dizziness, lightheadedness, fainting, irregular heartbeats, intestinal ischemia, ischemic colitis, and some others. Death of patients due to intestinal ischemia—the necrosis (death) of the intestinal tissue caused by insufficient blood flow—prompted the U.S. Food and Drug Administration's intervention,[13] which required Novartis, the maker of Zelnorm, to provide stronger warnings on the label about these side effects.

- *Hydro-C Colonic Moisturizer* is a safe alternative to Milk of Magnesia, Epsom Salts, or Zelnorm. I first identified this compound, a derivative of vitamin C, for myself and the readers of my earlier books who couldn't manage their chronic constipation, hemorrhoidal disease, or anal fissures in any other way. It's safe, effective, inexpensive, non-addictive, and has a range of healing properties which may benefit constipation-related disorders. You can learn more about Hydro-C's properties, composition, mechanism of action, and safety at www.AgelessNutrition.com.

If it upsets you that there isn't some neat trick that can somehow override years of colorectal damage, well, it upsets me too. But such is life. I would rather endure the hassle of a low-fiber diet for the rest of my life than let a high-fiber diet cut my life short. Speaking of hassles.

### Common rules of transition to a low-fiber diet

The following are the "must do" actions for anyone considering a low-fiber diet. These rules must be abided by not just daily, but for the rest of one's life. If you ignore them, either you'll slip back to a high-fiber diet, or get constipated, or both. In either case, some of the digestive disorders described in this book may eventually catch up with you. Consider these rules cheap health insurance.

### Don't miss the urge

While stools are still large and heavy, the defecation urge is more pronounced because of the strong pressure inside the colon and rectum. When stools are becoming small and light, there is very little pressure, so the urge becomes subtle and barely noticeable. But the urge is even more critical now, because if you miss or ignore it, the small stools will rapidly dry out, harden up, and may become even more difficult to expel than the large ones.

As you may recall from previous chapters and perhaps from your own experience, the urge sensation is related to eating: food stimulates the gastrocolic reflex, the gastrocolic reflex stimulates the mass peristaltic movement, the mass movement propels the colon's content toward the rectum. In turn, the rectum contraction propels stools toward the anal canal, which stimulates the nerve plexus, and that stimuli is what sends you flying to the bathroom.

When you switch over to a low-fiber diet, you should get to the bathroom as soon as you sense the first inklings of the gastrocolic reflex, because the stools are way too small and light to reach and stimulate the nerve plexus, unless you're already "in position"— meaning sitting down on the toilet bowl and ready "to go." If you aren't prepared, you may have to wait for another reflex. Unfortunately, a true mass peristaltic movement, also known as "peristaltic rush," occurs only a few times daily, usually during or shortly after a meal. If you wait too long or miss those reflexes too often, the stools will dry out, harden up, and you're back to square one.

Though all of the above sounds easy and logical, many cultural (can't go to the bathroom in the middle of a meal), logistical (bathroom is too close to the kitchen), behavioral (a habit of resisting stools), parental (Johnny, wait until we get back home) and other factors complicate things. Partial nerve damage complicates things even more, because the urge sensation is even less perceptible. Hopefully, you can overcome all of these obstacles, and discipline yourself to be in the bathroom not in the nick of time, but in advance. Eventually, this will become visceral and much easier to accomplish.

If you do have partial nerve damage, insert glycerin suppositories before sitting down for a meal. This way, when the gastrocolic reflex strikes, you'll have a double-action working in your favor— mass peristaltic movement from the top, and suppository stimulation from the bottom. Hopefully, as you get more and more disciplined and perceptive, unconditional reflexes will set in and you won't need suppositories.

Does reading material in the bathroom help? Yes, it does, a lot! First, it takes your mind off the conscious control of defecation. Secondly, it lets you pass the time easier. Finally, it relaxes you, because you aren't as tense as you might be if you were just sitting and waiting for something to happen. Just make sure whatever you're reading is fun and light. You don't want to read anything that may make you tense, because the tension spreads throughout the entire body, including the large intestine, and inhibits involuntary contraction of smooth muscles and defecation.

"Tight ass" isn't just a figure of speech—it's a bona fide obstacle caused by stress and mental tensions. In this context, meditation (especially in the lotus position) is a very effective "laxative," because it relaxes you and your anal muscles at the same time. A hot bath is also an effective relaxant, as are stretching exercises, a leisurely walk, relaxing music, or anything that takes your mind off of daily worries.

"Urge management" represents probably 80% of constipation prevention. Ideally, if you really get the hang of it, you'll have a bowel movement after each major meal. Inversely, "urge mismanagement" also represents 80% of the reasons why most people become constipated in the first place. That's why people in simple cultures, especially those living alfresco, are constipation-free regardless of their diet—they never have to resist the urge to move their bowels, and they don't have any particular shame associated with defecation.

When social mores and conditions override basic instincts, anyone can become severely constipated. You'd be surprised how many people search the Internet daily for the subject of dog or cat constipation. Nobody's immune, not even pets.

Speaking of pets, we have two wonderful cats, who have never been constipated. To keep it this way, we feed them only organic canned cat food. It took me just one sighting of their huge stools on a dry food diet, prescribed by a vet, to ban dry food as a "main course" forever. They do get 10–15 bits of organic dry food to snack on after evening meals, because we think (perhaps erroneously) that the chewing action helps keep their teeth clean.

Back to people... You're probably aware of the management postulate that the remaining 20% of any task requires 80% of the work. Indeed...

## Eliminate disbacteriosis

Easier said than done. You really can't replace 400–450 kinds of innate intestinal bacteria with supplements, which at best may contain up to ten common strains. Nonetheless, the regular use of good quality acidophilus supplements helps to increase stool mass, make stools softer, and also make them more water-retentive.

It's imperative to take high-quality brands without any additives, such as bovine colostrum. Some people are incredibly allergic to bovine colostrum, which may cause allergic shock (anaphylaxis). After all, bovine colostrum is intended for calves rather than people, most of whom have never tasted raw milk, and haven't had a chance to develop a limited immunity to bovine flora.

Logically, it may appear that liquid acidophilus preparations may be more effective than encapsulated supplements, because they have more bacteria per dose and contain live, rather then sublimated, flora. Unfortunately, some of these preparations are literally too effective, especially lactic acid bacterial strains, such as L. acidophilus, L. bulgaricus, L. casei, and others that are preceded with the capital L, which means *Lactobacillus.*

When these bacteria reach the intestines, they proliferate with dramatic speed, and produce both lactic acid and gas, which may sometimes cause severe distress, abdominal pain, and bloating. This pain may be easily confused with appendicitis, and if you have a low pain threshold, you may have to take antibiotics to wipe the pain out—not a desirable action because all the good bacteria will get wiped out as well.

Even though milk enhances the survival of intestinal flora, commercial yogurts and other fermented dairy drinks are rarely as active as therapeutic preparations, because they are often treated with high heat to stop fermentation and prevent spoilage, which kills bacteria.

To be effective, liquid preparations must be taken on an empty stomach, otherwise gastric acid kills bacteria. Quality encapsulated supplements are provided in *enteric* capsules, which disintegrate only inside the intestines. Keep in mind that lactic acid bacteria are

the main culprit behind dental caries (cavities), so it's a good idea
to brush your teeth with sugar-free toothpaste after drinking liquid
preparations, fermented dairy products, or eating naturally ripened
cheeses.[14]

If you'd like to try liquid preparations, proceed slowly and observe
their actions for 48 to 72 hours. If, during this time or shortly thereafter, you begin experiencing gases and bloating, discontinue using
them at once. Similar caution should be exercised when taking supplements in capsules or in any other form. A fiber-free diet won't
prevent bacteria from procreating, because bacteria get all the nutrients they need from the glycoproteins secreted with mucus.

If you aren't experiencing much bacterial action, you may add
supplemental doses of fructooligosaccharides (same as FOS), inulin, apple pectin, or acacia gum—soluble fibers intended to stimulate the procreation and development of bacteria. They are available in supplement form in health food stores. Follow the manufacturer's directions. Reduce the dose or eliminate it altogether if
you experience excess gas and bloating.

You can find a more detailed discussion of disbacteriosis and
recommended brands (the ones that myself, my family, and the
readers of my Russian-language books have been taking for many
years) at www.AgelessNutrition.com.

## Diet composition

Diet influences bowel movements in ways completely contrary
to conventional thinking. Let's repeat the quote from Chapter 5,
*Constipation*:

---

*Human Physiology:* [Colon] motility is influenced by the energy
content and composition of the meal, but not by its volume or pH.
Energy-rich meals with a high fat content increase motility; carbohydrates and proteins have no effect.[15]

---

Interesting! How much you eat makes no difference, fiber isn't
even mentioned, carbohydrates and proteins are irrelevant, and fat
rules! But why?

Fat in food initiates the release of bile stored in the gallbladder.
Bile stimulates the peristalsis of the small intestine, which in turn

stimulates the gastrocolic reflex, and so forth. This effect of fat on morning stools didn't escape enlightened Europeans: a cup of fresh-brewed coffee, heavy cream, fresh butter, triple-fat brie, and fat-laden croissants are customarily served for breakfast in much of Western Europe. Lo and behold, Europeans scorn fiber, and are much skinnier and healthier than Americans, despite the predominantly low-fat diet in the United States.

Bitterness in coffee is another strong and fast-acting stimulant of gastric and billiary digestion. For this reason drinking coffee on an empty stomach is a bad idea. When food isn't forthcoming, hydrochloric acid and gastric enzymes irritate the stomach's epithelium and find their way into the even less protected small intestine. When fats aren't forthcoming to utilize and neutralize the bile, the lower intestine is also affected by its high astringency, Gastroenteritis (chronic inflammation of the stomach and intestinal epithelium) is a common side effect of morning coffee. This condition is the precursor of peptic ulcers, irritable bowel syndrome, and inevitable intermittent diarrhea and constipation. For this and many other good reasons, I no longer drink tea or coffee, nor do I endorse them for the prevention of constipation.

If you do drink coffee, at least make sure it's always freshly-ground and brewed (to avoid trans fats in instant and packaged coffee) and consumed with fatty meals, or, at the very least, heavy cream. In addition to breakfast, Europeans drink coffee as an aperitif and digestive aid after meals. When dining out, I sometimes enjoy a cup of decaf espresso to complete a memorable meal. Since we dine out rarely,[16] and memorable meals are even rarer, this doesn't amount to very much.

### Mineral and water status

Potassium is *the* mineral that retains water in stools. Because it's found primarily in plant foods, low-carb diets are universally low in potassium. Supplemental potassium causes digestive distress and isn't desirable. To prevent potassium deficiency, drink one to two glasses of cucumber juice daily (with skins) an hour before a meal. Cucumber juice is rich in potassium (about 350 mg per 8 oz). Because it's practically free of sugars, refrigerated cucumber juice stores well. Juice a batch once or twice a week from large seedless cucumbers (each yields about a cup of juice).

Tomatoes are another excellent source of potassium, and should be consumed raw, preferably without skins (they contain indigestible fiber). One medium-sized tomato contains almost 300 mg of potassium and less than 4 grams of carbs. The rest is water (117 g). Commercial tomato drinks, such as V-8, are loaded with fiber to give them body, and should be avoided. Just squeeze a regular tomato to see the striking difference in taste, color and texture vis-à-vis supermarket tomato juice.

Other good sources of potassium are fermented dairy products (yogurt, buttermilk, kefir), slow-cooked beef or chicken broth, and vegetables with a low-fiber/low-carb content, such as zucchini, squash, and eggplant.

You do not need to drink more water to enhance stools' moisture. 100 g of stools require about 50–70 ml of water to stay moist—a tiny fraction of the total daily water turnover inside the alimentary canal. In fact, the more you drink, the more water and potassium you are going to lose through the kidneys. This issue was addressed in Chapter 2, *Water Damage*. Furthermore, stools become dry not because there isn't enough water, but because getting water out of stools is the primary job of a healthy large intestine. Expel them timely and regularly, and they'll never get dry.

### Moderate physical activity

Just like with any other organ, blood vessels and intestinal muscles benefit from a healthy workout and the vigorous oxygenation that any form of exercise brings. Exercise is particularly effective in expunging stress hormones, triglycerides, and excess glucose from the blood that directly or indirectly impedes circulation and muscular contraction. Just as exercise firms up the skeletal muscles, it also conditions, strengthens, and rejuvenates the vascular and intestinal smooth muscles. Even a brief daily walk brings a considerable improvement in bowel function.

You do not need to exercise your abdominal muscles to improve your ability to strain, because (a) with smaller stools you will not need to strain any longer, and (b) because you want to avoid straining as much as possible to prevent hemorrhoidal disease, anal fissures, bleeding, and pain. If you want to exercise to have great looking abs, that's fine. Just don't use them for the wrong tasks.

## Quality supplements to enhance overall health

A multivitamin formula by itself isn't going to do much to relieve constipation or improve stools. However, high quality supplements taken regularly improve overall health, restore damaged nerve receptors, improve digestion, circulation, and muscular health, stimulate metabolism, and serve a broad range of other positive functions. You can find additional recommendations at www.AgelessNutrition.com.

## What to do with small, hard stools

So you missed a stool or two because of a business trip, honeymoon, stressful event, or whatever. That's no reason for despair. Just take several reduced doses of an osmotic laxative, such as Milk of Magnesia or Epsom Salts, to rehydrate them. If you take too large a dose, you may get diarrhea before these hard stools have a chance to rehydrate. Hydro-C (see page 208) is an effective and safe alternative. Once your stools are normalized, try not to miss expelling them again.

As you can see, constipation is a complex syndrome, which tends to become more and more challenging with age. If your constipation hasn't advanced too far (i.e. just functional constipation, related to a change in diet), there is more information on these pages about managing it than you'll find anywhere. If you have a more complicated history of chronic constipation and associated intestinal disorders, such as chronic diarrhea, irritable bowel syndrome, Crohn's disease, ulcerative colitis, hemorrhoidal disease, anal fissures, and others, you may benefit from reviewing additional publications dedicated specifically to these subjects. Please check www.AgelessNutrition.com for more information.

Mother Nature, anticipating a thorny destiny for her offspring, made the stomach a much sturdier organ than the large intestine. But even she couldn't anticipate the onslaught of so much factory-made fiber in today's food supply while conceiving and executing the human body. And this brings us to the number two challenge of transitioning to a low-fiber lifestyle—indigestion.

## Indigestion

Indigestion is a broadly used term that encompasses numerous disorders, such as heartburn, abdominal or upper chest pain, nausea, belching, and a feeling of fullness. Over the past few decades, the pedestrian "indigestion" has been gradually replaced with the more respectable "dyspepsia." During the same time period the plebian "heartburn" became the impressive-sounding GERD, or gastroesophageal reflux disease.

This section, however, isn't about GERD or dyspepsia, but, literally, about incomplete digestion—the original true meaning of the term indigestion. Since the stomach digests nothing but proteins, indigestion also means the incomplete digestion of proteins. Paradoxically, a low-fiber diet is the best defense from indigestion, yet when some people suddenly drop fiber and carbs from their diets they may experience the temporary indigestion of proteins. After constipation, indigestion was one of the most common complaints from people who attempted the Atkins and similar diets.

What's the big deal? Well, even a brief episode of indigestion, especially in people past the age of 50, may cause stomach or esophageal inflammation. Inflammation can turn into ulcers and polyps, and some of these may eventually become cancerous. The presence of H.pylori bacteria inside the stomach speeds up ulceration. Since half of all people with peptic ulcers aren't infected with H.pylori, and half of those who are infected don't develop peptic ulcers, H.pylori probably plays second fiddle in the pathogenesis of ulcer. This means that you can take all of the antibiotics and acid blockers you want to eradicate H.pylori, and still get inflammation and ulcers, unless you guard yourself against indigestion.

A more immediate concern is the putrefaction (rotting) of undigested proteins inside the stomach and intestines. Some of the by-products of putrefaction are extremely toxic neurotoxins that can cause nausea, vomiting, diarrhea, paralysis, and even death. One such substance is called cadaverine—a deadly toxin that's present in all decaying animal flesh (i.e. cadavers). Because putrefaction inside the intestines is slow and gradual, full-blown poisonings are rare, but nausea, muscular apathy, and severe headaches are quite common among people affected by the indigestion of proteins.[17]

So it's best to prevent indigestion regardless of your diet, and even more so while transitioning to a low-fiber one, because a complete recovery from even a brief encounter with indigestion often requires medication that blocks gastric acid and produces... well, even more indigestion, because the acid was intended by nature not to harm the stomach but to digest proteins and to protect it from viruses and bacteria.

Why, then, does indigestion occur during transition? If you've been consuming high-carb/high-fiber fare for breakfast and lunch for many years, your stomach has adapted to passing them along to the intestines without secreting much, if any, gastric juices and enzymes. When you suddenly replace breakfast cereals with eggs and sausage, your stomach fails to secret enough gastric juices on a moment's notice, because, as Ivan Pavlov illustrated with his dogs, digestion isn't altogether conscious, but also a reflexive process.

So it takes some time to condition new digestive reflexes to respond to new foods. But there's more to it than just reflexes. Other, less obvious, factors that impede gastric digestion are: inadequate chewing (also a mostly unconscious action that requires retraining), dental problems, overconsumption of fluids, enzymatic deficiency related to malnutrition, chloride deficiency (hypochloremia) related to low-salt or salt-free diets, scaring of the stomach's epithelium, antacids (i.e. Mylanta, Pepto-Bismol, Tums) or acid-blockers (i.e. Zantac, Prilosec, Prevacid), stress, bland food, and others.

So the operative terms of a smooth transition are the **gradual** introduction of new foods, **elimination** of obstacles, and **awareness** of perils. Here are the rules:

- *Begin with the smallest possible amount of new foods*, particularly proteins, so the stomach can process them fully and completely. Keep increasing the amount in very small increments until the stomach is fully adapted.
- *Less processed foods are easier to digest*. Begin with sashimi instead of baked salmon, steak instead of meat loaf, brie instead of aged cheeses, and so on.
- *People in-the-know order their steak rare because it's juicier, tastier, and digests faster than well-done steak*. Use cooking techniques that yield the most digestible, succulent food: stewing instead of broiling, slow cooking instead of frying, finely

chopped instead of ground, rare instead of well-done, and so on.

- *Avoid ground meat.* On the surface, it may seem that ground meat will digest faster, but in reality it doesn't, because most people don't chew soft ground meat enough to break down the fibers. That's why there's more food poisoning related to hamburgers than steaks, and indigestion may cause some of them rather than just Listeria or E.coli bacteria. If you have difficulties chewing, use a food processor to chop meats.

- *Drink a glass of good-quality mineral water thirty to sixty minutes before a meal.*[18] If you consume lots of fluids with or after a meal, they may dilute the already insufficient digestive juices, and impede digestion.

- *Abstain from hard liquor*, because alcohol blocks gastric digestion. If you have any digestive disorders, or are predisposed toward them, or would like to lose weight, it's best not to have any alcoholic beverages, including beer and wine, because they stimulate overeating, impact the liver, kidneys, and blood sugar, lower the metabolism, and cause weight gain.

- *Avoid mixed meals* (i.e. carbs and proteins together) during the transition because excess carbohydrates interfere with the gastric phase of digestion. In other words, sandwiches and sides are out of the question.

- *Eat in a timely way.* If you eat protein-dense food outside of the usual time frame, indigestion is almost guaranteed for the same Pavlovian reasons cited above. That's why so many people get food poisoning while on an intercontinental vacation. The combination of abundant food and bad timing is a prescription for indigestion. Experienced travelers keep their food schedule close to their home schedule regardless of what and when the locals eat.

- *Chew well.* Unlike bananas or cereal, meats, fish, and seafood require thorough chewing, otherwise more gastric acid, more enzymes, and more time is required to break apart and digest large chunks of inadequately chewed flesh.

- *Avoid stress.* Stress inhibits gastric digestion regardless of diet composition. If you happen to be under a great deal of stress, you're better off skipping proteins altogether, and instead having a light dish such as broth, a cup of yogurt, or rice pudding. The pudding may sound like a sacrilege, but getting gastritis is even worse.

- *Give it time.* Unlike carbohydrates, proteins need time to digest—anywhere from 4 to 6 hours under normal circumstance, and much longer for older individuals. Do not eat close to bedtime, because once you're lying down, the gastric content spills down into the upper stomach chamber, which isn't protected from acidity as well as the lower chamber is. Ditto for the esophagus. At the very least, sleep on a raised pillow.

- *No antacids.* Antacids neutralize gastric acid or block its secretion. Acid is essential for proper digestion of proteins and to protect the stomach from pathogens ingested with food and water.[19] You aren't likely to have heartburn anyway if you follow all of these rules. Consult your doctor regarding any GERD-related prescription medication you may be taking.

- *Moderation.* Limit protein-based meals to once a day,[20] preferably with dinner, so that you have time to chew slowly, digest leisurely, and enjoy a stress-free meal. If you begin your day with scrambled eggs and sausage for breakfast, it will digest from 8 am to 2 pm. If you eat a chicken sandwich for lunch, it will digest from 2 pm to 8 pm. If you have a stew or hamburger for dinner, it will digest from 8 pm to 2 am. That's a grand total of 18 hours of non-stop digestion. And that's in an absolutely healthy individual. No wonder so few people enjoy healthy digestion past the age of forty, and are so drained for most of the day; the body needs a lot of energy for digestion.

- *Essential enablers.* Two ingredients are an absolute must for adequate gastric digestion. First, the body needs table salt (sodium chloride, NaCl) to make hydrochloric acid (HCl). Second, fat stimulates gastric digestion, enhances satiety, and is essential to neutralize the bile secreted by the liver.

- *The right attitude.* There's a tendency in all of us to look at people we know, and ask ourselves the question: *Why can't I eat just like he/she/they can?* That's a valid question that no book can answer. The right question to ask should really be: *What can I eat without causing harm to myself?*

Follow these simple, commonsense maxims, and your transition to a low-fiber/low-carb diet will be quick and trouble-free. In addi-

tion to transition, you may encounter unpredictable events, such as
trauma, surgery, or food poisoning, when your usual diet and routine suddenly goes down the drain. During moments like these,
you need all the nutrients you can get, and you don't need to create
even more problems. So keep these rules in mind while getting
back to your customary diet.

Where there's smoke, there's fire. Where there's fiber, there are
carbohydrates, a lot of them. So when fiber is shown to the door,
carbohydrates get thrown out as well. But not without putting up a
frantic fight to keep their usual place in your breakfast, lunch, and
dinner. Which brings us to the next peril of transitioning to a low
fiber lifestyle—an addiction to carbohydrates, and its nasty ac-
complice: hypoglycemia.

## Hypoglycemia

Carbohydrates are broadly promoted as "comfort food" because,
presumably, they alleviate bad moods, crankiness, and irritability
related to mild hypoglycemia—a medical term for *low blood sugar*
caused by elevated levels of insulin, which is the blood sugar's
regulating hormone.

The levels of insulin and blood sugar (plasma glucose) influence
a person's mood because (a) glucose provides energy for the brain
and oxygen-carrying red blood cells, and (b) insulin happens to
lower glucose levels more than any other factor. Naturally, when
(a) collides with (b), (a) falls down precipitously and impacts one's
mood just as much as failing light impacts one's vision.

This relationship between carbohydrates and mood has led to a
popular myth (a euphemism for nonsense, actually) about the connection between dietary carbohydrates and serotonin, commonly
known as "good mood hormone," while completely ignoring hypoglycemia. In reality, serotonin has absolutely nothing to do with
glucose metabolism or insulin production, and vice versa: carbohydrates have no influence whatsoever over the levels of serotonin.

Serotonin isn't even a hormone, meaning a regulating substance
secreted by an endocrine gland. Serotonin is a neurotransmitter, a
chemical agent involved in the transmission of nerve impulses. It is
synthesized from tryptophan—an essential amino acid that can be

obtained only from the diet. Tryptophan is abundant in meat and some plant proteins. Vitamin $B_6$ (pyridoxine) is also required for the synthesis of serotonin, and, just as with tryptophan, is available mainly from animal sources.[21]

For those reasons, depression, anxiety, and insomnia (the ingredients of a "bad mood" in otherwise healthy people[22]) have less to do with serotonin, and more to do with too much insulin, too little protein, or both. That's also why tryptophan supplements and selective serotonin re-uptake inhibitors (SSRIs), such as Prozac, are marginally effective alone, because they do not eliminate hypoglycemia, hyperinsulinemia, and malnutrition—true triggers of functional mental disorders.

The liver and muscles store glucose in the form of glycogen for use between meals. When these stores are completely exhausted, required glucose is synthesized from muscle tissue. This process is called gluconeogenesis. Because gluconeogenesis produces glucose on demand, the level of insulin remains very low. That's why carb-free diets don't cause hypoglycemia or create problems as long as you consume enough protein to prevent muscle wasting. The same mechanism allows a body to function normally during a fast, except for ongoing loss of muscle tissue.

Sugar cravings[23] are one of the most notorious and best-known symptoms of hypoglycemia. If a sugar fix reduces the cravings, it means that your pancreas is functioning well, and that your body's sugar uptake[24] is adequate. In other words, you're free from two primary components of the diabetic syndrome: insulin deficiency and insulin resistance. Paradoxically, the healthier you are, the more bothersome the symptoms of hypoglycemia become, precisely because your pancreas is able to produce so much insulin, and your body is able to uptake blood sugar so quickly.

A 70 kg (155 lbs) human body contains about 5 liters (5.3 qt) of blood. The glucose in blood is measured in milligrams (1/1000 of a gram) per deciliter (1/10 of a liter) of blood. At 80 mg/dl—an average normal concentration of glucose between meals—there are only 4 g of glucose in the whole bloodstream; a rather tiny amount. That's why a sudden surge of insulin in a healthy person can bring the level of glucose dangerously low before other regulatory mechanisms kick in to stabilize it.[25]

The leading causes of hypoglycemia in people affected by diabetes (whether diagnosed or not) are insulin resistance, insulin therapy, and drugs that lower blood sugar. Insulin resistance is a metabolic syndrome that describes an impaired body's response to both insulin and glucose. Simply speaking, it means that a person requires more insulin and glucose to maintain a level of blood sugar above the hypoglycemia threshold. It also means that "normal" blood sugar is a relative value: what may be normal level for one person, may represent hypoglycemia for another. That's why there isn't a specific fixed blood sugar level that tells you where normal blood sugar ends and hypoglycemia begins. Some people, for example, can function perfectly well at 60–70 mg/dl, while others may faint. In general, a level of 40–50 mg/dl is considered the cutoff point—meaning that the blood sugar level is low enough to cause severe symptoms of hypoglycemia.

Fainting (hypoglycemic syncope, coma) is the body's defensive mechanism of recovering from severe hypoglycemia and preventing brain damage. Most people recover from fainting in less than a minute. Nevertheless, the experience is quite jarring, especially when one is "operating machinery." By the time a recovered victim is presented to a doctor, the blood sugar and other vital signs are already normal. Diagnosing hypoglycemia from a blood test taken even minutes after the fainting episode, is, obviously, impossible.

The treatment of hypoglycemic syncope has became a profitable business for hospitals, whose emergency rooms receive a steady stream of relatively healthy people affected by it. The profit comes not so much from stabilizing a patient, but from admitting him or her to a hospital for a comprehensive checkup, often at the patient's or family's insistence. Besides wasted time, money, and nerves, this kind of testing is never without harm: a full-body CT scan or angiography, for example, exposes the patient to a huge dose of radiation, but without any worthwhile cause. Radiation exposure is cumulative, and can contribute to cancers down the road.

The symptoms of drunkenness—dizziness, blurred vision, muscle weakness, slurred speech, sugar cravings—are identical to the symptoms of hypoglycemia, because alcohol impairs glucose metabolism and affects our behavior by depriving the central nervous system (CNS) from its fuel. This, incidentally, is why very sweet cocktails, such as a Kamikaze (vodka, triple sec, sweetened lime juice) or Long Island Ice Tea (gin, vodka, rum, tequila, orange liqueur, and sugar syrup) keep your brain, at least for a while, quite sharp, while your wobbly legs can barely hold you: your brain is flooded with high blood sugar, but glucose uptake by the muscles is literally turned off.

If you do get tipsy from drinking, suck on sugar cubes or glucose tablets to recover your composure somewhat. If you're irresponsible enough to drive while drunk, this technique will make you a bit less dangerous to yourself and others. It will not reduce your blood alcohol level in any way, but will only increase the immediate availability of glucose to your brain. Correspondingly, this may slightly improve your vision, concentration, and reaction time. If you do get caught and lose your driver's license—you deserve it. So don't drink and drive. My family may be crossing the intersection in another car.

Diabetics are trained to anticipate and prevent extreme hypoglycemia. Similar techniques, sans measuring blood glucose with a personal glucometer, apply to healthy people. They are described at the end of this section.

You may not experience hypoglycemia while consuming carbohydrates as usual, but it may hit you over the head hard as soon as you cut down on them, or drop them altogether. That's what the Atkins and similar diets have done to hordes of unsuspecting people who went from a high- to zero-carb diet overnight, completely unprepared. You don't really want to repeat their unfortunate experiences: relentless migraines, severe fatigue, alarming drowsiness, intense depression, obnoxious irritability, impaired speech, blurry vision, lapsed memory, sometimes a scary bout of fainting. To prevent all that from happening to you, too, aren't you better off knowing why it's happening and what you could do to avoid it?

Let's address the *why* question first. It's simple: When you cut down on carbohydrate consumption, your pancreas, still unaware of the sudden change, releases more insulin than is now required. This happens because a healthy pancreas releases insulin in two stages. The first stage is an unconditional release of stored insulin in anticipation of, or in response to, a meal. The second, and much later stage, is a response to glucose as it gets assimilated from digested carbohydrates.

When you cut down on carbs, the unconditional release of stored insulin is adjusted to your new eating pattern gradually. While the adjustment is taking place, you may still experience moderate headaches, similar to ones that can happen while waiting for a meal or missing one. I call this condition the "hungry spouse syndrome," because, in addition to the headache, elevated insulin makes people irritable and angry. For the same reasons, hyperinsulinemia is often at work in abnormal behavior patterns such as road rage, spousal abuse, workplace violence, and the like. The more insulin and glucose in the system, the more violent and aberrant the behavior.

So if you don't rush things, and reduce carbs step-by-step, the pancreas will gradually adapt to your new diet, and insulin-induced hypoglycemia will go away for good. For a trouble-free transition, your strategy must be preventing hypoglycemia from occurring in the first place. Tactically, you have to be ready to address its symptoms without resorting to carbs. First, let's establish the strategic rules:

- Gradually exclude nutritionally marginal sources of simple carbohydrates, such as soft drinks, ice cream, candies, pastries, preserves, fruit juices, and fruits with a high sugar content, such as grapes or mangos. Spread this phase out over several weeks, until you no longer experience cravings.
- Substitute fresh milk with natural yogurt. One cup of milk, whether skim or whole, contains almost a tablespoon of milk sugar (lactose, 12.8 g per 244 g cup). Natural yogurt is practically lactose-free.[26]
- Gradually reduce the most "offensive" sources of complex carbohydrates, such as cereals, pasta, bread, baked goods, pizza, potatoes, beans, and the like.
- White rice is the least "offensive" source of dietary carbohydrates, especially during the transition to a low-fiber diet. In addition to a relatively low ratio of carbs-to-weight after cooking, it's also fiber- and gluten-free. Consumed in moderation, it is a versatile substitute for grains and potatoes.
- Avoid artificial sweeteners. The oral sensation of sweetness causes an almost identical (by volume) release of insulin, even

when the source of sweetness is 100% sugar-free. From a hypo-glycemia point of view, artificial sweeteners present a double jeopardy: lots of insulin in the blood on one hand, zero carbs coming from food on the other. This means no diet sodas of any kind, especially on an empty stomach.

Reducing needless carbs isn't rocket science. There aren't too many strategic rules, and these rules are plain simple and grounded in common sense. Just don't rush. If you've been consuming car-bohydrates for years, cutting them down in the too-quick span of a week or two isn't going to make any difference. Your goals are health and happiness, not coma and misery.

Let's get down now to the day-to-day tactical rules. While im-plementing the above strategy, concentrate on the following spe-cifics:

- Do not drop your morning tea or coffee while still reducing carbs, because the double impact of caffeine and sugar with-drawal is too severe. Once you're done with carbs, you may con-sider reducing coffee and tea consumption gradually, because caffeine stimulates metabolism, and contributes to hypoglycemia as well.

- In the overall scheme of things, one or two teaspoons of sugar (5–10 g) with your morning tea or coffee is safer than any fac-tory-made ersatz sweetener. I'm not encouraging sugar consump-tion, just emphasizing the obvious.

- Avoid alcohol[27] in any form, because it causes intense sugar cravings, as strong as those from too much insulin. If you still like your glass of wine with dinner, don't drink it on an empty stomach, only after you've eaten some food. This prevents the easy passage of alcohol into the intestines, ensuing quick absorp-tion, and a rapid sugar-lowering effect.

- Low-fiber (preferably skinless) vegetables, such as spinach, zuc-chini, squash, eggplant, tomatoes, and cucumbers are acceptable, because their carb content is low.

- If you don't have any digestive disorders, and chew your food well, leafy vegetables such as lettuce, spinach, chard, collard greens, watercress, and the like are acceptable in reasonable amounts. In larger amounts they should be avoided, because they may impede gastric digestion and intestinal transport.

- To keep your sanity intact, the occasional piece of bittersweet dark chocolate is acceptable to reduce strong sugar cravings. Just don't abuse it, and don't swallow the chocolate quickly, but allow it to melt under your tongue. This way the sugar absorbs right into the bloodstream, so you can quickly relieve the craving with the smallest possible amount of carbohydrates.
- If you do experience severe hypoglycemic symptoms as described previously, always carry sublingual glucose tablets. They are intended for people with diabetes to manage insulin overdosing, and are available at any drugstore.
- Each glucose tablet contains from 3 to 4 g of pure glucose, almost as much as the total normal volume of glucose in the blood. When placed under the tongue, the glucose rapidly absorbs into the bloodstream, and quickly relieves hypoglycemic symptoms.
- In an emergency, you may substitute glucose tablets with lollipops, hard candies, sugar cubes, grapes, grape juice, or non-diet soft drinks. All of these are acceptable substitutes, but only if kept in the mouth until hypoglycemic symptoms are reduced. Swallowing them will not have any rapid effect.

Keep in mind that drinking sweet juices or soft drinks after a meal is only marginally effective for hypoglycemia relief, because carbs can't get down quickly enough into the intestines where most of the glucose normally gets absorbed. The absorption of complex carbohydrates is even slower, because pancreatic enzymes must first break them down.

The relative speed of digestion and assimilation of carbohydrates is measured by the glycemic index (GI), which breaks them down into "fast" carbs (like glucose, at 100 GI) and "slow" carbs (like barley, at 22 GI). This measure is widely used by people affected by insulin-dependent diabetes to balance medicinal insulin with carbohydrate consumption.

The glycemic index doesn't measure carb content, meaning that consuming 28 g of sugar and 100 g of cooked barley will yield the same amount of carbs, but barley will take five times as long to digest and assimilate completely. For healthy people, low glycemic foods are even more harmful than sugar, because they force the pancreas to secret insulin for much longer periods of time, and are the primary culprits behind chronically high levels of insulin.[28]

The glycemic index isn't a helpful measure by which to manage hypoglycemia in diabetes-free individuals because carbs are carbs no matter what, and to curb insulin production you must first curb carbs. There isn't such a thing as "less offensive" or "healthier" carbs. After all kinds of carbs get digested, the blood "sees" nothing but glucose,[29] and it doesn't care in the least what the name of its original source was—sugar or barley.

Finally, keep in mind that stress, physical as well as emotional, lowers the blood sugar, and stimulates the rapid release of stress hormones, including insulin. That's what's happening to young, healthy girls during rock concerts—their blood sugar level goes down from mind-bending excitement, and they faint. If you, too, have been experiencing moderate symptoms of hypoglycemia, rock concerts or not, carry easily accessible glucose tablets with you at all times, and instruct people close to you where to find them, if needed.

Depending on your age and shape, a transition to a low-carb diet takes anywhere from a few weeks to a few months. To "uncondition" the pancreas from flooding the body with insulin in response to stress (a very palpable reaction in the area of the solar plexus) is a much longer process. When you're no longer experiencing a dry mouth, trembling fingers, bulging veins, and emotional rage in response to family disputes, job-related altercations, or to someone cutting off your car, you're finally "unconditioned."

As you can see, it's really very simple: common sense, a basic knowledge of human physiology, a small preventative (glucose tablet), and more attention to details. Do all this, and your transition to a low-carb diet will be easy, safe, and enjoyable.

When incompetence colludes with ignorance, good becomes bad, and vice versa. That's essentially how we got hooked on carbs and fiber in the first place. High-carb diets happen to be high-water diets. When carb consumption goes down, so does water consumption, and the mouth feels dry. If you ask carb advocates what's going on, they tell you that low-carb diets causes dehydration. If you ask me what's going on, I'll tell you: Drink a glass of water! Of course, there is more to this oddity than just a glass of water, and that's our next subject.

## Dehydration

A low-carb diet doesn't cause dehydration per se. It's quite the opposite. People who eat less carbs urinate less and perspire less because excessive blood sugar isn't affecting their kidneys as much, and their body temperature—one of the yardsticks of metabolism—isn't as high.

Nonetheless, a lot of unscrupulous or misinformed medical professionals claim that a low-carb diet does cause dehydration, because people who switch to low-carb diets experience certain dehydration symptoms, such as dry mouth, reduced output of urine, low blood pressure, fatigue, etc. So let's take a look at what's actually going on:

- When you are cutting down carbs, this often means reducing soft drinks, juices, fruits, milk, and so forth—all foods with a very high intrinsic water content. Naturally, when you are consuming so much less fluids, the urine output goes down as well.

- Low blood pressure is related to three factors: less fluids in the diet, a reduction of triglycerides, and a reduction of insulin. These are all cause for celebration, not concern. You may feel a slight dizziness for a short while because the body needs time to adjust to normalized blood pressure.

- Fatigue is more likely a function of transitional hyperinsulinemia than dehydration. To make sure you aren't fatigued from dehydration, just drink a glass or two of quality mineral water on an empty stomach.

- The temporary vestiges of hyperinsulinemia cause a dry mouth condition (xerostomia), because insulin action deprives the salivary glands of essential fluids. This creates a perception of dehydration.

- The assimilation of water from food and beverages among people who consume mostly carbs is different from people who consume mostly proteins or who eat a mixed diet. Since almost all water absorbs in the intestines, it can't get down there while the stomach is busy digesting. That may also cause temporary (while food is digesting) mouth dryness.

- Drinking more water after a meal doesn't alleviate a dry mouth for the same reasons. Hence you need to change your pattern of water consumption—not with a meal or after a meal, but always thirty to sixty minutes before a meal.
- The digestion of protein requires significantly more saliva, gastric and pancreatic juices than does the digestion of carbohydrates, up to 7–8 liters during one day. All of these fluids are derived from interstitial fluid, plasma, and lymph (collectively, *extracellular fluids*).
- When all extracellular fluids are mobilized for digestion, a person may temporarily feel some symptoms of dehydration. Most of the water is absorbed back after digestion is completed.
- A moderate to high consumption of proteins requires more innate fluids for the digestive process, while carbs require almost none, because of their intrinsic water. Some people fail to compensate for this difference, and experience dehydration.
- A low-carb diet is often a low-potassium diet. The deficiency of potassium may cause a dry mouth condition, and create the perception of dehydration, even when the levels of water in the body are adequate.
- People who consume low-sodium diets may experience dehydration, because sodium is an essential electrolyte responsible for water retention. People on low-carb diets usually increase the consumption of proteins, but fail to adjust their salt intake.

As you can see, transitional dehydration is partly perceptual, partly actual, but easily correctable and preventable. Here are the steps, some of them already mentioned in other chapters:

- *Hydrate in advance.* Get used to drinking liquids before a major meal to build up the water reserves needed to produce saliva and digestive juices. Most of the water that you consume with a meal will not get absorbed until it gets into the small intestine hours later, especially if your meal contains protein.
- *There are no rules.* The volume of liquid very much depends on what you are going to eat and drink, i.e. the water content of food, and how much food. Just experiment until you hit a sweet spot—your mouth is neither getting dry, nor are you constantly running to the bathroom.

- *Supply base liquids for digestive functioning.* If you haven't had soup or a salad containing water-rich vegetables, such as tomatoes or cucumbers, wash down a protein-rich meal with a glass of mineral water, preferably noncarbonated. This water will be used by the stomach to concentrate the gastric juices. If you don't provide enough liquid, the stomach will draw water from the blood plasma. This is one of the reasons why certain meals make you drowsy—it's a response to lowered blood pressure.[30]

- *Limit liquids with meals.* Do not consume too many liquids with meals, because an excess of liquids lengthens digestion, delays stomach emptying, and may cause heartburn. Also, the more liquid you ingest, the more hydrochloric acid and digestive enzymes your body must produce to properly break down food.

- *No liquids after meals.* If you are experiencing thirst an hour or two after a major meal, don't drink. First, water will not relieve your thirst anyway, because it can't get assimilated while food is still churning in the stomach; second, excess water will prolong digestion and will make it even more difficult and inefficient. Wait from four to six hours before taking any liquids.

- *Keep the mucosa moistened.* To relieve dry mouth and the perception of thirst after a meal, take small sips of carbonated, sugar-free mineral water and swirl it around—bubbles stimulate the saliva glands and break down dense saliva. There are some other methods, such as chewing gum, lozenges, mouthwashes, and saliva replacements, but I can't vouch for any of them.

- *Don't abuse salt.* Once the meal begins to be absorbed, excessive sodium chloride can cause thirst and dry mouth, even though you may already have plenty of fluids inside the body. To avoid overhydration and resulting edema, swelling, excessive urination, potassium depletion, and other perils, be aware of the hidden salt in all processed food.

- *Add natural potassium.* Drink one to two glasses of cucumber juice (with skins) daily, an hour before meals. Salt to taste. Cucumber juice is rich in potassium (about 350 mg per 8 oz) and practically free of carbs. Because it's free of sugar, refrigerated cucumber juice stores well. Juice a batch once or twice a week from large seedless cucumbers—each yields about a cup of juice.

- *Watch out for alcohol.* A dry martini isn't called "dry" for nothing. After one too many the mouth indeed feels quite dry. Beer, wine, and spirits represent triple jeopardy to the digestive process: alcohol is a potent diuretic (drying factor), excess water (with drinks such as beer and wine) disrupts digestion and electrolyte levels, and alcohol is a major stimulant of appetite, because it disrupts glucose metabolism (lowers blood sugar). The outcome of too much alcohol, too much food, and too much water all at once is as predictable as nightfall—indigestion causes vomiting, vomiting causes dehydration, dehydration causes hangover. More temperate drinking spares you of the vomiting, but causes all the same side effects nonetheless (indigestion, dehydration, hangover). If you can find a way of drinking that causes none of the above, here's to you, pal!

Finally, if anyone tells you that a low-carb diet is dangerous for the kidneys, that's simply not true. You may hear two ubiquitous arguments:

- *A low-carb diet causes dehydration, and dehydration is dangerous for the kidneys.* Well, we already debunked that myth above. To neutralize that nonsense, instead ask why kidney disease, kidney failure, and dialysis are the most common conditions among people who are overweight or diabetic, and are consuming a high-carb diet?
- *Elevated protein in urine results from consuming too much protein.* That's an interesting deception. "Protein in urine" is actually an albumin, a blood protein manufactured by the liver. Albumin maintains proper osmotic pressure in order to prevent blood plasma fluids from flooding and exploding the blood cells. When the kidneys are healthy, large molecules of albumin can't pass its filtration membranes. Damaged kidneys let albumin out, and that's what's being measured and detected during a test for "urine protein." This condition is called albuminuria.[31] It's true that digestion breaks food proteins down into amino acids, but albumin isn't one of them. To neutralize that "protein in urine" nonsense, ask what kind of proteins are detected in the urine, and in what way are they related to proteins in food?

Live and learn! No wonder the well-learned live longer.

Rejecting fiber and reducing carbohydrates also means giving up lots of processed foods that are artificially fortified with iron, calcium, and A, D, and B-complex vitamins. For most people, whose diets have already been sub-optimal for some time, this final step will cause malnutrition related to the acute deficiency of those nutrients, unless they are replaced with quality supplements. That's our final challenge.

## Malnutrition

Does the above mean that a high-carb diet is better and safer, nutritionally speaking? No, it doesn't. Cereals, orange juice, and skim milk—foods you are close to giving up—are all considered "health foods." Here is the rational behind this thinking, and the actual results:

- *Wheat cereals,* nutritionally speaking, are useless—just starch, added sugar, and extra fiber. To make cereals a "health food," synthetic vitamins $B_1$ (thiamin), $B_2$ (riboflavin), $B_3$ (niacin), folic acid, and iron (ferrous sulfate or fumarate) are added to flour during milling. The fortification of wheat flour is mandated by the U.S. government in order to prevent deficiency-related diseases, particularly birth defects, iron-deficiency anemia, and developmental problems in children. Ironically, the widespread allergy to gluten—a protein in wheat—blocks the digestion of iron and folic acid, and is one of the leading causes of pernicious anemia among millions of young and old Americans alike. That's on the one hand. On the other, if gluten causes you no harm, according to the research team from the Center for Food Safety and Applied Nutrition (a division of the Food and Drug Administration), the remedy is worse than the problem:

Twenty-one of the 29 breakfast cereals had iron levels of 120% or more of the labeled value, and eight cereals had values of 150% or more.

[…] It is possible that iron overload may outweigh iron deficiency and may be a more serious problem in adult males and non-pregnant females in the U.S.

[…] …with recent increases in fortification, public health officials in the US are concerned that excess intake of specific nutrients such as iron and folic acid may result in toxic manifestations.[32]

And these are problems on top of the already certifiably harmful content of breakfast cereals: gluten (allergies), sugar (obesity), fiber (digestive disorders), and trans fats (cancers). Some "health food," isn't it?

- *Skim and reduced fat milk*[33] is fortified with synthetic vitamins A (retinyl palmitate) and vitamin $D_3$ (7-dehydro-cholesterol), because natural vitamin A is lost during the removal of fat, and milk is naturally low in vitamin D. Some dairy products are also fortified with calcium, because natural calcium is bound by milk proteins, and digests poorly. The fortification of dairy with vitamin A is mandated by the U.S. government in order to prevent blindness and poor immunity, both vitamin A deficiency disorders. Vitamin D is supposed to protect children from rickets, teenagers from scoliosis, and adults from osteomalacia. Ironically, the fat-soluble vitamins A and D found in skim and reduced fat milk are mostly useless, because they don't digest without fat. Adding insult to injury are widespread allergies to casein (milk protein), and lactose intolerance, which affects tens of millions of Americans. Both conditions cause intestinal inflammation, and render vitamins A, D, calcium, and everything else futile. In addition to zero health benefits from drinking skim or low-fat milk, kids are getting fat:

Children who drank the most milk gained more weight, but the added calories appeared responsible. Contrary to our hypotheses, dietary calcium and skim and 1% milk were associated with weight gain, but dairy fat was not. Drinking large amounts of milk may provide excess energy to some children.[34]

That's the conclusion from a survey of 12,000 children between 9 and 14 years of age, conducted by Harvard University researchers, and published in the *Journal Archives of Pediatrics & Adolescent Medicine* in June of 2005.

- *Orange juice* is routinely fortified with synthetic vitamin C to
  compensate for oxidative losses of natural vitamin C during its
  manufacturing, packaging, storage, and transportation. To make
  additional health claims, some producers of orange juice have
  begun adding supplemental calcium. There is a trend toward adding vitamin D to orange juice as well, even though it wouldn't
  get absorbed from a zero-fat beverage. Besides, the high sugar
  content and high acidity of orange juice causes more minerals to
  get depleted through the urine than what's added at the factory.
  The problem is so acute that the American Academy of Pediatrics has been telling parents to avoid excessive juice consumption:

---

4. Juice is not appropriate in the treatment of dehydration or
management of diarrhea.
5. Excessive juice consumption may be associated with malnutrition (overnutrition and undernutrition).
6. Excessive juice consumption may be associated with diarrhea, flatulence, abdominal distention, and tooth decay.[35]

---

The authors don't specify what's excessive. Well, here's the math:
on a body weight-basis, a glass of juice for a three-year-old at
40 lbs is equivalent to four full glasses for an adult at 160 lbs.

It doesn't sound like a description of a "health food," does it?
Nonetheless, a bowl of cereal with skim milk and a glass of orange
juice has become more American than the proverbial apple pie.

If that's your breakfast, check out the table below. As you can
see, along with a meager fix of mostly synthetic vitamins, inor-
ganic iron, and supplemental calcium, this kind of breakfast also
"delivers" 15 g of fiber and 61 g of carbohydrates, or the equivalent of 5 tablespoons of sugar. That's over one half the daily total
requirement for an active 7-year-old, and over one third for an
adult, all from just one breakfast which, by conventional standards,
is pretty paltry and more like a sustenance ration for prisoners of
war than your average American breakfast.

| | Unit of Measure | Orange Juice Raw | Skim Milk | Kellogg's All-Bran With Extra Fiber | Total |
|---|---|---|---|---|---|
| NDB No: [36] | | 09206 | 01085 | 08253 | |
| Servings | | 1 cup | 1 cup | 0.5 cup | |
| Weight | g | 248.00 | 245.00 | 30.00 | |
| Water | g | 218.98 | 222.56 | 0.90 | 442.44 |
| Fat | g | 0.50 | 0.20 | 1.05 | 1.75 |
| Protein | g | 1.74 | 8.26 | 3.39 | 13.39 |
| Carbohydrates | g | 25.79 | 12.15 | 23.10 | 61.04 |
| Fiber | g | 0.50 | 0.00 | 15.00 | 15.50 |
| Iron | mg | 0.50 | 0.07 | 5.40 | 5.97 |
| Calcium | mg | 27.00 | 306.00 | 124.00 | 457.00 |
| Vitamin A | IU | 496.00 | 500.00 | 614.00 | 1,610.00 |
| Vitamin D | IU | 0.00 | 101.54 | 63.00 | 164.54 |
| Vitamin C | mg | 124.00 | 0.00 | 7.50 | 131.50 |
| Thiamin | mg | 0.22 | 0.11 | 0.45 | 0.78 |
| Riboflavin | mg | 0.07 | 0.44 | 0.51 | 1.02 |
| Niacin | mg | 0.99 | 0.23 | 6.00 | 7.22 |
| Folate, total | mcg | 74.00 | 12.00 | 126 | 212.00 |

Not surprisingly, most adults who start their day with this kind of "healthy" and "natural" breakfast are fatigued from hypoglycemia by the time they get to work, while many children can't concentrate or sit still at school because they've already ingested over half of their daily energy requirement. Adults counteract this problem with a cup of strong coffee, children—with Ritalin.

It's easy to understand and appreciate the intentions behind the fortification of basic food. A humane society must take care of all of its citizens, no matter what their income, social status, education, or age. So, beginning in 1941, the U.S. government begun formulating paternalistic nutritional policies for society's most disadvantaged—inmates in prisons and psychiatric asylums, children in orphanages, patients in nursing homes, conscripts in the army, underprivileged kids in urban ghettos, and so on. Had the government failed to provide its less fortunate citizenry with a sustenance ratio of essential nutrients, the budgetary burden of treating scurvy, rickets, and birth defects, providing dogs for the blind, or funding more and more nursing homes would be enormous.

That's what the standard "healthy nutrition," promoted by the so-called "Dietary Guidelines for Americans,"[37] represented by the Food Guide Pyramid[38] (called *MyPyramid*, after 2005) is all about—sustenance, and the prevention of birth defects and degenerative diseases. It isn't about maintaining good looks, youthful bodies, vibrant sexuality, ageless minds, boundless longevity, and, of course, a healthy and functional large intestine. There is absolutely no way to get "quality out" of a diet developed for the impoverished.

But, then, you read this book, take its reasoning to heart, and decide to reduce carbs from your diet and cut out the fiber. No more bread, no more pasta, no more cereals, no more orange juice, no more milk, no more food that harms your digestive, endocrine, nervous, and reproductive systems. You avoid eating too many obesity-causing carbs, too much gut-busting fiber, too much allergenic gluten, too much diarrhea-causing lactose, and too many cancer-causing trans fats, while finally getting enough essential fats and primary proteins.

There is just one problem with this smart decision—just as a high-carb diet without fortification would be, a low-fiber diet is also notoriously deficient in iron, water-soluble vitamins, minerals, and microelements. And that's on top of the distinct probability that your body is already seriously lacking essential nutrients from years and years of dietary neglect. Where do you get these indispensable nutrients from, if fortified cereals, breads, pasta, juices, and milk are no longer desirable or acceptable? Well, there are two options:

- *Best:* Move to the countryside, drink unprocessed well water, eat pristine, organically grown produce, and hope that your neck of the woods isn't deficient in iodine, affected by acid rain, or contaminated by dioxin and DDT.
- *Second best:* Take quality supplements to augment the essential vitamins, minerals, and microelements lacking in the low-carb diet you've adopted.

If the first option isn't yet a viable one for you, then the question is: What kind of supplements should you take for best results? Now you have three options:

- *Consumer-quality supplements* that contain USDA Recommended Dietary Allowances (RDA)—the standards similar to those found in fortified food. These are your typical One-A-Day, Centrum, Therargram, and the like. To minimize price and maximize profit, most of them are made in Asia, compressed into one large tablet, and covered with artificial coloring to mask oxidation and enhance shelf life. These supplements are available just about anywhere, are inexpensive, and are definitely better than nothing. Just like with iron and folic acid in wheat flour, they're intended to prevent degenerative disease, not to promote vigorous health and longevity. If you believe you can get long-lasting health benefits from a single daily tablet, you may as well ignore much of what you've learned in this book.

- *"Natural" supplements* from well-known brands, such as Twinlab, Country Life, Schiff, Solgar, and others, which use the *Optimal Daily Allowances* (ODA) to formulate their products. ODA is a set of more evolved nutritional standards, which recommends a higher intake of essential nutrients well within the upper limits of safety. These supplements have been used for decades by tens of millions of Americans without side effects or objections from the Federal Drug Administration, U.S. Department of Health & Human Services, the Surgeon General, or the National Institutes of Health. The "natural" designation has more to do with marketing than content. Quality, value, and effectiveness-wise, these supplements are in the middle.

- *"Professional" supplements.* Also formulated around the *Optimal Dietary Allowances* (ODA), these are made from pharmaceutical-grade ingredients, and marketed primarily through nutritionally-oriented medical professionals. They're optimized for maximum bioavailability, meaning the best possible safety, assimilation, and effectiveness. Doctors who specialize in performance medicine, preventive healthcare, and longevity, recommend and distribute these type of supplements, hence their "professional" designation. Not surprisingly, the majority of big name celebrities, big league athletes, big shot politicians, bigwigs in business, and medical professionals big on knowledge (the kind of people whose careers are built on their energy, vigor, and healthy appearance), take these kinds of supplements to protect their biggest asset—themselves.

A great many degenerative conditions that stem from malnutrition, such as nerve damage, muscular dystrophy, mucosal atrophy, endocrine disorders, emotional problems, and atherosclerosis, can be partially reversed by using quality supplements. Besides, anything that can make sick people well again, makes healthy people great. Here's the basic list:

### Professional-quality multivitamins

The key to professional-quality multivitamins is flexibility. Unlike consumer or natural brands, they aren't packaged into a one-size-fits all one or two hard tablets, but into easy-to-digest capsules. These type of supplements usually don't include iron. This way, to prevent iron overload and associated toxicity, women who are pregnant, lactating, or of child-bearing age, women past menopause, children, teenagers, and adult men (all of whom have varying needs) can safely supplement iron on an individual basis.

Other considerations are safety-related: the type of manufacturing, the quality of components, and the level of testing used for professional supplements is similar to the pharmaceutical industry, where the stakes are higher and the oversight of safety is more rigorous than for food-grade supplements.

Professional supplements are usually obtained through medical professionals. They are manufactured in small batches to avoid adding fillers, preservatives, stabilizers, glazing, and artificial coloring. For these reasons they're considered hypoallergenic.

Nutritionally-oriented doctors, nutritionists, and dieticians can point you in the right direction. Or you can consider using Ageless Protection multivitamins that myself and readers of my earlier books have been taking since 1999. They are manufactured in the United States by a top-tier professional supplement company, which is considered the leader in this area.

Additional information about Ageless Protection multivitamins, including a list of components, warnings, dosage, and other considerations, is available at www.AgelessNutrition.com.

In addition to Ageless Protection multivitamins, three ubiquitous supplements are recommended for people recovering from fiber dependence, constipation, and more serious digestive disorders, such as irritable bowel syndrome, ulcerative colitis, and Crohn's disease:

## Dietary iron

Unprocessed water from springs and wells, red and organ meats from pasture-fed animals, and cast iron cooking utensils used to provide dietary iron to our ancestors. Not anymore. Tap and bottled water has little or no iron; red and organ meats are out of vogue, consumed infrequently, or kosherized (the blood—a main source of iron—is removed); non-stick and stainless steel cookware has replaced cast iron; and people with intestinal disorders aren't able to digest iron even when it's plentiful.

Hair loss is one of the most prominent symptoms of low-carb diets, which is caused by iron deficiency. Actually, a low-fiber diet is great for one's mane, because it supplies the essential proteins and fats required for the maintenance of a healthy scalp and hair. Besides, a low-fiber diet inhibits the production of dehydrotestosterone—the hormonal trigger for age-related male pattern baldness.

The prevention of iron-deficiency anemia is essential for overall health and well-being in general, and intestinal health in particular. Conventional iron supplements are known to cause constipation and digestive distress, which makes them unsuitable for people with intestinal disorders, who need extra dietary iron the most.

Water-soluble *iron carbonyl* is considered the most efficient and the least side-effects prone form of iron. You can obtain iron carbonyl supplements at better health food stores or from www.AgelessNutrition.com.

## Vitamin B$_{12}$

Normal intestinal flora on the inside, and red and organ meats in the diet, used to be primary sources of vitamin B$_{12}$. Digestion of dietary B$_{12}$ is complicated by the need for the *intrinsic factor*—an actual term used in medical books, meaning an enzyme whose biochemical nature is unknown. This intrinsic factor is produced by the stomach and intestines during digestion and absorption, and is usually missing in people with digestive disorders.

A deficiency of vitamin B$_{12}$ affects the formation of red blood cells (pernicious anemia), causes nerve damage, intestinal malabsorption, Crohn's disease, and is implicated in chronic alcoholism and indirectly in an array of other degenerative disorders.

Here are the most prominent deficiency symptoms of vitamin B₁₂, grouped by the affected systems:

- *GI track:* sore mouth and tongue, loss of appetite, anorexia, diarrhea, and constipation.
- *Nerve damage:* loss of anorectal sensitivity, inability to have an orgasm, numbness and tingling of hands and feet, ringing in the ears.
- *Anemia:* weakness, fatigue, paleness, and shortness of breath.

A healthy person won't have any problem assimilating vitamin B₁₂ from an adequate diet or oral supplements. But for someone with a history of digestive disorders, constipation, and fiber-dependence, a regular diet and oral supplements may not be effective because of an intrinsic factor deficiency and compromised absorption through the intestinal mucosa.

In those cases the most efficient path for Vitamin B₁₂ into the body is via intravenous infusion, which isn't practical on a day-to-day basis. The second best is a sublingual form of vitamin B₁₂, because it absorbs through the mouth's mucosa directly into the bloodstream.

You can obtain *sublingual vitamin B₁₂* at better health food stores or from www.AgelessNutrition.com.

### L-Glutamine for intestinal recovery

The amino acid glutamine is the principle metabolic fuel for the intestinal mucosa, or, more specifically, for the cells that line the intestinal epithelium (enterocytes). For this reason, the small and large intestines require more glutamine than any other organ.

A deficiency of glutamine causes the atrophy of the intestinal mucosa, a condition commonly associated with chronic enteritis, irritable bowel syndrome, ulcerative colitis, and Crohn's disease. All of these disorders, in turn, are associated with chronic constipation, something you want to prevent and avoid during the transition.

Glutamine is readily synthesized in human cells. It is also the most prevalent amino acid in intestinal tissue, blood, skeletal muscles, the lungs, liver, brain, and stomach. When the demand for glutamine exceeds the internal supply—because of trauma, disease, infection, medical treatment, digestive impairment, dietary deficiency, starvation, and similar circumstances—the body must get it from the diet or from supplements. For this reason glutamine is designated as a "conditionally essential" amino acid.

Just like with any other amino acid (except essential), when the diet lacks the adequate amount of protein required to synthesize glutamine, the body draws it from itself. Muscle and bone-wasting (i.e. osteoporosis) is one of the first and most prominent symptoms of acute glutamine deficiency.

Meats, fish, poultry, dairy products, and beans are the main dietary sources of glutamine for people with normal digestion. Because beans cause flatulence and bloating related to their high-fiber content, they are an inappropriate source of glutamine for anyone but the young and healthy.

For people who already suffer from intestinal disorders, regular diets can't provide adequate glutamine regardless of the source, because they have difficulties digesting dietary protein to begin with. Ironically, this impasse is caused in part by... glutamine deficiency. There is only one way to break this vicious cycle: by using glutamine in supplemental form.

Glutamine supplements are available in three forms: (1) as *L-Glutamine*, a free-form amino acid, which means it's identical to the glutamine present in the body; (2) as *glutamine peptides,* which means it is bound with other amino acids; and as (3) a mix of both.

Glutamine peptides are considered more stable during storage, but are known to cause constipation and bloating, and are contraindicated for people with kidney disease, and women who are pregnant or nursing. For these reasons glutamine peptides aren't appropriate for the treatment of constipation and digestive disorders.

There are no known side effects associated with pharmaceutical-grade supplemental L-Glutamine, because, as has been already said, it is identical to naturally-occurring glutamine in the body, and doesn't need to be predigested, as glutamine peptides do.

Glutamine supplements are especially popular among athletes and body builders, and are broadly available in health food stores in the form of water-soluble powders, tablets, or capsules. Depending on the degree of intestinal damage, you may require from 15 to 30 g of L-Glutamine daily, hence neither tablets or capsules are practical or economical for this purpose.

Pharmaceutical-grade L-Glutamine is best for supplementation because of its purity and exceptional digestibility (bioavailability). For best results it must be taken on an empty stomach, so it gets down into the intestinal tract without being held up by gastric digestion. Most of the supplements for athletes sold in health food stores contain food-grade L-Glutamine, or are mixed with glutamine peptides.

You may want to consider the *Ageless GI Recovery* brand of L-Glutamine. It is manufactured in the United States by a professional supplement company from pharmaceutical-grade L-Glutamine. It is specifically formulated for intestinal recovery, particularly during the transition to a low-carb diet, and for improving the retention and survival of intestinal flora on fiber-free diets. To better accomplish this task, it contains small quantities of natural soluble fiber (acacia fiber and inulin) which are preferred by normal flora, but do not "appeal" to pathogenic bacteria. In these small amounts, neither causes the bloating or flatulence associated with soluble fiber.

*Ageless GI Recovery* isn't available in stores. You can obtain it from www.AgelessNutrition.com, or substitute pharmaceutical-grade L-Glutamine, which is available at better health food stores.

And that brings us to the final challenge of transition...

## What's for dinner?

If you are slightly bewildered by the "what's for dinner (breakfast, lunch)?" question, don't be! This book isn't about what to eat, but about what NOT to eat!

Thus, if you like an Italian-style diet—reduce the fiber! If you prefer a French-style diet—reduce the fiber! If a kosher diet is your thing—reduce the fiber. If you love Japanese food—keep loving it, because it is naturally low in fiber. Whoever you are, whatever your heritage, no matter what your means are, you don't need to change anything in your diet, other than reducing the darned fiber. No fiber equals no menace; no menace equals no harm.

Granted, this book (particularly this last part) sounds like a sermon for a low-carb diet. But not because I particularly care for a low-carb diet, or hate carbs—not at all. To the contrary, I love bittersweet chocolates, enjoy luscious strawberries with heavy cream, can't resist the crunchiness of a fresh baguette smeared with a dollop of triple-cream brie, eat a dish of plain rice twice a day, can't say no to a raspberry mousse at the end of a good dinner, and even indulge in a scoop of homemade ice cream from time to time.

So what? If you're of normal weight, full of energy, free of diabetes, hypertension, heart disease, depression, and insomnia, as I am, keep doing what you've been doing. But if not, it's critical to do the right thing: drop the fiber, reduce the carbs, be patient, and eventually, you'll be able to have your cake and eat it, too!

Still not sure what to eat? Following the acclaim of the Atkins and South Beach diets, more books have been written about the low-carb/low-fiber lifestyle than about any other "dietary" subject. Get any one you like. Fortunately, this time around, you wouldn't have to suffer through constipation, indigestion, hypoglycemia, dehydration, or malnutrition.


Bon Appétit!

# Footnotes

[1] T. Fukawa, N. Izumida; Japanese Healthcare Expenditures in a Comparative Context. The Japanese Journal of Social Security Policy; Vol 3, No. 2 (Dec 2004).

[2] Rice, white, medium-grain, cooked; NDB No: 20051; USDA National Nutrient Database for Standard Reference.

[3] Kellogg's Raisin Bran; NDB No: 08060; USDA National Nutrient Database for Standard Reference.

[4] Obesity, percentage of adult population with a BMI>30 kg/m2 (2003); Organization for Economic Co operation and Development; www.oecd.org

[5] Ibid.

[6] There is a commonly held misconception that native Africans consume a high-fiber diet. That may very well be true for very poor Africans living on some form of public assistance, but in traditional African tribal societies all of the food came from ranching, herding, hunting, and fishing, and not from land cultivation, which was taught to Africans by European missionaries and colonizers quite recently. Land overdevelopment for agricultural use has led to continent-wide environmental disaster, which brought along starvation, epidemics, and genocidal wars.

[7] Morbid obesity is defined as being 100 lbs over ideal body weight or having a BMI (body mass index) above 40. According to his first book, a 6' tall Dr. Atkins weighed 135 lbs when he graduated high school—a weight that was close to his ideal. At the time of his death Dr. Atkins weighted 258 lbs, a significant enough difference to qualify him for gastric bypass surgery, which is only approved for morbidly obese individuals.

[8] Philip S. Schoenfeld, MD, MSEd, MSc; Guidelines for the Treatment of Chronic Constipation: What Is the Evidence?; Medscape Gastroenterology. 2005;7(2) ©2005 Medscape; http://www.medscape.com/viewarticle/507545.

[9] Ibid.

[10] Ibid.

[11] To learn more about food additives consult "A Consumer's Dictionary of Food Additives" by Ruth Winter, M.S. Its 6th edition lists 12,000 additives that are routinely added to food. The 5th edition contained only 8,000 entries. At best, I am familiar with just 2 to 3% of them. There are so many additives because concocting and selling ersatz foods from factory-made ingredients is immensely more profitable than dealing with perishable, natural foods.

[12] There are six types of laxatives: bulk-forming (fiber, psyllium), lubricant (mineral oil), emollient stool softeners (Colace), hyperosmolar (lactose, sorbitol), stimulant (sena, castor oil, aloe juice), and saline. All of them have side effects, and none are suitable for people affected by IBS, Crohn's disease, or ulcerative colitis. This represents a particular challenge for people with severe organic constipation. In that case, the brief use of saline laxatives to normalize stools is the lesser evil.

[13] U.S. Food and Drug Administration; Questions and Answers on Zelnorm (tegaserod maleate); http://www.fda.gov/cder/drug/infopage/zelnorm/zelnorm_QA.htm

[14] Most sliced cheeses that are sold in supermarkets are factory-made (processed) from various dairy and non-dairy components. Natural cheeses are made from fermented whole milk and are gradually ripened to the desired consistency. Most of them still retain live bacteria. Softer cheeses, such as brie, contain more live bacteria.

[15] R.F. Schmidt, G. Thews. Colonic Motility. *Human Physiology, 2nd edition.* 29.7:731.

[16] Resisting good food and fine spirits while dining out is a challenge. The price for indiscretion is paid the morning after: fatigue from poor sleep, dry mouth from alcohol-related dehydration, headache from sulfites added to wines, bloating from overeating, etc. These after-effects, even the minor ones, ruin my ability to research and write, sometimes for days. For these reasons, I avoid parties and conventional restaurants like the plague. We do eat out often, though, but mostly in sushi bars or simple restaurants, which serve the most basic food. It's hard to overindulge in sashimi, lobster tail, or a piece of rotisserie chicken. As Spartan as it may seem, ours isn't an austere existence, but a preferred lifestyle dictated by professional and personal necessities. In other words, I do it for the same reasons other responsible professionals (models, actors, athletes, anchors, surgeons, pilots, etc.) watch their diets, take supplements, and go to bed early: to walk the walk, talk the talk, look the part, and move ahead.

[17] Similar symptoms may accompany severe hangovers, because excess alcohol blocks gastric digestion. If you feel nausea after too much food and too many drinks, it's best to throw up immediately to prevent further putrefaction and ensuing poisoning.

[18] To make digestive juices, the body draws water mainly from the blood. A dry mouth an hour or so after a meal means that your body is partially dehydrated, because it needed to use a lot of intrinsic fluids to make up the digestive juices. Drinking while the meal is digesting isn't going to relieve dehydration, because the water you just drank can't get down into the duodenum and get assimilated back into the bloodstream. This water can, however, dilute digestive juices, extend digestion, and cause indigestion. So it's best to swish a sip of mineral water and spit it out. Also, chewing something sweet stimulates saliva secretion, and relieves a dry mouth condition. It's a good idea not to drink liquids at least 4–6 hours after a protein-based meal, longer for older adults.

[19] Smith J.L.; The Role of Gastric Acid in Preventing Foodborne Disease and How Bacteria Overcome Acid Conditions; Journal of Food Protection, Volume 66:7, 1 July 2003, pp. 1292–1303(12).

[20] It's a challenge to have just one protein-based meal a day because we are conditioned to variety from childhood. In reality, variety is the enemy of good digestion, because your digestion can never adapt well to an ever-changing array of food. It works fine in the young and healthy, but as we get older, variety causes all kinds of digestive problems. To avoid this trap, I adapted to a Japanese style of eating. In Japan, a communal bowl of warm cooked rice is

available all day long for breakfast, lunch, and snacking. Proteins are consumed mostly with dinner. I boil myself 2.5 oz (70 g) of regular white rice each morning, add 50–60 g of butter (82% fat), and eat the first batch around 12 pm, the second around 4 pm. That's about 50 g of carbs and almost zero fiber. We have dinner between 7 and 8 pm, which usually consists of a small piece of herring (a source of salt) with a slice of butter, and a simple dish without sides, such as lamb or beef stew, grilled chicken, lamb chops, or filet mignon. We don't cook fish at home, because once you get used to sashimi, home-cooked fish isn't very tasty. I may have a glass of wine with our meal, but prefer not to, because it stimulates too much appetite and tires me out for the rest of the evening. For desert, I may have two-three small butter Danish cookies, a scoop of natural ice cream, or a small shot of port. Bite-size sweets, especially when chewed very slowly, raise the blood sugar back up, and suppress appetite. It took me about five years to gradually adapt to this little food, and to enjoy it. I'm rarely hungry, nor do I experience any kind of distress before or after a meal. My weight stays stable at 155 lbs (5'7") plus or minus 2–3 lbs. My exercise routine is limited to daily walks, and brief morning stretches, yet my body is quite fit and muscular for a relatively sedentary writer who is over 50. I work 12 to 15 hours every day in front of the computer, mostly writing, reading, or researching the Internet. My wife, who is much more active physically and emotionally, has a slightly more varied diet (banana, morning coffee, occasional bagel, and one or two European beers daily). Tatyana is also 5'7," weighs 125 lbs, and has never been to the gym or dieted. We both take professional-quality supplements, because our diet is certainly deficient in many essential vitamins and minerals. We drink primarily European bottled water with a high mineral content, about three to four glasses daily—one in the morning, one with supplements, and one before dinner. Obviously, we drink more when outside in the heat, mowing the lawn, etc.

[21] Rare organ meats (liver, kidney), soft eggs yolks, raw fish, and caviar are the most abundant dietary sources of vitamin $B_6$. It is easily ruined by cooking. Quality supplements are the optimal source, because the consumption of rare organ meats, soft yolks, and rare fish is generally discouraged for sanitary purposes. Raw carrots and brewer's yeast contain a great deal of B-complex vitamins. However, their widespread consumption is a nutritional novelty.

[22] The healthier you are, the higher the probability of a foul mood, because even a slightly elevated insulin level in healthy people lowers glucose faster than in people already affected by metabolic disorders, such as diabetes or insulin resistance. That's also why younger, healthier people are impacted by severe depression more often than middle-aged adults, who are either not as healthy, or have already begun counting carbs for health and weight reasons.

[23] In people such as myself and my wife, who are accustomed to a low-carb diet, fatigue and the occasional bad mood are associated with cravings not for sugar, but for sashimi, rare steak, raw oysters, foie gras, or eggs Benedict—all abundant sources of tryptophan and vitamin $B_6$ (except oysters).

[24] "Sugar uptake" is a clinical term which describes the relative rate of change (dynamics) of measurable blood sugar. Slower uptake indicates the presence of a metabolic disorder, such as diabetes. On the other hand, a very fast uptake in healthy people may cause hypoglycemia.

[25] The liver, muscles and cells store excess glucose as glycogen, a complex carbohydrate represented by a very long chain of linked molecules of glucose. When the blood's glucose gets too low, and none is coming from food, the pancreas releases the hormone glucagon, which in turn stimulates the breakdown of glycogen into glucose. The glucagon also stimulates the release of triglycerides from adipose tissue (body fat). Cells, other than the brain's, can metabolize triglycerides into energy via the process known as lipolysis, which Dr. Atkins made famous by incorrectly naming it "ketosis" in his first book (1972). He somewhat correctly called it "ketosis/lipolysis" in his second (1992), and, correctly used the term "lipolysis" in his final (2002) book. This error cost him dearly, because ketosis is a shorthand for diabetic ketoacidosis (DKA)—a deadly condition specific to hyperglycemia (extremely high blood sugar), dehydration, and acidosis (elevated blood pH). Naturally, doctors were up in arms, because "safe ketosis" for them is akin to "safe coma."

[26] Natural yogurt is almost lactose-free, because most of the lactose is consumed by bacteria during fermentation. Supermarket-variety yogurts are literally cooked from skim milk, milk solids, and soluble fiber additives to create body rather than fermented naturally. They still retain most of the lactose, and aren't suitable for low-fiber diets or people with allergies and lactose intolerance to dairy.

[27] Alcoholic beverages contribute to obesity not just from their energy content, estimated at seven calories per gram of pure alcohol, but from lowering the blood sugar, which causes intense sugar cravings and stimulates the appetite. Because of its potent sugar lowering effect, alcohol also stimulates insulin release. That's why some mildly drunk people are so aggressive and rage-prone. Alcohol's influence on the blood sugar/insulin dynamic is behind the dumb-ass recommendation that people affected by diabetes drink wine. Considering alcohol's impact on the liver, kidneys, hypertension, and triglycerides, wine for diabetics is as poisonous as sugar syrup.

[28] This isn't what you're going to read in books dedicated to this subject, because the glycemic index concept was originally developed for people with insulin-dependent diabetes, but was later transferred to healthy people without adequate thought and analysis. In automotive terms, the engine that runs on low RPMs (revolutions per minute) will outlast the same engine that runs at high RPMs, assuming that both run the same amount of time. However, if you run your low RPM engine for five hours at a time, and your high RPM for only 10 minutes, guess which engine will last longer?

[29] Technically, digested carbohydrates enter the body as either glucose, fructose, or galactose—the three basic molecules that make up all carbohydrates. For example, table sugar (dextrose) is made from one molecule of glucose and one of fructose. Milk sugar (lactose) is made from glucose and galactose, also one of each. Glucose was originally called *grape sugar,* because grapes contain pure glucose. Both the fructose and galactose get converted into glucose by the liver; however, their exact metabolic path is murky even today. Many processed foods add fructose instead of sugar as the main sweetener. Because sugar (dextrose) must be listed on the label separately from total carbohydrates, this little trick allows manufacturers to label a product as "low sugar" or "no sugar added," which is true in a formal, legal sense, but a blunt deception in terms of human physiology and metabolic im-

pact. The hypoglycemic effect of fructose is similar to glucose. Fructose is made from cornstarch.

[30] Another reason for after-the-meal drowsiness is, of course, hypoglycemia. If you can't afford a snooze after lunch don't eat mixed (i.e. protein and carb) meals. The meal must be either pure carbs to speed up digestion and utilize insulin (just like water, carbs don't get assimilated until they reach the small intestine) or carb-free to prevent the release of stored insulin, which shoots blood sugar down as soon as you begin eating. This approach requires some time to adapt your endocrine system to a new eating pattern.

[31] The following conditions are associated with albuminuria: bladder tumor, congestive heart failure, diabetic nephropathy, glomerulonephritis, nephrotic syndrome, polycystic kidney disease, interstitial nephritis, membranous nephropathy, necrotizing vasculitis, glomerulonephritis. reflux nephropathy, renal vein thrombosis, malignant hypertension, heavy metal poisoning, and others.

[32] Paul Whittaker, et al.; Iron and Folate in Fortified Cereals; Journal of the American College of Nutrition, Vol. 20, No. 3, 247–254 (2001); http://www.jacn.org/cgi/content/abstract/20/3/247

[33] Newer Knowledge of Dairy Foods; National Dairy Council; http://www.nationaldairycouncil.org/NationalDairyCouncil/Nutrition/Products/milkPage5.htm

[34] Catherine S. Berkey, et al.; Milk, Dairy Fat, Dietary Calcium, and Weight Gain: A Longitudinal Study of Adolescents; Arch Pediatr Adolesc Med 159: 543–550.

[35] The Use and Misuse of Fruit Juice in Pediatrics; American Academy of Pediatrics; Committee on Nutrition; Pediatrics 2001;107:1210–1213.

[36] Agricultural Research Center; USDA National Nutrient Database for Standard Reference; http://www.nal.usda.gov/fnic/foodcomp/search/

[37] Dietary Guidelines for Americans 2005. The U.S. Department of Health and Human Services; http://www.healthierus.gov/dietaryguidelines/

[38] United States Department of Agriculture; http://www.mypyramid.gov/

# CHAPTER TWELVE

## THE LOW-FIBER ADVANTAGE

Your body is the only "authority" you can trust unconditionally. It lets you feel and evaluate the advantages of a low-fiber diet literally "by your gut." If that's not enough for you, or if it seems too subjective, consider comparing your past and current blood tests. You should observe a drop in your triglycerides and HbA1c (the average amount of blood sugar over the past six to eight weeks), and most likely, a rise in your HDL ("good") cholesterol.[1] If you want to investigate things even further, ask your doctor to review your past and present metabolic (kidney- and diabetes-related) and hepatic (liver-related) test results, and you should see them normalizing as well.

Just keep in mind that it takes years, perhaps decades, to develop diet-related health disorders. Hence, it would be nuts to expect that any diet—low-fiber or not—can magically undo all of the damage in a day, a week, or even a year. Still, all things considered, getting better, even slowly, is a far better option than getting nowhere.

So what's so magical about a low-fiber diet? In a nutshell, two things: (1) it makes the digestive process quick and efficient, and (2) it's naturally low in carbohydrates. Here's a brief summation of its most important advantages. First, in terms of your digestion:

## The healing properties of a low-fiber diet

The impact of a low-fiber diet on the digestive process is recognizable from the relatively rapid reduction of functional (reversible) side effects caused by excess fiber: the disappearance of heartburn (because there is less indigested food inside the stomach), the absence of bloating (because there is less bacterial fermentation), the easy passing of stools (because the stools are smaller), the reduction of hemorrhoids (because there is less straining), and the gradual vanishing of nagging abdominal discomfort (because of all of the above). You can't miss these signs.

The progress doesn't end with just the relief of side effects: as the quality of digestion improves, your body begins to absorb more essential nutrients from pretty much the same diet you consumed before, because fiber is no longer there to impede their assimilation. The improved availability of nutrients accelerates tissue regeneration throughout the body, rejuvenates the endocrine system, and increases the output of digestive enzymes. This, in turn, accelerates the healing of the digestive organs, which in turn improves digestion, and in turn accelerates the healing... well, you get the picture.

This process of recovery is the direct opposite of the harm fiber causes. The harm starts with fiber's interference with digestion: as digestion becomes less efficient, so does the body's ability to resist harm. As the harm increases in scope, digestion becomes even less efficient, and the harm more apparent. This step-by-step decline of health accelerates with aging. Therein lies yet another important advantage of the low-fiber diet:

A LOW-FIBER DIET DECELERATES
AGE-RELATED DECLINE

The decline may be slow and imperceptible in the case of young people, and precipitous and apparent in older people, but the aspects of the decline caused by fiber come to a halt the moment you stop overconsuming it.

I emphasize this point to instill a dose of optimism in you: it doesn't matter how old you are, nor does it matter how far this or that disorder has progressed. What really matters is that as soon as you take action, you put a stop to the self-inflicted downfall, because you remove one of its most prominent causes. This in itself, even when complete recovery may not be feasible, is worth the effort.

Diseases aside, the impact of fiber's reduction on satiety is yet another important advantage of the low-fiber diet. While appetite makes you want to eat, a lack of satiety causes you to overeat. The mechanisms behind satiety are mainly physiological—you don't feel satisfied from eating until the stomach is filled to a certain capacity. That's why stomach-reduction surgeries are so effective for morbidly obese people: after surgery they need just a fraction of food to feel "stuffed."

But we aren't actually born with huge, hungry stomachs. They stretch out gradually as we keep filling them with a high-bulk diet. In fact, fiber advocates hawk this phenomenon as an advantage: fiber fills you up and promotes satiety, they claim. But that's a devil's benefit, as each new "fill-up" keeps stretching your stomach a teeny bit more, so that the next time around you need a teeny bit more food to fill it to satiety again. Do this for some years, and eventually you "grow" a stomach that's indeed hard to please. This is yet another aspect of fiber addiction.

Fortunately, it also works in reverse: as soon as you stop consuming a high-fiber diet, your stomach begins to gradually shrink in size, and with each new meal you'll need less and less food to feel satisfied. All this without a gastric bypass (GBP) or a stomach band (LAP-BAND®) squeezed around it—the two most popular surgical options to reduce the stomach's capacity and "speed up" satiety.

The advantages of a low-fiber diet don't stop with just no longer overeating. Here's a brief recap of its other undeniable benefits:

- *Oral health.* A low-fiber diet improves dental health, because it reduces bacterial fermentation inside the oral cavity. The by-products of fermentation are the leading cause of dental caries, periodontal disease, and tooth loss.
- *Esophagus.* A low-fiber diet prevents heartburn. In turn, this eliminates the causes of esophageal inflammatory disease (esophagitis), which may result in the development of *dysphagia* (difficulties swallowing), *Barrett's disease* (irreversible change of the esophageal epithelium), and cancer.

- *Gastric digestion.* Meals without fiber and carbohydrates promote rapid and complete stomach digestion. The improvements are particularly apparent in people over the age of 50 (the group most often affected by indigestion, GERD, gastritis, and peptic ulcers).

- *Duodenum.* A low-fiber diet prevents duodenitis and duodenal ulcers. The extended contact of the duodenal epithelium with fiber soaked in hydrochloric acid and gastric enzymes is a primary cause of these inflammatory conditions.

- *Pancreas.* A low-fiber diet protects the pancreatic ducts from obstruction and from ensuing pancreatitis. Acute pancreatitis is a leading cause of type I diabetes symptoms in children, whose small organs can get clogged by fiber quite easily.

- *Gallbladder.* A low-fiber diet prevents cholecystitis, which is the obstruction of the billiary ducts, through which the gallbladder and liver discharge bile into the duodenum. Again, fiber is the only outside substance capable of causing the primary obstruction (the secondary obstruction comes from gallstones and bile salts). Acute cholecystitis is a leading cause of gallbladder disease caused by gallstones, gallbladder inflammation, or both. Each year over half a million Americans undergo a cholecystectomy (gallbladder removal surgery). As you might expect, obesity and diabetes—both conditions brought about by a high-carb/high-fiber diet—are the leading causes of cholecystitis. And yes, women are twice as likely as men to have gallstones. No surprise there: women consume more fiber than men because twice as many women are also affected by constipation.

- *Intestinal obstruction.* Intestinal obstruction isn't possible with foods that digest completely. The small intestines are supposed to transport liquid chyme only, not large lumps of undigested fiber. Intestinal obstructions on a low-fiber diet are as likely as a rainbow during a snowstorm.

- *Hernia.* A low-fiber diet prevents herniation of the abdominal wall by the small intestine, or its protrusion inside the scrotum. These two conditions are likely to occur when the intestines expand beyond the capacity of the abdominal cavity to retain them. There is only one food component capable of causing this kind of expansion: indigestible fiber.

- *Enteritis.* A low-fiber diet protects the intestinal epithelium from inflammation caused by mechanical contact, from chemical irritation caused by gastric juices and enzymes (absorbed by fiber while in the stomach), and from obstructions caused by lumps of fiber.

- *Malnutrition.* Enteritis, whether caused by the mechanical properties of insoluble fiber, chemical properties of soluble fiber, or allergenicity of plant proteins, blocks the digestion of nutrients, including essential, health-sustaining amino acids, fatty acids, vitamins, minerals, and microelements. This causes a broad range of degenerative diseases, ranging from pernicious anemia to kwashiorkor, osteomalacia to birth defects, and everything in between. A low-fiber diet, especially one free from wheat (a source of gluten) is essential for the proper assimilation of nutrients.

- *Bloating and flatus.* The fermentation of fiber inside the large intestine produces copious gases, which cause pain and bloating. A fiber-free diet eliminates intestinal bloating and the source of the pain (from pressure). Flatus is particularly bothersome in terms of social interactions for all people, and it's outright painful for most. A low-fiber diet reduces the presence of gases to the barely perceptible.

- *Appendicitis.* A low-fiber diet is key to preventing appendicitis. The accumulation of fiber inside the cecum obstructs the appendix, and causes its inflammation. There is no other dietary factor that can cause appendix obstruction, because under normal circumstances the cecum's content is fluid. Children are particularly vulnerable because their cecum is tiny, taut, and prone to obstruction.

- *Diarrhea.* A low-fiber diet prevents diarrhea. Without exception, all kinds of soluble fiber are diarrhea-causing agents. For this reason fiber is widely used in medicinal and home-made laxatives. Intestinal inflammation caused by insoluble fiber blocks the absorption of fluids, and causes diarrhea, too. Combine both irritants, add (as widely recommended) even more fiber to treat diarrhea, and you're assured of chronic diarrhea.

- *Constipation.* A low-fiber diet eliminates constipation caused by large stools. If you don't want your children to ever experience constipation, eliminate fiber-rich foods from their diets. Unfortunately, a low-fiber diet alone isn't sufficient to treat constipation after the large intestine has already been irreversibly transformed by large stools. This complicated subject is discussed throughout this book.

- *Hemorrhoidal disease and anal fissures.* A low-fiber diet is key to the prevention and treatment of these two conditions (caused by large, hard stools, and the straining required to expel them) and their numerous side effects.
- *Irritable bowel syndrome.* A low-fiber diet relieves IBS symptoms as soon as large stools "depart" the bowel. No irritant inside the bowel equals no irritable bowel. It's as simple as that.
- *Crohn's disease.* Crohn's disease is IBS gone too far. A low-fiber diet is key to treating and preventing Crohn's disease.
- *Ulcerative colitis.* This tragic disease is the final straw—the sum total of all of the above. Naturally, the treatment of ulcerative colitis must begin with a zero-fiber diet in order to eliminate its diarrhea-, constipation-, and inflammation-causing effects.
- *Cancers of the digestive organs.* A low-fiber diet reduces the chances of the digestive system getting struck by cancer, because it eliminates the major dietary cause of digestive disorders. It's axiomatic that healthy organs are less likely to get affected by malignancies than unhealthy organs. The unfortunate fact that ulcerative colitis increases the risk of colon cancer 3,200% provides us with all the proof we need about the fiber-cancer connection.

A low-fiber diet alone isn't a guarantee of vibrant health and boundless longevity. It is, however, an important step toward attaining these treasured things. And it's never too late to make it happen. Besides benefiting your digestive system, a low-fiber diet works wonders for your endocrine system and metabolism.

### The metabolic advantages of a low-fiber diet

While the endocrine system governs the metabolism of energy, it's you who governs the supply of nutrients that provide the energy in the first place. A true breaking down of the metabolism is a rarity: only about 5% of diabetes victims, for example, suffer from a failure of the pancreas to produce insulin. The other 95% overpower the body with so many carbohydrates that their pancreas either can't keep up with the demand (for insulin), or their bodies simply ignore the insulin, which is already plentiful.

Thus, true recovery from metabolic disorders like diabetes lies not in taking more drugs to trick the pancreas into producing even more insulin, or taxing the liver into converting excess blood sugar into even more body fat, but in balance. The plain, simple, elementary balance between how much energy you really need and how much you're actually getting from food.

Most people can't find that balance, not because they aren't willing, or are foolish, but simply because they're misinformed about the role of dietary carbohydrates and natural fiber in health and nutrition. That's why so many well-meaning and health-conscious individuals prefer getting their fiber from abundant "natural" sources, believing it's healthier,[2] while in fact it's as far from the truth as New York is from Paris.

Natural fiber—both the soluble and insoluble kind—is present only in plant-based foods, such as grains, nuts, seeds, legumes, fruits, and vegetables. It's also found in foods processed from these plants, such as cereals, bread, pasta, and baked goods. All of these foods contain anywhere from ten to twenty times more carbohydrates than fiber, which is enough to overpower even the most robust endocrine system with excess energy. Thus, when you cut down on the fiber-rich foods in your diet, you're also cutting out accompanying carbs, and bringing the energy supply and demand back into balance.

Assuming you won't be rushing to replace these excluded carbohydrates with refined sugar, fruit juices, and soft drinks, your diet will become not just low in fiber, but decidedly low in carbs as well. Thus, serendipitously, you'll be accruing the benefits of a low-carb diet, too.

While simple carbs (i.e. mono and disaccharides, such as sugar) digest rapidly and cause a brief spike in blood sugar, complex carbs (i.e. polysaccharides, such as starches in grains) digest for hours at a time. All along, while digestion is taking place, the pancreas secretes insulin to keep up with the steady supply of glucose entering the bloodstream.

A chronically elevated level of insulin is called *hyperinsuline-*

*mia.* Besides extremely rare pancreatic tumors and extraordinary stress, there is only one factor that can cause hyperinsulinemia: dietary carbohydrates. The more carbohydrates you eat, the more insulin your pancreas produces to utilize them.

Elevated insulin is a potent vasoconstrictor, meaning it narrows major and minor blood vessels throughout the body. When this happens, blood pressure and pulse rates go up, while the supply of oxygenated blood delivered to the essential organs and extremities goes down. For these reasons, hyperinsulinemia is a primary cause of elevated blood pressure, heart disease, atherosclerosis, diabetes, liver disease, kidney failure, nerve damage, blindness, peripheral vascular disease, dementia, migraine headaches, chronic fatigue, attention deficit/hyperactivity disorder, hypoglycemia (low blood sugar), incessant appetite, and obesity. And that's just the big ones.

Not so long ago, the sum of most of these symptoms was called *Syndrome X.* Now it's called "prediabetes,"[3] because the "*X*" in the syndrome is no longer a mystery. It stands for hyperinsulinemia, which is obviously caused by too many carbohydrates in one's diet. Consider an average "healthy" breakfast: a glass of orange juice (26 g of carbs), a cup of Kellogg's Crispix (25 g) with a cup of milk (12 g), and one medium-sized banana (27 g). That's 90 g of carbs, or the equivalent of six tablespoons of sugar, which is almost half the daily requirement for the average adult. While this modest breakfast keeps digesting, the body keeps secreting insulin, almost half the daily dose. And that's before several snacks, sodas, lunch, and dinner.

Of course, if you don't consume prodigious amounts of carbs, the pancreas doesn't flood your body with insulin. So as soon as your consumption of carbs goes down, the state of your health goes up, and you can expect to see the following improvements just from taming the hyperinsulinemia:

- *Hypoglycemia.* When blood sugar drops down below 40–50 milligrams per deciliter of blood (mg/dl), a person loses consciousness (i.e. coma, syncope), and may actually die, often not from the coma episode itself, but from an ensuing accident, such as a fall or car crash. Hypoglycemia occurs when there is more insulin in the system than available glucose to satisfy demand by the central nervous system. Its symptoms are hard to miss: fatigue, drowsiness, irritability, hunger, headache, memory loss, vision disturbances, speech impairment, unsteadiness, dizziness, tingling in the hands or lips, dilated pupils, rapid pulse, low blood pressure, and some others. When insulin levels are normal, hypoglycemia isn't likely even on a zero-carb diet, because the body can maintain a steady level of blood glucose from other sources of energy, such as dietary fats and proteins, or stored energy in the form of glycogen in the liver, fat from adipose tissue, protein from muscle tissue, and so on.

- *Elevated triglycerides.* A high level of triglycerides is considered to be a more objective marker of advancing heart disease than any other factor. As soon as carbohydrates are reduced, the level of triglycerides follows suit, because the liver no longer needs to convert excess blood glucose into triglycerides, which, incidentally, becomes body fat. Chronically elevated triglycerides increase blood viscosity, which is another major cause of elevated blood pressure.

- *Hypertension.* Your blood pressure will normalize because insulin no longer constricts your blood vessels, and no longer forces your heart to pump more blood more vigorously to overcome the resistance of narrow vessels as well as viscous (from triglycerides) blood.

- *Heart disease.* Your heart condition will improve because your heart muscles will get more well-oxygenated blood, and also because it will not have to pump the blood extra hard to overcome the counteraction of constricted blood vessels and the friction caused by triglycerides.

- *Atherosclerosis.* If you suffer from atherosclerosis, it may gradually reverse itself because insulin no longer contributes to vascular inflammatory disease, which damages the vessels on the inside and leads to the accumulation of vascular plaque—a primary cause of permanent narrowing of the affected vessels. The reversal of atherosclerosis is described in detail in mainstream medical literature.

- *Migraine headaches.* The two most prominent dietary causes behind migraine headaches are the constriction of cerebral blood vessels by insulin, and cerebral edema caused by excess dietary potassium. Carbohydrate-rich foods are at once the largest source of dietary potassium and the triggers of insulin. In this respect, a low-carb diet is truly the best headache "medicine." Alcohol, monosodium glutamate (MSG), naturally occurring and added sulfites in wine, and the amino acid tyramine, found in aged wines, cheeses, and many other foods are also triggers for head-aches, unrelated to insulin or carbohydrates. When these are added on top of too many carbs, a headache can become one gi-ant migraine.

- *Attention deficit disorder in adults.* This condition is caused by impaired cerebral circulation, low-blood sugar, and general fa-tigue. These three factors depress the central nervous system (CNS), and interfere with normal day-to-day functions and ac-tivities.

- *Attention deficit/hyperactivity disorder (ADHD) in children.* Since both elevated glucose and insulin are potent stimulants of the CNS, children respond to them with alternating patterns of hyperactivity and fatigue. Both states interfere with concentra-tion and cause behavior patterns that are considered abnormal. Shortly after affected children are placed on a low-carb diet, the symptoms of ADHD gradually diminish and eventually disap-pear. It just takes time for a child's pancreas to reduce the pro-duction of insulin and adapt to a new pattern of behavior.

- *Insomnia.* A combination of elevated levels of insulin (an energy hormone) and elevated levels of blood sugar (a fuel for CNS) are the primary causes of functional (i.e. reversible) sleeplessness. How can one sleep when the body is so overstimulated with en-ergy? That's why you've been told from childhood not to eat se-veral hours before bedtime. As people get older, digestion and utilization of energy stretches from the customary 4–6 hours to 8, 10, or even 12 hours. So even if you've completed your dinner by 7 p.m., it may continue digesting until 3, 5, or even 7 a.m. When you finally doze off, the sleep is superficial, because the level of insulin remains high long after the blood sugar has gone down. Not surprisingly, the quality of sleep goes up as soon as the amount of dietary carbs goes down. As with ADHD, it takes time to tame and adjust the unconditional (not dependent on the diet) release of insulin.

- *Chronic Fatigue Syndrome.* A combination of fatigue from low-blood sugar, mental and muscular apathy related to constricted blood vessels (i.e. inadequate supply of blood), and general weariness stemming from chronic insomnia are the primary ingredients of chronic fatigue syndrome. The reduction of dietary carbohydrates eliminates the causes of low blood sugar, blood-vessel constriction, and insomnia, and brings welcomed energy back. If this doesn't occur, seek out and eliminate other possible causes, such as celiac disease, anemia, dehydration, low thyroid function, chronic infections, autoimmune disorders, depression, and so on. Not surprisingly, a high-carb diet contributes mightily to all these conditions.

- *Susceptibility to colds.* An elevated level of glucose in healthy children stimulates metabolic rates and raises body temperature, which causes profuse perspiration. When children perspire, they're more likely to get chills from the ensuing rapid evaporation—a condition that makes them susceptible to colds. Adults may get colds for similar reasons, except that in their case constricted blood vessels lower body temperature, and facilitate bacterial infections. In addition, elevated levels of blood glucose provide plentiful feed for fledging bacteria to invade, procreate, and overpower the immune system of children and adults alike. In essence, excess carbs make you a walking Petri dish, ready and willing to shelter, feed, and grow any bacterial pathogen that happens to be around. A reduction of dietary carbohydrates in the diet significantly reduces the chance of bacterial infections.

- *Acne.* Hormonal changes in teenagers has little to do with acne. Puberty happens to coincide with the appearance of fully-functional sebaceous glands on one's face and body. Excess oil excreted by these glands clogs them, while the bacteria lodged within them causes the infection and eruption. A zero-carb diet is one of the most effective means of acne control because (a) it curbs oil production by reducing the level of triglycerides in the blood, and (b) it doesn't stimulate bacterial growth as much because of a reduction in the level of blood sugar.

- *Seborrhea.* Besides "dandruff," the term *seborrhea* means "too much oil." A low-carb diet controls seborrhea for the same reasons it "treats" acne: it eliminates excess triglycerides (derived from glucose and fermentation of fiber), which are the leading

source of "too much oil." The dietary fats from plant oils found
in dressings and mayonnaise also contribute to seborrhea and
acne. A low-fiber diet, along with a moderate consumption of essential fats from animal sources, helps control dandruff and acne
without resorting to medical treatments.

- *Yeast infection. Candida albicans,* a yeast-like fungus, is commonly present in the mouth, vagina, and intestinal tract. In
  healthy people its proliferation is kept well under control by
  symbiotic bacteria and other immune co-factors. It's believed
  that a deficiency of vitamins $B_{12}$, folate, zinc, and selenium contributes to *candidiasis,* an abnormal growth of fungus. This
  growth is further sustained by an elevated level of blood sugar.
  Intestinal inflammation caused by gluten (a wheat protein) and
  the fermentation of fiber (a source of elevated acidity), are the
  two primary causes of vitamin and mineral deficiencies even
  among people who take supplements or eat a "balanced" diet. A
  reduction of carbohydrates (especially from the grain group) and
  the elimination of fiber is an effective preventative from recurring yeast infections, especially when combined with quality
  supplements.
- *Liver disease.* A condition known as fatty liver, which is caused
  by the continuous onslaught of carbohydrates, is reversible in
  people who adopt a low-carb diet. Its reversal greatly benefits
  those who have been affected by hepatitis, because a healthy
  liver has a high degree of resistance to these viruses.[4]
- *Type II Diabetes.* If you have type II diabetes (non-insulin dependent), its symptoms should gradually reverse. You may be
  able to get off side effects-prone medication, because the nor-
  malization of blood sugar is an almost immediate response to a
  low-carb diet. Don't judge your recovery progress just on self-
  testing, or on fasting plasma glucose tests. Take the HbA1c (gly-
  cosylated hemoglobin) test instead. Unlike the fasting plasma
  glucose test, which takes a direct snapshot of widely fluctuating
  daily levels of glucose, the HbA1c reflects the average concentration of glucose in the blood during the preceding six to eight
  weeks. It presents a true picture of diabetes, irrespective of external circumstances such as a fast, medication, or recent meal.
  Wait for at least two months from the day you begin a low-carb

diet before taking this test.

- *Type I Diabetes.* If you have type I diabetes (insulin-dependent), you should be able to significantly reduce your doses of insulin to a much safer level. In many cases, you may find that you have been misdiagnosed, that your pancreas is still functional, and that it can manage blood sugar on its own. According to some experts, the rate of misdiagnosis of type I diabetes among children is up to 50%.[5] It isn't just elevated blood sugar that's eventually harming these children, but also the large doses of insulin prescribed to support their high-carb diets.[6]

- *Blindness.* Your eyes aren't as likely to succumb to diabetic retinopathy, a condition commonly related to diabetes, hypertension, hyperinsulinemia, and elevated triglycerides, and the leading cause of blindness among adults with either type of diabetes, and (even more often) with undiagnosed diabetes.

- *Impotence.* A low-carb diet may boost your libido just as well as Viagra does, because both things dilate and relax the blood vessels that govern erections. In addition, unlike Viagra, a low-carb diet will not cause headaches or blindness. If you recall Graham's and Kellogg's rational for vegetarian, high-fiber diets, it wasn't to keep people from screwing up their health, but to keep people away from having sex, even with their lawful spouses.

- *Nerve damage.* Low-carb diets protect you from nerve damage caused by hyperinsulinemia. Diabetes- and prediabetes-related nerve damage is associated with a loss of sensitivity in the extremities. Nerve damage of the anal canal is one of the primary causes of constipation, and dependence on fiber to move the bowels. Penal and vaginal nerve damage affects intercourse, because the victims aren't able to reach orgasm. Premature ejaculation also results from indirect overstimulation of the nervous receptors by elevated insulin. That same overstimulation eventually causes the receptor's demise.

- *Appetite control.* Insidious hunger and incessant appetite are very much the symptoms of hyperinsulinemia, both of which are provoked by low blood sugar. This narcotic-like effect of insulin is also hard to overcome, because the urge to consume carbohydrates is beyond simple conscious control, but driven by the body's survival instincts and unconditional responses. For anyone wanting to lose weight, or at the very least wishing to not gain any more, this effort-free curbing of the appetite is one of the most pleasant aspects of a low-carb lifestyle.

- *Obesity.* If you are overweight, you may stop gaining weight, and may begin to gradually lose body fat, because body fat is made almost exclusively from the carbohydrates in your diet. If you consume less than 200 g of carbohydrates daily (an average for the medium-sized adult), the balance is drawn from body fat (the physiology of weight loss). If you consume more than 200 g, you just get fatter, and fatter, and fatter.

- *Low weight.* If you're underweight, you may begin gaining weight gradually. The combination of your genetics, insulin resistance, and hyperinsulinemia is the primary cause of weight loss. Genetics determine the ability of your adipose tissue to store fat. Hyperinsulinemia causes insulin resistance, or the inability of cells to respond to the insulin signals in order to start absorbing glucose. In turn, this metabolic disorder turns on lipolysis (a conversion of body fat into energy), and gluconeogenesis (a metabolic function that produces glucose from muscle tissues). The simultaneous inability to accumulate fat, and the use of body fat and muscle tissues for energy, causes weight loss and prevents weight gain. The process is similar to the weight loss experienced by people with type I diabetes, except in their case the elevated insulin comes from the injections.

- *Kidney disease.* If you have kidney disease, you'll see an improvement for two reasons: (1) When the level of glucose in the blood exceeds 200 mg/dl, the hyperosmotic pressure forces the kidneys to filter out excess sugar with urine. (2) Hyperinsulinemia causes increased blood pressure, which destroys delicate kidney tissues. The combined onslaught of both forces (hyperosmotic pressure and blood pressure) doesn't give the kidneys a chance to regenerate and recover from the preceding damage.

- *Nocturnal Polyuria.* You'll no longer get up in the middle of the night to urinate as often, if at all. Children, whose sleep is so much deeper than that of adults, aren't as likely to have embarrassing episodes, either. Bedwetting and nighttime urination occur because of two factors: (1) elevated levels of glucose cause hyperosmotic pressure and a correspondingly high urine output;

and (2) a frequent urge is caused by inflammatory bladder disease, resulting from elevated levels of acidity and glucose in the urine. Both conditions contribute to bacterial infection of the bladder and ensuing inflammation.

- *Cancer.* As you recall from Chapter 10, *Colon Cancer*, researchers determined a direct connection between the intake of dietary carbohydrates and cancer. All malignancies begin with just one cell. The likelihood of this cell taking hold and growing into a full-blown tumor increase substantially when the immune system is suppressed by disbacteriosis, by carbohydrate-related disorders, and when blood circulation is impeded by hyperinsulinemia. It's also a well-known fact that blood sugar (glucose) is a primary metabolic fuel for cancerous cells: the more glucose in the system, the faster the proliferation of primary cancer and secondary metastases. When the onslaught of carbs is reversed, the greenhouse conditions for cancers are also reversed, however indirectly.

Should I go any further? Even this long list is far from comprehensive. You may read a good deal more about the benefits of low-carb diets from numerous diet books. Luckily, a low-carb diet happens to be a low-fiber diet as well. Finders keepers!

## Summary

- Human digestive organs can accommodate a limited amount of undigested fiber, but aren't intended for its unlimited consumption across the span of many years.
- When the digestive organs are exposed to large volumes of indigestible fiber, they experience numerous disorders from chemical, mechanical, and fermentative damage.
- A low-fiber diet is the least taxing diet for the digestive organs, because it doesn't impede gastric digestion, doesn't affect the transport of digested food, doesn't interfere with the assimilation of nutrients, and doesn't obstruct the elimination of biological waste.
- A low-fiber diet is effective for the prevention and treatment of most digestive disorders, because it enables the natural healing and recovery of the digestive organs.

- A zero-fiber (i.e. low-density) diet is prescribed to all patients before and after any surgical procedure related to the digestive organs, in order to prevent harm and to speed up recovery. Similarly, a low-fiber diet protects healthy digestive organs from harm and illness.
- A high-fiber diet happens to be a very high-carbohydrate diet, because most natural foods contain ten to twenty times more carbohydrates (by weight) for every unit of fiber. The extended overconsumption of carbohydrates causes metabolic disorders such as hyperinsulinemia, hyperglycemia, hypoglycemia, diabetes, and others.
- A chronically elevated level of insulin causes extended constriction of the blood vessels. Constricted blood vessels resist blood flow, and cause elevated blood pressure. Elevated blood pressure is associated with heart disease, atherosclerosis, and stroke.
- The adoption of a low-fiber diet coincides with a significantly reduced consumption of dietary carbohydrates (low-carb diet). Low-carb diets are an effective preventative for cardiovascular and endocrine disorders, including diabetes and obesity.
- Effective and lasting weight loss is one of the most desirable aspects of a low-fiber diet. When fiber is removed from the diet, weight loss is aided by a general reduction of appetite and faster satiety—two factors crucial for permanent weight loss.
- The advantages of a low-fiber diet come from the combined effects of better digestion and improved endocrine functions, which impact health, well-being, and longevity.
- Quality of life and the preservation of health should be key considerations for anyone considering a low-fiber diet while they're still relatively healthy. The reversal and prevention of disease should be a key concern for people who are already experiencing digestive and metabolic disorders.

\*\*\*

# Footnotes

[1] The level of LDL ("bad") cholesterol is determined primarily by age and genetics. Normally, it goes up as people get older, and has no direct bearing on your diet, because LDL cholesterol (as measured) is produced exclusively by the liver regardless of your diet's fat and cholesterol content. Actually, a falling level of cholesterol, including LDL, indicates liver disease, and is in fact one of the first symptoms of impending liver failure and death. According to The Merck Manual of Diagnosis and Therapy (2:15. Hyperlipidemia), the average (that means 95th percentile) level of cholesterol (LDL+HDL) for healthy people "ranges from 210 mg/dL (5.44 mmol/L) in Americans < 20 yr old to > 280 mg/dL (> 7.25 mmol/L) in those > 60 yr old." http://www.merck.com/mrkshared/mmanual/section2/chapter15/15a.jsp

[2] Paradoxically, if your goal is to add bulk to your diet, you are better off taking a supplemental fiber, than consuming a high-fiber natural diet, because supplements don't add any digestible carbohydrates to an already bad mix.

[3] "Prediabetes" is a recently concocted term that describes people who have most or all of the symptoms of type II diabetes, except that their blood test is still below the threshold for diabetes. Please note that diabetes itself is a "syndrome," which means a group of symptoms that make up a disorder. Because most physicians still rely on highly unreliable "fasting plasma glucose" blood tests, a great deal of people with diabetes aren't diagnosed at all, are diagnosed with the incorrect type (i.e. type I or II), or are wrongly diagnosed (don't have any diabetes). My second Russian-language book, "Disorders of Carbohydrates Metabolism," addressed these issues in depth. Since a version of it in English isn't available, I encourage you to read "Dr. Bernstein's Diabetes Solution: The Complete Guide to Achieving Normal Blood Sugars," which covers similar issues. Dr. Bernstein is a practicing physician in the United States, who became a doctor just to prove that a low- or zero-carb diet is all that's needed to recover from type II diabetes or to endure type I without dying from its side effects. Needless to say, his "discovery" hasn't become popular among his peers, who still prefer drugs, insulin, and more carbohydrates to "treat" diabetes. (For more information see http://www.diabetes-normalsugars.com/)

[4] I am acquainted with someone who experienced a remission of hepatitis C infection (determined by the absence of antibodies) after following a near zero-carb diet for about five years. He adopted that diet after reading my Russian-language books, because he was affected by type II diabetes, which is now also in complete remission. By current yardsticks, a recovery from hepatitis C is considered a miracle. I'm not surprised, however: just as antibodies from most vaccines eventually wear off, apparently hepatitis C antibodies can also vanish. You just have to create a proper environment for healing. Apparently, a zero-carb diet did it for this man. Keep in mind that just one case like this, even well documented, is still considered anecdotal and unrepresentative, and is in no way indicative of what may transpire in any other case.

[5] U.S. Center for Disease Control, Special Focus: Diabetes; http://www.cdc.gov/nccdphp/cdsum99.pdf; page 11.

[6] Richard K. Bernstein, M.D.; Dr. Bernstein's Diabetes Solution: The Complete Guide to Achieving Normal Blood Sugars; ISBN 0316099066.

# CONCLUSION

---

## IN HEALTH WE TRUST!

---

I never wanted to be a doctor because I'm too squeamish, too impressionable, and too fastidious—not exactly the qualities called for to examine and care for sick people. Nonetheless, I went to medical school to yield to my mother wishes, chose the pharmaceutical track to make this experience as short and sterile as possible, and left the field for greener pastures (computer science, investment banking, business management) as soon as I graduated.

Despite my enormous curiosity about the workings of the human body, medical school didn't teach me anything truly useful about preserving health and vitality. That wasn't the goal of my curriculum: doctors and pharmacists are trained to take care of the sick, not the healthy.

And that's one of life's strange ironies—throughout the formative years we study many complicated subjects that rarely become useful in adulthood, but not simple and indispensable matters such as health, manners, or relationships. These life- and career-defining skills are primarily implanted by our parents and peers and to a lesser extent by pop culture (movies, television, books, periodicals, and, nowadays, the Internet).

The parental influence is by far the strongest influence simply because of a parent's lengthy "ownership" of our young, imprintable minds, and their control over what gets inside our stomachs. If your parents are healthy, you're lucky. If not, you're likely to carbon copy most of your parents' bad habits and related ills.

That's why I often chuckle while reading studies that blame life-style diseases on genetics, forgetting (or ignoring) the fact that 18–20 years of sharing the same dinner table with a constipated mom or diabetic dad has nothing to do with genetics, but everything with what was on that table. Not that genetics aren't important, but food choices originate in the supermarket aisles, not in the genes.

In any event, by the time you begin reading this kind of book, you must have already been making your own dinner for some time, and it's already too late to change your parents or improve your genes. But it's never too late to drop excess carbs and fiber from your diet.

Nothing discredits fiber better and faster than the people who re-cover by dropping it from their diets. We survived millions of years of merciless evolution despite fiber, not because of it. It's no accident that the American frontier culture, with its reliance on ranching, and not fiber-rich crops, went on to build a great nation.

Finally, please realize that I am not a doctor, nor am I playing one on these pages. This book distills generally available informa-tion about fiber-related disorders. It doesn't, however, provide medical advice on how to diagnose and treat diseases. For that, you need a caring, open-minded, and competent doctor. Once you find one, just follow these simple rules:

- *Be an equal.* The more you know about your body and your health, the more attention, respect, and care you'll get back from your doctors. And if you don't get respect and attention from any particular one, just choose another. A doctor who doesn't respect your grasp of his field is even less likely to respect your body, your health, and your wallet.
- *Don't expect specialists to be know-it-alls.* A top-flight gastroen-terologist knows as much about forensic nutrition (my field of expertise) as I know about anorectal surgery (not much). This isn't his or her chosen specialty, area of primary interest, or the subject of vigorous study spanning many years. You wouldn't ask an eye doctor to examine your anus, would you?
- *Don't seek diet advice* from a board certified gastroenterologist. At a huge expense of time, money, and resources, he or she has

been trained to operate on you, not teach you how and what to eat. You wouldn't ask Mario Andretti to teach you drive around town, would you?

- *Don't stick this book in front of your doctors.* Professionals don't study medicine from popular books no matter how relevant or well written they may be. Appeal to basic facts. No one will argue with you that the anal canal is too small and too tight to effortlessly pass large stools, period.

Of course, not ever needing a doctor is best. For that, be proactive. Drop the fiber. Reduce the carbs. Don't drink more water than your body needs. Don't take lifestyle drugs, change the lifestyle. Take quality supplements. Enjoy a daily walk. Don't eat anything that your great-great-great-grandparent wouldn't have eaten. Pray to God to give you health while you have it, and not when it's gone.

***

A good deal of peripheral research didn't make it into this book, and there isn't a better addendum than the Internet. Please visit www.FiberMenace.com often for more information and insights.

# INDEX

## A

abdominal cramps, 16, 33, 107

abscess, anal, 136

acid-blockers, 217

acidity

  intestinal, 89

  normal, 89

Acidophilus milk, 88

acne, 259

adenocarcinoma, 178

adenoma, colorectal, 178

adipose tissue, 47, 64, 247, 257, 262

agar-agar, 18

Agatston, Dr., 61

albumin, 69, 231

alcohol, avoidance, 225

alcoholic beverages, 247

amalgam fillings, 88, 90

American Dental Association, 90

American Dietetic Association, 14, 43, 46, 115, 187

American Gastroenterological Association, 87, 114

American Heart Association, 41

American Institute for Cancer Research, 185

American Medical Association, 87

aminosalicylates, 169

anal abscess, 34

anal canal, 31

anal canal, functions, 110

anal cushions, 133

anal exams, 110

anal fissure, causes, 162

anorectal pain, 202

antibacterial agents, 153

antibiotic-associated colitis, 87

antibiotics, 89

anticholinergics, 170

Appendicitis, 32

appendix, 30

appetite control, 261

Armenia, cancer risk, 188

arsenic, 90

artificial food coloring, 90

artificial sweeteners, 224

atherosclerosis, 257

Atkins diet, 60

Atkins, causes of death, 53

Atkins, diet failure, 199

attention deficit/hyperactivity disorder, 258

Author

  on eating out, 245

  personal diet, 245

## XYZ

## Back Cover Footnotes:

- Every tenth adult American (over 21 million) has been diagnosed with an ulcer at least once in his or her lifetime.
  - "Number of noninstitutionalized adults with diagnosed ulcers: 14.5 million (2003)"; "Percent of noninstitutionalized adults with diagnosed ulcers: 6.8 (2003)"

    Calculation: Over 18 years old: approximately 210 million adults. Total adults diagnosed with ulcers: 21.3 million, or about every 10th adult.

    Summary Health Statistics for U.S. Adults, 2003, tables 7, 8; http://www.cdc.gov/nchs/data/series/sr_10/sr10_225.pdf

- Every fifth American (up to 60 million) suffers from irritable bowel syndrome.
  - "In fact, irritable bowel syndrome (IBS) affects approximately 10-20% [30 to 60 million – ed.] of the general population.";

    Source: About Irritable Bowel Syndrome (IBS); International Foundation for Functional Gastrointestinal Disorders; http://www.aboutibs.org/index.html

- Every second adult over age fifty (about 38 million) is affected by hemorrhoidal disease.
  - "Hemorrhoids are very common in both men and women. About half of the population have hemorrhoids by age 50."

    Source: Hemorrhoids; NIH Publication No. 02–3021; Feb. 2002; http://digestive.niddk.nih.gov/ddiseases/pubs/hemorrhoids/index.htm

- Every second adult over age sixty (about 23 million) suffers from diverticular disease.
  - "About half of all people over the age of 60 have diverticulosis."

    Source: Diverticulosis and Diverticulitis; NIH Publication No. 04–1163; 4/04; http://digestive.niddk.nih.gov/ddiseases/pubs/diverticulosis/

- Depending on who's counting, over 80 million Americans endure chronic constipation.
  - "The exact prevalence of constipation depends on the definition used; prevalence estimates range from 2% to 28%."

    Calculation: 297 million (as of Sept. 2005) * 28% = 83.1 million.

    Source: Talley NJ; Definitions, epidemiology, and impact of chronic constipation; Rev Gastroenterol Disord. 2004;4 Suppl 2:S3-S10. PMID: 15184814; http://www.ncbi.nlm.nih.gov/

- Besides impaired digestion, over 137 million adult Americans are overweight or obese...

  – "Results from the 1999-2002 National Health and Nutrition Examination Survey (NHANES), using measured heights and weights, indicate that an estimated 65 percent of U.S. adults [over age 20 – ed] are either over-weight or obese."

  Calculation: Over age 20: 71.4% of population; Population in 2005: 297 million; Total overweight adults: 297 million * 71.4% * 65% = 137 million.

  Source: Prevalence of Overweight and Obesity Among
  Adults: United States, 1999-2002;
  http://www.cdc.gov/nchs/products/pubs/pubd/hestats/obese/obse99.htm

## U.S. Census Bureau (population breakdown):

Source: QT-P1. Age Groups and Sex: 2000
Data Set: Census 2000 Summary File 1 (SF 1) 100-Percent Data;

http://factfinder.census.gov/servlet/QTTable?_bm=y&-geo_id=01000US&-qr_name=DEC_2000_SF1_U_QTP1&-ds_name=DEC_2000_SF1_U&-_lang=en&-_sse=on